Books by Laura Bradbury

Grape Series
My Grape Year
My Grape Québec
My Grape Paris
My Grape Wedding
My Grape Escape
My Grape Village
My Grape Cellar

The Winemakers Trilogy
A Vineyard for Two

my

grape

Quebéc

my grape quebec

LAURA BRADBURY

Published by Grape Books

Visit: www.laurabradbury.com

This book is dedicated to Pam, my favorite Montrealer. She's a stellar human being, a cherished friend, and my life is one hundred times better with her in it.

Je reviendrai à Montréal
Dans un grand Bœing bleu de mer
J'ai besoin de revoir l'hiver
Et ses aurores boréales
– Robert Charlebois "Je Reviendrai à Montréal"

chapter one

I stopped crying somewhere over Greenland. This plane was taking me an ocean and a continent away from France, where I had built a life for myself over the past year. Worse, it was taking me away from Franck.

I suspected he might be the love of my life, but I knew how skeptical our friends and family were that the two of us would manage to stay together. I might harbor a romantic heart, but I was also a realist—circumstances were stacked against us.

First of all, there was the sheer geographical distance between France and the extreme west coast of Canada where I was returning home after my exchange year in Burgundy. The entire Atlantic Ocean and the vast expanse of Canada separated us. At least that would be lessened by half a continent when I flew to Montréal at the end of the summer to start studying at McGill University.

Money was also a problem in that neither Franck nor I had any. I was a mere student, and he'd just finished his year of indentured military service required by the French government. He had been living and working on the Air Force base in Dijon, but the military service year wasn't a time when anyone could save. His living expenses were paid but the standard government stipend was next to nothing.

Getting Franck to Canada would require a plane ticket and those cost a significant sum, at least by our broke standards.

But money wasn't the most daunting obstacle. The immigration conundrum held that top spot, hands down. Canada was known to be scrupulously fair in its immigration laws, which wasn't a good thing for us. While Franck had the equivalent of an undergraduate degree from the Sorbonne, he would practically have to have a Ph.D, in some specialized subject in order to make him qualify to be an eligible immigrant.

I'd heard it was possible to "buy" one's way into Canada with a significant investment in the local economy, but that wasn't even worth dwelling on. Another thing Canada looked for in its immigrants was the ability to speak both of its official languages, French and English. Obviously French wasn't a problem for Franck, but he spoke virtually no English besides the smattering of words I had taught him. As these were mostly swearwords, I didn't think they would be much help in his immigration application.

I glanced at the map on the seatback screen in front of me and wrinkled my nose at the dry, canned airplane air. Somebody was eating peanuts nearby, because everything smelled vaguely of peanut butter, something I hadn't eaten during my twelve months in France. Our route had us going down over Greenland and then skirting the northern tip of Québec before flying south over Winnipeg and Calgary, then into Vancouver.

Part of me was excited to eat a peanut butter sandwich on fresh sourdough bread and see the friends and family I hadn't seen for an entire year. At the same time apprehension scratched at me.

Who was I now? My year in France had changed me completely. I was scared the person I'd been in Burgundy would cease to exist once I was outside of France. I liked the person I'd become there: deeply in love for the first time in my life and determined to forge my own unconventional future. I much preferred her to that good girl I'd been before I left for France, full of intentions to follow the rules and make everybody happy.

Maybe it wasn't back home on my island in the Pacific that I could live my new self fully. Maybe that would have to wait until my plane landed back in the province I was flying over right now. I pressed my forehead against the window to see if I could catch a glimpse of Québec below me, my future home, and hopefully my future home with Franck. All I could see was a blanket of clouds as impenetrable as my future.

A few days later, I began crying again in the Thrifty's grocery store parking lot. My grief had come out of nowhere. One second I was happily going on a shopping trip with my mom and enjoying that cozy feeling of doing familiar things with people I loved, and the next I was struck with the reality that my life-changing year in Burgundy had somehow managed to bring me back here to my old life in Victoria, exactly where I had started. All of a sudden, I was openly weeping over the realization that perhaps my year in France hadn't changed anything at all.

My mom rubbed my back and unhooked my hands from around the bar of the shopping cart I was pushing in front of me. I could tell from her bewildered expression she was trying to understand what the hell was going on, but I couldn't stop the tears long enough to explain. My breath came in ragged gulps.

"How about you stay in the car while I get the groceries?" she suggested. "I'll be quick."

I nodded and she passed me the keys.

I slid into her Subaru that smelled the same it had always smelled—of warm plastic and mint chewing gum—and tried to collect myself.

Franck and I had talked on the phone that morning, and he told me that he'd visited all the Canadian embassies, consulates, and immigration offices in Paris before returning to Burgundy. His determination hadn't wavered one iota, but the news was not good. As we suspected, he did not fit the profile of an eligible immigrant to Canada. No-one he'd talked to had given him even the slightest sliver of hope.

There was comfort in seeing my family again and catching up with friends, but at the same time it felt like each minute I spent here in Victoria made my life in France—and my life with

Franck—recede a little bit further. Franck was slipping away like an ebb tide, and soon he would be beyond my reach. I tried to reason myself out of this panic that tightened around my chest like a rope, but I could only think of one thing. I couldn't get to Montréal fast enough.

chapter two

My father had accompanied my older sister Suzanne out East to help get her settled when she started university in Ontario three years before. With me, my parents figured after an entire year in France on my own this could be dispensed with. I was not offended in the slightest.

My plane left at an ungodly hour from the Victoria airport, but I was ready to be on it. Leaving for Montréal felt safer than staying in Victoria. After a summer of longing for Franck and being unsure who I was anymore in the context of my old life, I was headed to a new place where I could start completely fresh, and hopefully begin a new life with Franck. That was, if we could ever manage to get past the hurdles that still stood, seemingly impenetrable, between him and a permanent residency visa.

My family were a bit shiny eyed, but it was a pale imitation of when Suzanne had left for university the first time. After being away for a twelve-month stretch a mere term away felt like no big deal at all. I was wearing a jaunty suede Panama hat I had just bought, and had a hard time feigning sadness and containing my excitement. The past two months had felt like a parenthesis, but comfortable just didn't sit right anymore.

The flight sped by. I spent it ignoring the man beside me who showed every sign of being keen to grace me with an exegesis on Québec language politics. I clapped on my massive headphones and listened to a tape of Francis Cabrel Franck had sent me, while writing a letter telling him all my dreams of our future together in this city that was new for us both.

I practically skipped off the plane and grinned when I saw the "Bienvenue à Montréal" sign painted over the arrivals door. This was going to be *our* city. We had to make this work.

Outside the terminal, I took off my jaunty hat. It was a humid thirty or so degrees, something I wasn't expecting. I'd heard so much about the punishing winters in Montréal, but nobody had bothered to inform me about the summers.

I struggled to keep my massive suitcases from toppling off the trolley in the taxi line-up. Franck and I had a hell of a time getting my luggage through the metro turnstiles in Paris when he took me up to Charles de Gaulle to catch my plane back to Canada just eight weeks before, but apparently I was incorrigible when it came to overpacking.

As I waited in line, trying not to breathe too deeply because of the exhaust in the humid air, I remembered how Franck had heroically carried my bags almost single-handedly. The need to see him made my knees turn to rubber. I gazed back at the sliding arrivals door I had come through. Would he be arriving soon through there? I tried to conjure up how it would feel, seeing him again. I'd be nervous, because my heart whooshed at the mere thought. Behind that excitement though was a doubt—would we work as well here in Montréal as we had in Burgundy?

"*Bonjour!*" I greeted my taxi driver cheerily. "*Je vais à l'Université de McGill.*" Pleasure rippled through me at being able to speak French. Besides talking to Franck on the phone—and never for very long as the long-distance charges were stratospheric—I had barely spoken two words of French in Victoria. It made me feel closer to Franck to be conducting life in our shared language again.

The driver rubbed his scruffy beard and scowled at me. "Where are you from?" he asked me in heavily-accented English.

"British Columbia," I admitted. I was usually proud of my

beautiful province, but the way he asked made me feel ashamed that I was not a born and bred francophone. "But I can speak French."

He made a guttural sound of disapproval. "English Canadian, going to McGill?" he said, finally. "We will speak English."

His English accent was so terrible I was tempted to argue that my French was far better than his English (which it was), but then I thought better of it. I was vaguely aware there were tensions between the francophone and anglophone communities in Québec, and I knew that McGill, as a well-known anglophone university right in the heart of Montréal, was a controversial choice to many French-speaking Québecois. Before I decided where to plant my flag in the sand, I needed to get familiar with my new home. Maybe I should have listened more to my seatmate eager to discuss language politics on the flight.

"Fine," I said.

I decided to ignore the taxi driver's surly attitude. I watched the outskirts of the city roll by as I vacillated between hope and despair. So far all of Franck's attempts to find a way into Canada had failed. On the other hand, neither of us had ever mentioned giving up … yet.

I had told my parents about Franck, of course, but I had never given them details about what was going on in my personal life. I told them Franck was going to try to immigrate to Canada which, if it did come to pass, would freak them out. As things stood, however, I doubted they took the prospect any more seriously than anyone back in France did.

The taxi began to climb a steep hill. I caught a glimpse of the street sign, rue Université. We were driving alongside the McGill University campus. I had been in Montréal only once before—the previous year with my father when he combined a business trip to Toronto with a tour of eastern Canadian universities for me. I'd fallen in love with the crazy cultural fusion of Montréal and the traditional, yet wildly international feel of McGill.

The McGill campus could not have had a better location. It was nestled right downtown, at the foot of the glorious Mont Royal which provided a backdrop of trees—snowy when my dad and I had been there in January, but now a lush green.

The driver dropped me off at the very top of the hill, in front of a cluster of three buildings. They were all identical, and none of them would have looked out of place in a catalogue of communist architecture. The same dreary curtains in the windows, some shut, some open, and the same industrial materials used in an era when a heavy-handed use of asbestos was considered a selling point.

These were the three residences on the hill, all of which had a reputation of being ugly but extremely fun places to live. I had been assigned to Molson Hall, named after one of Canada's well-known breweries. I personally found it hilarious to live in a university residence named after a brand of beer—that smacked of the blatant flouting of rules I had fallen in love with in France.

The taxi driver turned around in his seat and grimaced at me. "Thirty dollars."

Even though he was being an asshat I still couldn't bring myself to leave no tip. I couldn't decide if the decent tip was a result of my moral conscience or my pushover heart. As I plucked out two twenties from my wallet I caught a glimpse of the beautiful fifty franc bill I kept in there. It was a stunning color of cornflower blue with an illustration of Antoine de Saint-Exupéry and Le Petit Prince on it. I'd kept it as a talisman, promising myself that I would get back to France and spend it. I tucked it away again and passed the Canadian bills to the driver.

He counted it, then went around to the back of the taxi, where he hauled out my two enormous suitcases.

"*Bonne chance*," he muttered in French, making it sound as though he knew I was already doomed, then roared off. I stared after him, wondering if it was the tip that had made him change his mind about speaking to me in English.

I studied my surroundings. I had been left on what looked like a concrete driveway about fifty feet from the front door of my residence. The block letters above the front door spelled out MOLSON HO SE. The silver "U" in HOUSE had fallen off at some point, or maybe been wrenched off and spirited elsewhere as a prank. I glanced down at my two massive bags. How on earth was I ever going to get these inside Molson Hose, my new home?

Franck, my luggage-whisperer, wasn't here, so I would have to figure this out myself. I half pushed, half dragged the first suitcase into the lobby, and walking out to the second my arms felt like they were going to drop out of their sockets and I could feel sweat dripping behind my ears. It was *so* humid. There seemed to be almost nobody else around. I knew I was arriving two days earlier than most people, but I never expected to arrive to a ghost town.

I stood for a minute by my second suitcase, pausing to take a bracing breath before dragging it inside.

I felt a tap on my shoulder and turned to see a tall, lanky girl with chocolate brown eyes and a chestnut bob. "Jesus," she said, looking down at my bag. "Did you pack a corpse in there?"

I sighed. "I know. I know. I packed way too much."

She stuck out her hand. "I'm Anne. Which house are you in?"

"Molson."

"Molson Hose?" *Ah. So I wasn't the only one who found the missing U amusing.* "Me too. There's almost nobody here, you know. My university experience has been seriously anticlimactic so far. I bought a giant box of condoms at Costco, but I haven't been getting my money's worth, that's for sure."

"Oh … bummer." I wasn't exactly shocked about the sudden turn of the conversation, but it did catch me off guard. Oh well. If Anne was a sexually liberated woman, all the more power to her. This was university after all. To each their own. "Do you know where I sign in?" I asked.

"Yeah." She pointed to the round, equally Stalinequse building behind us. "That's the cafeteria. You need to check in there. Do you need help? I'll come with you. I'm really bored."

Twenty minutes later, Anne and I shoved my suitcases into my new room on the seventh floor. I felt grateful for two things: Anne lived on the same floor, and the freight elevator in the building was working. My luggage seemed to take up all the space in the room, which with its cinder block walls and humming ceiling light, did boast a certain prison-cell *je ne sais quoi.*

"Pretty bad, eh?" Anne said, hands on her hips. "At least all the rooms are equally appalling." She threw open the grungy yellow curtains that had some sort of unidentifiable brown spots all over them and looked out. "At least you look onto Mont Royal. That will be nice when the leaves start to turn."

I grew up on an island of ancient rainforests, so the green that filled my window was a welcome sight. I turned around to take in the full effect of my room. I shook my head at the concrete block walls. "You'd think they could have at least painted them over."

"I know," Anne agreed. "Maybe making it look like a priest's cell is supposed to make us study harder?"

"Maybe."

"I don't know about you, but I'm going to work hard and have *a lot* of sex."

I wasn't sure what to say. "So … no boyfriend, I'm guessing?"

She guffawed. "In my first year of university? I'm not crazy. I'm free as a bird and I like it that way. I love sex."

"Um … good for you." I couldn't really think of what else to say to that.

"Do you have a boyfriend?" she asked, and then her eyes lit up. "Or maybe you're a lesbian?"

I shook my head. "Sorry to disappoint." I felt like I was letting her down by being straight, just like I had let down the taxi driver by being anglophone. Good God. I hated that I was such a WASP. "I do have a boyfriend, but unfortunately he's still in France. We're doing everything we can to get him here, though."

"Why?"

I was cracking open the window to let in some fresh air. This place smelled like Windex overlaying stale beer farts. "What do you mean *why*?"

"Why on earth would you want a boyfriend in university? Or a girlfriend for that matter? This is our time to play the field, have fun. You will be denying yourself the smorgasbord and that, my new friend, is tragic."

I didn't know what to answer. I knew that getting so serious about someone at eighteen wasn't exactly ideal. I had been brought up to be capable and independent and I understood in theory that my exclusivity with Franck would mean I was bypassing a lot of other formative experiences.

"I wasn't planning on meeting someone this early," I said. "I never thought this would happen to me so soon but … well … we fell so hard for each other. I just can't throw that away."

Anne drew her eyebrows together. "I still don't get it, especially when he's not even here."

I shrugged. "It's hard to understand myself sometimes. Anyway, apologies for not being a lesbian."

She twitched her right shoulder. "I guess it's not your fault."

I took my hat off and put it down on the melamine counter of my built-in desk. Everything was built in—the desk, the drawers, the closet. At least I didn't have to buy any furniture. I ran my fingers through my hair to fluff out my sweaty hat-head. Anne plopped herself down on the bed. A thrill ran through me. Maybe Franck would join me in that bed sometime soon, although it seemed awfully narrow.

"Is that bed *smaller* than a regular twin bed?" I asked.

Anne peered down on the bare mattress she was perched on. "Yup. They're also super lumpy and uncomfortable. Not easy for sex, especially with tall guys, let me tell you."

"I thought you said you hadn't used your Costco condoms?"

She flipped her shiny chestnut hair. "Well, maybe a few, but not nearly as many as I hoped … yet."

I wasn't sure if this was bravado or the truth, but Anne was the only person around to show me the ropes, and I didn't really much care. There was a knock on the door.

"Come in?" I said, but it came out as a question rather than an invitation. I didn't know anyone in the residence besides Anne.

The door creaked open and a tall guy with wavy blond hair poked his head in. "I heard your voices," he said. He looked over at me and paused for a few seconds, then shook his head. Maybe he was travel-weary and feeling a bit spacy like me. "Hi. I'm James. I live down the hall and I heard Anne's voice."

Anne waved her hand between me and the newcomer. "Laura,

meet James. James, meet Laura. James and I have been hanging out because we've been pretty much alone in this ghost town."

The puzzle piece clicked. Here was the tall person who was tricky to have sex with on the tiny residence bed.

"It's a pleasure." He nodded at me with a gleam in his eye. Uh oh. This guy was a player. "You guys hungry? I'm heading over to Saint Laurent to find some dinner. Wanna come?" His brown eyes stayed fixed on me. "The food service at the cafeteria doesn't start until next week."

I put my hand over my stomach. I hadn't eaten since Vancouver with all the excitement of arriving and moving in. Reminded, my stomach rumbled. "Actually, I'm starving. I guess I haven't eaten since British Columbia."

Anne stood up and brushed dust that must have come from my mattress off her jean shorts. "You ready?" she asked me.

I gazed over at my still unpacked suitcases. "I guess I can deal with those later."

"There's plenty of time for that," James said. "Besides, Mont-réal is waiting for you, Laura."

chapter three

It was a fifteen-minute walk to the boulevard Saint-Laurent. I didn't know the way, of course, but I just tagged along behind Anne and James, who had apparently been going there for most of their meals.

We'd been accosted by Sam, my floor fellow, on the way out. He was one of those overly enthusiastic sorts. I could just tell he'd be guilty of abusing exclamation marks in his written assignments. He was obviously thrilled to be a floor fellow and was the type that would likely stay in residence for all four years of his degree, despite the fact that rental accommodation was dirt cheap and plentiful in Montréal.

Anne was skillful in getting rid of him and told us as we walked along that she had already slept with him on her first night in town but wasn't interested in a repeat performance.

The air smelled so different. It wasn't saturated with the salty tang of the ocean like it was back home, or rich with the mineral scent of limestone as in Burgundy. Montréal was redolent of birch trees and hot sidewalks.

As we walked, we exchanged basic details about ourselves such as where we came from and where we'd gone to high school. Coincidentally enough, it turned out James had also just come back from an exchange year with Ursus, but he'd been to Portugal. He'd been sent by one of the Ursus clubs in Ottawa, where he lived with his parents who were diplomats. We compared our experiences and mine was hands down the better one.

He had been placed with a series of disastrous families and

he'd never been able to win over the other students at his high school. I found this hard to believe, as he was an unquestionably handsome guy. He was someone I might have found attractive if I wasn't already in love with Franck. That, and the fact he was a player who had already slept with Anne.

I laughed. "Surely some of the girls liked you?"

James stopped in his tracks, and my face burned. Maybe I didn't know him well enough to joke like that yet.

"Why would you say that?" he said.

"Nothing." I shook my head, cursing my overfamiliar sense of humor. "I was just kidding around. Forget it."

He smiled then. "Sorry. You just caught me off guard."

We started walking again, much to my relief.

"There were a few girls who followed me around everywhere," he continued, looking at his feet. "But they were never the ones I actually wanted to talk to."

"What kind of girls interest you then, James?" Anne asked, with a certain arch playfulness. "I got the impression you have extremely high standards."

Why had I even brought this up? Maybe it hadn't ended amicably when James and Anne got together. I certainly had no desire to stir up a lovers' quarrel.

"I suppose you speak fluent Portuguese now," I said, desperate to change the subject.

"I do." He smiled "Although I'm not sure how useful that's going to be for me here in Montréal."

I started peppering Anne with questions as we crossed over Aylmer and Durocher and Hutchinson streets. I had a terrible sense of direction, so I was trying to commit street names to memory. Meanwhile, I learned Anne hailed from Toronto and had done a fascinating sounding thesis for Grade 13 on the poetry in the lyrics of Leonard Cohen.

We heard the buzzing voices and music spilling from the boulevard Saint-Laurent about a block away.

"The street is shut off to cars one week a year," Anne said. This explained why the restaurant tables spilled and people were sitting cross-legged on the yellow line between the two lanes, drinking glasses of wine.

We decided on a pizza place just off the junction between Prince Arthur and Saint-Laurent.

Right at the junction there was an oddly dressed woman wearing a massive black hat that looked like it had been snatched directly off the head of Miss Havisham in Dickens's *Great Expectations*. She was playing a harmonica tunelessly, just sliding it from one side of her mouth to the other in a strange, two-toned dirge.

"What's that all about?" I asked as we waited to be seated.

"That's the harmonica lady," James said. "She's a bit of a local legend. She's there most of the time, even in winter."

"How strange," I said.

"Montréal is strange," Anne said. "That's probably the thing I love most about it. It's like nowhere else."

We were pointed to a table and I asked for their wine list. I perused it and decided on a simple Côtes du Rhône–to be honest, there wasn't much choice. I was beginning to realize how my time in Burgundy had turned me into a wine snob. I didn't like feeling pretentious, but the truth of the matter was that I had tasted so much fine wine, my taste buds were now difficult to satisfy. Before I left for France, I would have been perfectly delighted with plonk from a box.

"Is that OK?" I asked them after the waiter had taken in orders.

"It's more expensive than I'm used to," said Anne. "But I'm in a celebratory mood tonight."

I reminded myself I had to quickly adjust to my new budget as a university student. I had worked as a bank teller during my six weeks home to pay for my tuition, books, and some of my living expenses. I was grateful my parents helped me with money every month for groceries as well as covering my rent.

"Did you drink any good wines in Portugal?" I asked James. I was eager to dispel any awkwardness between us because of my dumb joke.

"Some, but the port ..." He sighed. "I drank some amazing bottles of that."

The wine came and it went down nicely. It went down even better when our pizzas arrived fresh from a stone pizza oven. As dusk began to fall, the noise and frenzy of the street seemed to amp up, and the scent of spilt cocktails and beer mixed in the warm air. I was buzzing with energy for the first time since leaving France. Maybe it was the French wine, maybe it was being in a city halfway closer to him, but I felt as though Franck was so close I could almost reach out and touch him. I could imagine him here, sitting beside me, enjoying this city that was brand new for both of us. An ache of longing washed through me, but it had an edge of sweetness as well as pain. I was lucky to have found someone I loved enough to miss this much.

Our conversation began to get more personal as we ordered another bottle of wine and some tiramisu for dessert. I poured out my story of Franck and me and our thunderbolt love affair and how we were both determined to get him to Montréal so we could be together.

As I talked, James seemed to get quieter and quieter, and Anne eventually seemed to be getting bored of my love story.

"Don't tell me you have a girlfriend back in Portugal," Anne said to James.

"No." He looked down into his wine glass and blushed.

"At home in Ottawa?"

He shook his head. "Nope. Why?"

"Then why wouldn't you sleep with me?"

"Wait," I said, laughing. "I thought you two *had* slept together." I turned to Anne. "Weren't you talking about James when you were saying how difficult it was to have sex with a tall guy in a residence bed?"

"What?" James yelped.

"No!" Anne said.

"Who then?" I asked.

Anne waved her hand. "Someone else. A guy from the basketball team who got here early for pre-season training. Aren't you going to tell her, James?"

"Tell me what?" I asked.

"No, I wasn't." James sighed. "Because I happen to be gentleman."

"Well, thank God I'm no lady." Anne cocked her head at me without a trace of embarrassment. "I propositioned James the first night we met. He turned me down. Can you believe that? The nerve."

"But … why?" I asked James.

"He's not into guys, if that's what you're wondering," Anne answered.

"I wasn't, but I still don't get it," I said. "Most men I know around our age don't usually turn down no-strings-attached sex."

"I have my reasons," James said, giving me an odd look. "And they're private."

Anne hissed to me in a whisper so loud that it defeated the purpose of a whisper in the first place. "I think he's a closet romantic. He's waiting for Mrs. Right." She stuck a finger in her mouth and mimicked vomiting.

"Do you really think your boyfriend will be able to get his immigration papers for Canada?" James asked, ignoring Anne. "Living in Ottawa, I've heard that's extremely difficult. Impossible, sometimes."

I began picking the label off our almost empty wine bottle. "I know it's going to be hard. We both do, but what we have between us … well, we can't just let it peter out." The idea that this was even a possibility stabbed my heart like a sword. "It's too good, what we have."

"Well, good luck," James said.

Anne snapped her fingers as the waiter returned to tidy up the dregs of our table and bring us our bills. "I don't feel like going back to Molson Hose yet. How about a club?"

James groaned.

I was still on West Coast time, which was three hours earlier, so I was feeling surprisingly energetic. "I'm in." Besides, I had to get to know this city so that I could show it to Franck when he came.

"I've heard there's a fabulous one on the rue Saint-Denis," Anne said, standing up and adjusting her breasts in her bra. "It's only a few minutes' walk from here."

"What's it called?" James asked.

"The name is in French and my French isn't very good, but it's called Les Foufounes Electriques. She butchered the pronunciation, but there was no mistaking it.

Both James and I burst out laughing.

"You know what that means too?" I asked him.

He nodded, still grinning. "My French slang is pretty good, having grown up in Ottawa."

"What does it mean?" Anne stamped her foot.

James and I exchanged a look and then started laughing again.

"I'm not explaining that," I said, gasping for breath. "You go right ahead."

"Are you kidding me?" James said. "Forget it."

"Come on!" Anne pleaded. "Now you have to tell me."

I shook my head. "Nope. I wouldn't even know where I'd begin."

"Come on." James got up and reached down for my hand to help me up out of my seat. Maybe it was an odd gesture between friends, but somehow it felt natural. "Let's go. Anne, I'm sure we can find someone there who will explain it to you."

Off we went, three new friends into the warm, loud Montréal night.

chapter four

A week later, I had managed to arrange to have a phone line set up in my room, which meant I no longer had to talk to Franck on the pay phone in the not-at-all-private residence lobby anymore. Sam the floor fellow always seemed to be lurking around the lobby of our floor, and unfortunately he spoke French.

We talked every day and I was growing desperate for a glimmer of hope. He had just arrived in Paris the day before to take another stab at the Canadian consulates and immigration offices. So far, nothing. It was almost torture to hear his voice when I longed to feel his arms around me and the light touch of his lips on mine. We ended our phone call with promises of our love for each other and forced positivity. We reiterated our determination to be together again soon.

After I hung up, I sat on my bed with my back against the cinder block wall, fighting a tight feeling around my heart. I took another sip of the cider in my hand. The guy in the next room was blasting ACDC's "Back in Black" on repeat and it sounded like he had at least twenty people partying in there—all yelling at one another over the punishing thumps of the bass.

I hated this weird limbo. It was frosh week at McGill, and everyone except me was partying and having random hook-ups with new people. I had fun with James and Anne—the three of us had become fast friends after that hilarious night at Foufounes Electriques, dancing with drag queens and all of Montréal's glorious variety of people, but I still felt as though my life as a university student in Montréal hadn't truly begun. I was stuck in this weird limbo until things with Franck were clearer. Until then, half of me, and more than half of my heart, was still with him in France.

He'd told me he was taking odd jobs: packing boxes full of wine at a local winery at night, as well as sticking labels on wine bottles at another winery and he was geared up to do the grape harvest as soon as that started. He was trying to put as much money aside as he could for a plane ticket.

I finished my cider and then got another from the mini-fridge that sat under my window with the view out to Mont Royal. There was the huge residence-wide party tonight and it sounded like it was getting into gear from the noise outside my room. I supposed I would venture out in the halls in a while, but I just needed a little longer to work through my heartache.

After a few minutes, there was a knock at the door.

"Come in!" I yelled.

It opened, and James walked in. He gave me long look and then sat down on the bed beside me. "What's up?" he asked.

I let out a gusty sigh. "I'm sad and a bit drunk."

He reached over and squeezed my arm. "What are you doing drinking alone in your bedroom? That's not like you."

I was finding friendships here at university formed fast. We spent so much time together, and one thing we learned about each other early on was our drinking habits. I was not a heavy drinker. I seemed to possess an internal off switch after two or three drinks. James was right, this was maybe the first time in my life I had ever drunk alone.

"I wasn't exactly alone. I just got off the phone with Franck."

"Oh," James said, looking down at my turquoise duvet. "And?"

"He's gone back up to Paris trying to find some way to be able to come to Canada, but he's striking out again. I just don't know what to do. I'm so frustrated I can't really do anything from here."

James looked up at me again. His eyes held a strange expression. "That's a shame. When I saw you with that cider I thought maybe … I thought maybe you guys broke up."

That notion shocked me to my core. No matter how much despair I felt, I had never considered breaking up with Franck. I was quite sure from our conversations and letters that he hadn't considered breaking up with me either. I shook my head. "No. Why would you think that?"

James shrugged, squirming a bit on the bed. "What you two are trying to do is so difficult. I don't know. Maybe it was just wishful thinking."

I nudged him playfully with my foot. "What are you talking about? Why would you want Franck and I to break up? Are *you* drunk? Unless—"

James was looking at me, an intent expression sharpening his features. His true motivation finally sunk in.

"Oh." Now it was my turn to look down at the duvet. I could suddenly feel the tension in the room, tension I had been oblivious of until that moment. "You mean … do you mean you like me? That can't be it—"

But James nodded. All at once, he looked as sad as I had been feeling. "I am crazy in love with you, Laura. Did you really have no idea?"

Still in shock over this surprise confession, I thought back. "No. None." All my romantic feelings had been so focused on Franck that perhaps I wasn't picking up on other signals. "But how? When?"

"From that first moment I saw you when I popped into your dorm room to ask you and Anne if you wanted to go eat dinner. He put his fist to his chest. "It hit me out of nowhere."

"But we're just friends," I insisted, feeling tipsy and disoriented and wanting more than anything to go back to the simplicity of our friendship.

"You were friends with me," he said. "But I've been falling in love with you since that first night."

I was certainly not a woman who was used to surprise declarations of love from men. Maybe the fact that I was already taken and not interested radiated from me, giving me some sort of newfound allure. "Is it because I'm already taken? I know some men like a challenge."

He jerked back as though I'd slapped him. "Even if you don't feel the same, don't mock me."

Chastised, I reached out and touched his cheek. "James, that came out wrong. I'm sorry. I guess I just can't understand the why of it."

"You mean, why do I want to kiss you right now?" he asked, frustrated. "Because your eyes change color every few minutes and you've read all of *Les Misérables* in French and you come out with these witty zingers that make me laugh and look at the world differently."

I don't know exactly what I'd expected for an explanation, but not that. Not something so heartfelt. If there had never been a Franck, I might have been tempted. I wondered briefly what it would be like to come here as a single person, and then to have James confess that he loved me. I would have been interested. Definitely.

"I am so, so flattered—" I began.

James closed his eyes and put out his palm to stop me. "I shouldn't have said anything."

But I owed him the truth. "If there was no Franck, I would probably feel the same about you."

He opened his deep brown eyes again. "I hate to admit this, but I sort of hate Franck and I've never even met him."

Given what James had just told me, I felt it would be a good thing if the two never met. "I'm so sorry," I said, meaning it. As long as there was Franck, there could never be anything between me and James.

His eyes softened. "I know you are. Can you make me one promise though?"

"Of course," I said, hating to see my friend like this, and hating even more that I was the cause.

"If you and Franck do break up, can you … Can you just let me know?"

"We're not going to break up," I said, trying to put it gently.

"Maybe," he said. "Maybe not. But can you promise me that?"

I nodded. "Sure." It was an easy enough promise, as Franck

and I were going to stay together whatever it took. It was the only solace I could give James in that moment. Still, after making it, I wondered if I wasn't being disloyal to Franck somehow.

"C'mon." I stood up. Nothing good could come from the two of us in my room together after what James had just confessed. "We should go out and be social, even if we don't feel like it."

He stood up reluctantly. I was suddenly acutely aware of his height and his eyes on me. They were full of a yearning that I realized with confusion had to do with me.

I needed to break this spell. "Let's go and find you an interesting girl," I said, giving him an awkward push on his shoulder. "I'm sure I'm not the only person around here who has read *Les Misérables*."

"In French."

"Maybe there's a person out there who has read it in Chinese. Who knows?"

"There's no point," he said, shaking his head. He turned the doorknob. A guy in a profound state of inebriation lurched down the hallway wearing a gold party hat and no pants. I was grateful to this strange, drunk student—the spell was now broken.

"C'mon." James turned and gave me a final, sad smile. "Let's go find Anne."

I was grateful that classes started two days later as things remained awkward between me and James, and I figured it would be easier when we were both busier. Neither of us had told Anne and went along with the pretense that the friendship between the three of us was exactly as it was before.

I avoided being alone with James. I would often get away by saying I had to go and call Franck or write him a letter. James would inevitably shoot me a wounded look, but he needed me to remind him to realize that Franck and I were still very much together. Maybe I needed reminding too, because there were moments when the idea of Franck was becoming frighteningly abstract.

At the end of my first week of classes, I confessed to Franck what had happened with James, reiterating that I had unequivocally turned him down.

Instead of being mad, he sighed. "Something similar happened to me."

"It did?" I demanded, jealousy clamping down on my lungs.

"*Oui*. My friend Nathanial called me up a few days ago and invited me to go out with him. He was down from Paris, in Dijon visiting his parents and I hadn't seen him in forever, so I said yes. He gave me no indication that it wouldn't be just the two of us. Sneaky bastard. I had a night off from my job packing boxes and borrowed my parents' car to meet him in Dijon that evening."

"And?" I said. I was tense with dread. "He wasn't alone?"

"No. He came with a date—his new girlfriend, I guess, although it doesn't seem serious. A blonde girl with huge French braids—I can't even remember her name, just that she looked like a milkmaid in one of those Swiss chocolate commercials."

"And?" I could sense Franck was putting off telling me the next part.

"She brought a friend of hers as a blind date for me."

A blind date? That needled my heart. Franck and I had met on a blind date set up by his sister Stéphanie. The blind date thing was *our* story, not his story with this other girl. "What was her name?" I asked, my voice coming out strangled.

"Ahhhhhhh ..." Franck said. "Aurélie? Or maybe Amélie? I can't remember."

"What was she like?" I better understood James in that moment. I didn't know this girl, but I hated her with all my heart.

Franck sighed. "She wasn't you, Laura. That's all that matters to me."

A surge of love broke through the jealousy. "*Je t'aime*," I whispered.

"Anyway, I explained to her right away that I was not interested in a date, and that Nathaniel had set this up without my knowledge. I told her all about you. I don't think it was at all the kind of night she was hoping for, but she was gracious about it. I have to give her credit for that."

On second thought, I hated Nathaniel in that moment more than Franck's blind date. "How did Nathaniel react? *Conard*."

Franck didn't disagree with my insulting epithet for his best friend. "I got angrier with him than I ever have. I told him off and demanded why he would do such a thing behind my back when he knew I was still with you."

"And?"

Franck sighed again. "He basically said what I've been hearing from everybody else: that he didn't believe things between you and me could last, given the distance, and he thought he was doing me a favor to stop me from miserably pining."

"Bastard. I bet he was surprised." Nathaniel was a notorious womanizer.

"He was. But the night wasn't a complete bust. Like I said, I spent the entire evening talking about you and how I was trying to get to Canada, and my blind date gave me a tip that I'm going to follow up on next week in Paris. I've already bought my train ticket."

Hope raced through me. "What is it?"

"She said she had a second cousin who, like me, didn't qualify as an immigrant when he applied to the Canadian embassy, but that he got in another way. Apparently there is this organization in Paris called La Délégation du Québec and they help franco-phone immigrants interested in moving to Québec. Something to do with the need to preserve the French language. Apparently if I go through them the standards applied to me won't be the same as if I went through the main Canadian offices."

"That's amazing. Do you think it could work?"

I could almost hear him give one of his trademark shrugs over the phone. "I can't know, but I know that I'm going to try. I'm not going to give up until I find that one person that will get me in so that we can be together. *Je t'aime*, Laura."

"I love you too," I said. "And I'm not going to give up either. But this distance thing. This is hard."

"I know *mon amour*," he whispered. "But we are going to

make this work. *D'accord?*"

"*D'accord*," I agreed.

The line went quiet for a moment, which left just the static of transatlantic phone calls.

"I have to say," he said finally, in a rougher voice. "I'm not in love with the thought of this James guy living on the same floor as you."

"Don't worry," I said. "I was very clear when I turned him down. I don't think he'll try again."

Franck didn't say anything for a moment. "I wouldn't be so sure."

"Don't worry. I'm with you."

"I'm coming for you," Franck said, his voice strained. "You have to believe that, Laura."

"I do."

chapter five

The leaves on Mont Royal above the University had begun to change color into a riotous mix of scarlet, yellow, and orange.

On the West Coast leaves stayed green until the fall rains started, at which point they fell off the deciduous trees in sodden, moldering clumps on the sidewalks. I had never before experienced the glory of an East Coast fall and I wished that Franck was there to see it with me.

I walked up the avenue McGill College from the post office, where I had just mailed off a second care package for Franck. This one was full of McGill swag—a keychain, a mug, and a hoodie, plus love letters and a cassette tape of Spirit of the West and the Tragically Hip—two Canadian bands that I loved and felt would help in Franck's eventual cultural immersion into Canadian life.

All my classes were well underway, and I was academically happier than I had ever been in my life. The English professors at McGill were charismatic and brilliant, and I was also trying out courses in History, Religious Studies, and Philosophy of Feminism to dabble in a few other things. None of my essays were due for another month, so basically, I just had reading for homework. For my English classes, that was a complete joy. I had never looked at learning as a means to an end. I loved learning for its own sake, and for that delicious sensation of my mind growing and becoming more insightful.

I paused at the gray stone university gates that flanked the entrance to the main campus and took a lungful of crisp fall air. The sky was pure blue without a cloud in sight. It provided a stunning backdrop to the blaze of color on the mountain. Even though I still felt like I was leading a split life—my heart in France with Franck and my mind and body here in Montréal—I adored being a McGill student.

Someone tapped my shoulder. I spun around to see Anne and James. Anne was smiling at me, and James's eyes were darting around, trying not to land on my face.

"Are you day-dreaming about Franck?" Anne asked with a grin.

"Yes," I answered bluntly, aware that James might need to hear this. "I'm just coming back from mailing him a care package."

James wore a pained expression on his face. "Lucky guy."

"Anyway, enough with the drippy love stuff. Do you have time for a coffee before your next class?" Anne linked her arm around mine.

I smiled back. "Always."

We began to walk up the central pathway up to the Leacock building, where there was a coffee vendor in the basement.

"Are you going to the English survey next?" James said.

I remembered he was in the same class as me. It was a typical first year class in an amphitheater with at least two hundred and fifty students. "Yup."

"Great. We can go together."

"Awesome," I said, though I wasn't really thinking that. More than anything, I wished James had kept his feelings to himself. He had been a wonderful friend, and I missed that.

James and I made our way into the amphitheater for our English class after we left Anne downstairs at the coffee stand. She barely waved us goodbye, as she was busy flirting with the cute barista.

"I have to admire Anne's stamina," James said, keeping pace beside me. "She seems inexhaustible in her capacity to pick up men."

I chuckled. "It's a shame there's not an Olympics for that. She'd win a gold medal for sure."

A whoosh of relief made me feel giddy. Things, for the first time since that night in my res room, felt normal between us. I remembered how much I enjoyed James as a friend.

"Sometimes I wonder if she'll ever settle on one person, or if she'll just continue experimenting for the rest of her life," I mused as we found some seats near the aisle around halfway up the amphitheater.

"I don't know," James said, taking his notebook and huge textbook out of his backpack. "I suppose if she's going to experiment, we're in the prime years for doing that. Most people aren't as committed as you are at this stage in their lives." His tone was completely neutral. Finally. We were on safe ground again.

I sighed. "You know what's strange? I never expected this to happen to me. I never had a serious boyfriend in high school. It just kind of ... all came together all at once." I still wondered at this sometimes. Meeting Franck had been such a lightning bolt out of nowhere. Part of me was still in shock that I had met and fallen in love with someone at eighteen. "Nobody was as surprised as me. Did you have a girlfriend in high school?"

James bit his lip as he turned to the first page of the Beowulf excerpt we were studying. "Yup. Isabella. We went out for about a year but things ended naturally between us at the end of Grade Twelve. We're still friends though."

"It's nice when things can end amicably."

"It is." He gave me a warm smile. I was going to take that as a peace offering.

Objectively, I could see how crazy it sounded to be in my first year of university with a twenty-two-year-old boyfriend abroad. Sometimes I worried I was doing myself a disservice somehow by limiting myself to one man during these years when I should be discovering all sorts of people. Not like Anne—I just didn't think such a ... varied ... love life was part of my emotional hardware— but some experimenting anyway. The thing is, it wasn't just some twenty-two-year-old foreign boyfriend. It was Franck, and that made all the difference. But a nagging doubt circled back into my head: here in Montréal, would Franck and I be able to recapture the magic we'd had in France?

"What are you so deep in thought about?" James nudged me with his arm.

"Beowulf," I lied.

He snorted.

"Believe it," I said, deadpan. "That Old English or Norse or whatever it is. Riveting. "Hwæt. We Gardena in geardagum, þeodcyninga, þrym gefrunon, hu ða æþelingas ellen fremedon." I recited from the textbook, surely massacring the pronunciation.

James stared at me, a smile hovering at the corner of his mouth. "Speaking Old Norse is so sexy, Laura. Is that how you got Franck to fall in love with you?"

Finally! We were joking around like I would with Anne. I was awash with relief to have James back—the old James. I'd missed him. "Actually, I didn't seduce him with Old Norse," I said. "It was tapdancing."

"Tapdancing?" He leaned forward towards me, his fist under his chin. "OK, this I have to hear."

Unfortunately, the professor called the class to order, so I wasn't able to expand on that night I'd first met Franck in Nuits-Saint-Georges, when he and Stéphanie and their gang of friends came to pick me up just as I'd finished a tap-dancing recital at the town theatre. The Beowulf lecture commenced. This prof was known to dump huge amounts of information fast, so we both furiously had to start taking notes.

For the next hour I was sucked into the world of warriors and Norse gods until the man finally finished up his lecture and James and I collapsed back in our seats. I shook out my right hand to stop the cramping in my fingers.

I looked over to see James scribbling something on his note-book, probably some last thought that he needed to get down before it escaped his mind. I massaged my palm and then stretched out my back. It ached from being hunched over for so long.

"Do you have anything after this?" I asked James. I had to go to my Philosophy class.

"Art History," he answered, and ripped off the bit of paper he'd been writing on. "I'll see you later I guess." He collected his books and slid them into his backpack.

"Yup," I said, gathering my things together. He was closest to the aisle, so got up first. The last thing he did before leaving was drop that crumpled bit of paper on the desk in front of me.

"That's for you," he said.

"What?"

"Just read it," he said, his brown eyes pleading. "Please."

He sprinted down the amphitheater stairs, away from me.

With a sinking heart I opened the piece of paper.

On it was written in James's messy writing, "I've tried, but I just can't stop being in love with you. I'm sorry."

chapter six

As the days wore into weeks and the leaves on Mont Royal reached their peak and then began to drop, Franck slipped further and further away. His trip to Paris hadn't been entirely fruitless. He had met a woman who told him he needed to talk to a different woman—her colleague—who was currently vacationing in Turkey.

"If anyone can help you, she can," the woman at the Délégation du Québec had told Franck. "I'll make an appointment for you in three weeks' time when she gets back."

Franck agreed, of course. We had to grasp onto hope wherever we found it, even when it felt flimsy. James didn't say anything further to me after leaving me the note, but I could tell from a look he would give me, every once in a while when others weren't paying attention, that he was still interested and biding his time. I could have used his friendship. My despair grew with every day that went by without Franck.

My parents and my little sister Jayne were due to arrive that afternoon for a visit. My older sister Suzanne and her boyfriend were coming from Ottawa to meet us in Montréal. None of them asked about Franck anymore. I supposed they all thought our break-up was inevitable and they didn't want to stir up sadness for me.

They were wrong.

We were not giving up. I held on to that. Maybe that woman Franck had an appointment with would be our savior. The three-week wait was almost over and he was going up to Paris the next day. If this didn't work out, I wondered what else we could try. We were running out of avenues.

That night, all together for the first time since the summer, we enjoyed a spectacular family meal at a fabulous restaurant called Les Filles Du Roy in the cobblestone streets of Old Town Montréal. The food was all local, and we finished up with caramelized maple tarts—something I had never eaten before.

I laughed inwardly, thinking about how Franck would find it amusing to hear my parents gush about the unthinkable age of the building that housed the restaurant, which dated back to 1750 or so. For someone who was used to using stones in his slingshots from Gallo-Roman ruins in the woods where he played as a boy, 1750 was practically modern.

We were well into the maple tart at the end of the meal when my mom slid me a look. "No news about Franck coming?"

I shook my head, surprised that she ventured to ask me about it. Something stopped me from sharing the news that he was imminently meeting with the woman who may hold the key to getting him his papers. It was superstitious of me, but I didn't want to jinx this last hope. Besides, I knew my parents would probably be happier to hear that Franck and I had abandoned our plan to stay together. I could hardly blame them. Given what they had seen of my past boyfriends, scarce as they had been, I could understand why they were wary of this mystery Frenchman.

"Nothing yet," I said.

"Maybe for the best?" she said gently.

I shrugged. I couldn't put into words how I ached for Franck or make them understand why we needed to be together. I knew it would all sound like nonsense from a lovestruck teenager. Besides, I had found that in my relationship with Franck, and I wanted those words to just be between the two of us anyway. I supposed that was part of moving from dependence to independence:

keeping some of my head and heart for myself alone.

The next day, Franck and I scheduled a phone call for just after he met with the woman at the Québec delegation. With our six-hour time difference between Paris and Montréal, I was pacing around my dorm room ten o'clock in the morning, skipping my Philosophy of Feminism class and cracking my knuckles—something I only did when I was extremely nervous.

Thank God I had finally managed to get my own phone line installed in my residence room. Franck had told me the Délégation du Québec where his meeting was set at three o'clock in the afternoon was located in the posh 16th arrondissement. He would find the nearest pay-phone as soon as he got out.

Ten o'clock Montréal time ticked by, then ten fifteen, then ten thirty … Was Franck not calling because the meeting had been yet another dead end and he didn't know how to tell me he was giving up on us? Still, he had promised that he would call, *no matter what.*

Maybe that first meeting had led to another meeting, or perhaps he'd been sent somewhere else … or maybe he was sitting on the Paris sidewalk with his head in his hands, trying to find the right words to let me down easily. I felt like I was going to explode from all the possibilities roiling inside me.

I willed the phone to ring, then willed it not to ring if the call contained bad news. But still, even bad news would be better than being stuck in this terrible limbo.

Finally, the shrill jangle of the phone sliced through the torture. I grabbed it before the first ring had even finished.

"*Allô?* Franck?" I yelped down the line.

"*C'est moi,*" he said, sounding cheerful. That was good, wasn't it?

"*Alors?*" I asked. *So?*

"We did it!" The tone of his voice told me he was bursting

with emotion. All of a sudden, his essential Franck-ness rushed back at me. I could see that sparkle in his eye and the quirk of his mouth like he was here in my room with me.

"What?" I gasped. "Tell me everything or I'm going to die."

As it turned out, all the hopes we had pinned on this woman at the Délégation Québec had been justified. Franck had gone into the meeting determined, but still shaking with nerves.

"I told myself that all I could do was speak from the heart and tell her the truth about why I needed to get to Canada," he said.

So that's exactly what Franck did. He told this woman how he and I had met one fateful night in Nuits-Saint-Georges, and how we were making out on the dance floor a mere two hours after we'd met. He told her how motivated and smart I was, and how I needed to be in Canada for university, but how he needed to be there with me, to support me and love me, and so that we could build our lives together. He explained how we had tried everything but had so far come up short in getting him legally into Québec.

"I'm afraid I didn't leave her much time to talk." Franck sounded rueful. "I was so nervous."

"What did she say?"

"When I finally finished, she sat back in her chair and looked at me with a smile. I didn't know how to react; nobody has smiled at me so far in this process. Then she said, "Of all the reasons I have ever heard to immigrate to Canada, your story of true love is one of the best."

"What?" I gasped on the other end of the line. "Are you serious?"

"Yes. Then do you know what she told me?"

I yelled. "You're killing me, Franck!"

He chuckled. She said, 'I'm going to give you two a chance and make sure you get your permanent residence papers. Take this to the office downstairs and they'll get you started with the administrative part of it."

"What!?!"

"I know. I couldn't believe it either, so I just sat there, staring at the piece of paper she passed me," Franck said. "Finally, she said to me, 'the longer you wait in that chair, the longer it will be until you can see your girlfriend'."

I laughed, joy bubbling up inside me.

"Finally, I looked up at her and said, 'I'm going to Canada?' I couldn't believe it. 'You're going to Canada,' she said. 'And if you two eventually have children, I'd like to see some photos please.'"

I leapt around my little room, shrieking. I was finally giving my AC/DC-loving neighbor a run for his money. "I love you. I love that woman. We're going to be together!"

Franck laughed down the phone line. "I love you too *ma* Laura. Now I have to go buy my plane tickets before the travel agency closes. If I get there in two weeks or so, can you come pick me up at the airport?"

"Shut up!" I yelled. "Of course! Get here as soon as you can!"

"I will. Promise," he said. "I'll call you in a few hours, OK?"

"Yes, *Oui*. I love you. This is like a dream."

"If it is, then let's make a pact never to wake up."

I took at least half an hour to sit on my bed and hug the news around myself before going out in public. Eventually, though, I had to make my way to an English Literature tutorial. I couldn't, however, wipe the grin off my face.

Unfortunately, I bumped into Anne and James as I was leaving the lobby.

"What's up?" Anne asked. "You look as though someone lit a lightbulb inside you."

There was no point in lying. The sooner James got used to the idea of Franck's arrival—I felt like I needed to pinch myself that this was now reality—the better.

"I just got off the phone with Franck," I said. "He's finally met with someone in Paris who has agreed to give him the immigration papers he needs to come here to Montréal. He'll be here in a few weeks! Can you believe it?"

Anne wrapped me in a hug. "Aw. I still think you're crazy, but you seem so happy."

I nodded. "I feel like I'm about to explode."

James tried to force a smile but wasn't quite successful. "So, we finally get to meet this famous Franck. I never thought it would actually happen—"

"I told you it would."

A muscle in his jaw twitched.

I resolved then and there to keep the two of them as far apart as possible. I did not need Franck's arrival marred with any of James's misplaced jealousy. "Finally."

"I can't wait to meet him!" Anne said.

James cleared his throat. "Me neither."

The next two weeks passed in a blur. Franck and I talked to each other at least once a day, if not more. There were so many things for him to organize. His papers would be arriving after he had left France, but his parents would forward them on and we would get them validated once they arrived here, although I didn't know all the details about that. He had bought his plane tickets and was due to arrive at the Mirabel airport at eight o'clock at night.

His family was having a hard time accepting his imminent departure, he told me. Mémé, his grandmother, in particular. She was convinced she would never see him again.

"I've tried to convince her that now with planes it's not that difficult to see each other, but when I explain that to her she just pats my hand and tells me she's going to die before my return."

Franck was the first in his family to move outside of France. It just wasn't done. I knew Michèle and André and Mémé would far rather Franck met a nice village girl in Villers-la-Faye and stay close to them. They didn't dislike me, and seemed to find my Canadian-ness entertaining, but the fact of the matter was that I was taking their son far, far away.

My parents, on the other hand, had no problem with me living away from them. Independence was highly prized in our family culture. They did, however, worry about what Franck was like now they knew his move to Montréal was, much to everyone's bewilderment, actually happening. They worried about me getting serious about someone at such a young age because that didn't harmonize with the whole independence thing.

There were only two people who believed Franck's move was a good idea – Franck and me.

I scanned my tiny dorm room and my even tinier dorm bed and wondered yet again about the feasibility of a Frenchman living in my room unnoticed. I would have to solve that problem eventually, but now I had to leave to buy my bus ticket to meet him at Mirabel airport. Would the reality of seeing him again live up to my hopes? I couldn't know, but I was about to find out.

chapter seven

It was hard to act nonchalant as I boarded the airport bus. I trembled with adrenaline and there didn't seem to be enough room in my chest for my heart anymore. This was really happening.

In two hours, I would be able to reach out and touch Franck. He had existed in the realm of fantasy and memory for so long that I no longer remembered precisely how that would feel.

Montréalais always groused about the Montréal airports—the Dorval airport closest to downtown handled mainly domestic flights whereas most international flights landed at Mirabel, which was a good hour drive out of town. Everyone grumbled about the amount of time it took to travel to and from Mirabel, but I was thankful for a parenthesis to mentally ready myself for Franck's arrival.

I fidgeted on my seat for the first half hour, unable to settle. Who was I kidding? This was too huge an event to prepare myself for. My body and mind were bursting at the seams, trying and failing to plan for being catapulted into an entirely new life. A new life that I couldn't possibly know the ending of. It terrified and thrilled me at the same time.

This choice to be together could either be the best thing that ever happened to both of us, or it could be a disaster. Those months we had been together in France had a quality of being suspended in time, but here in Montréal we would be living an actual life together with no end-date in sight. Would the magic we had be able to survive in the real world?

With moist palms I smoothed my skirt over my tights for the hundredth or so time. I had put a considerable amount of thought into my outfit, which was out of character for me. November brought with it a new chill in the air, so I wore a soft purple chenille sweater and a brand new floaty black skirt covered with tiny white polka dots. It was far too cold now to have bare legs, so I opted for a pair of thick black tights and under-the-knee black boots. The whole ensemble felt very me and très Montréal at the same time. I twisted my hands in my lap, wondering what Franck would think.

I checked my watch. Franck was most likely flying somewhere over Hudson Bay at that moment. I tried to imagine him, peering out the window. He told me he was going to try to do everything he could to get a window seat as this would be his first ever flight. I couldn't remember a time when I hadn't regularly flown on airplanes. Was he getting his first glimpse of his new home beneath him? I wondered if he was doing a better job of keeping his emotions in check than me.

To keep my mind occupied as the city gave way to fallow fields, I listed all the things I wanted to do with Franck during his first few days in Montréal. We had to go to Bens Diner, of course, and eat a smoked meat sandwich on rye. We'd finish it off with one of their slices of New York cheesecake smothered in strawberries. We'd also have to go and get freshly baked bagels up on the Plateau from the Fairmount Bagel Factory. I wanted to show him around the campus of course and get him oriented. There were so many things, but my mind kept looping back to that moment when I would finally be able to reach out and touch him for the first time—that moment when he—we—would become real again. That moment that was drawing closer by the second.

With a long squeal of the bus brakes we finally pulled up in front of the airport. I had always flown in and out of Dorval so far, so it was my first time there.

The building was huge and white and, from what I could see of its surroundings, built in the middle of nowhere. Dusk was falling, and I got the impression when I walked through the sliding glass doors that it was strangely deserted for an international

airport. There were none of the multicultural crowds and teetering
luggage carts that I saw in Charles de Gaulle on landing in Paris,
and none of the bustling crowds going to and from Asia like in
Vancouver. Mirabel felt like a ghost town. It would be a mislead-
ing first glimpse for Franck of the lively, eclectic vibe in Montréal.

Anyway, it didn't matter. Once we were together again I
doubted we would be paying much attention to our surroundings,
not for the first little while, anyway.

I found a screen in the echoing hall and saw his flight from
Paris was due to arrive on time. This meant I still had at least
forty-five minutes to wait. Me being me, I had given myself plenty
of margin to eliminate any chance of being late.

*What was I going to do with myself to keep from going stir-
crazy in the meantime?* My hands felt empty. I decided on a whim
to go and find some flowers or some other type of welcome gift. It
would keep me busy and would give me something to grip onto as
I waited for Franck to come off the plane.

There appeared to be no flowers on offer except some hideous
dyed carnations in lurid shades of neon yellow and improbable
blue. Carnations were the flowers everyone put on the gravestones
during All Saints on November first every year in France. They
would definitely send the wrong signal.

As I headed out of the flower shop, I spotted a stand where a
man was filling up balloons with helium. There was a bag of
crimson balloons with white X's and O's stamped all over.
Perfect. Franck would be welcomed by me and balloons.

So it was with a bouquet of seven helium balloons tied together with a white ribbon that I finally made my way over to the
arrivals door. People sent me amused looks, but I didn't want to
talk to anyone. It required every ounce of my focus to watch that
arrivals door and wait for it to slide open and bring Franck back
into my life.

"Arrivé / Arrived" flashed in red letters on the screen after Franck's flight number. I shifted my weight from foot to foot. He was here. We were finally in the same city again. I couldn't seem to wrap my mind around this new reality. Beyond all reason we had made this wild dream happen. Now we had to make it work.

The sliding doors stayed shut for what felt like an impossibly long time. Finally, they slid open and my heart tried to leap out of my throat, but it was an elderly lady being pushed in a wheelchair by someone who looked like her son.

Slowly, people began to trickle out. I had noticed on the screens that three transatlantic flights arrived within five minutes of each other. One from London. One from Germany. And Franck's flight from Paris. I squinted, trying to find evidence of a French person in what had become a steady stream of arriving passengers.

After an unbearably long wait, a man strutted through the doors with a pink scarf knotted around his neck, perfectly round spectacles, and a cigarette already between his fingers. He *had* to be Parisian. I knew it in my bones. I scanned the figures emerging from the doors with even more intent, looking for the one who meant so much to me.

I shifted the balloons from my right hand to my left. Blood pounded in my ears and my breath was coming in short staccato bursts.

Then … there he was. He strode towards me with his khaki military issue gunny sack slung over his shoulder and that mischievous grin.

I opened my mouth to shout his name but only a strange, strangled sound emerged. I wanted to run to him, but I was blocked by the metal bar in front of me. Besides, my feet were frozen to the spot.

I watched him come closer, bouncing on my toes now. He was wearing his denim jacket and a white T-shirt. He would be chilly, but I could warm him up. He drew close enough for me to discern the shadow of stubble on his face from the long trip. I could almost reach out and touch him.

He ducked underneath the bar in front of me, and I seemed to stop breathing altogether. It didn't matter, because all at once I was swept up in his arms. His scent surrounded me. Apples and bonfire. Home. He felt like home. I was never conscious of doubting that, but relief made me almost let go of the balloons.

Enfin. Enfin. His lips brushed against my earlobe, sending shivers up my spine. Finally. Finally.

I kissed him then, a fumbling, frantic kiss as if to convince myself that he was really there. "I missed you." My voice caught. "I missed you so much."

"Are the balloons for me?" he finally asked after a long while.

"Yes," I said, blinking back tears. I passed the bunch of white ribbon to him. "Welcome to Montréal."

"I love them," he laughed, kissing me again. "They're perfect, but not as perfect as kissing you *mon amour.*"

I slid my now free hand underneath his jacket and his T-shirt, where I could feel the smooth, muscular planes of his back. All of a sudden, making out with him in the middle of Mirabel airport wasn't enough.

"Let's get you back to your new home."

I'm not exactly sure how I managed to lead us to the bus back into Montréal. Walking was difficult. We couldn't seem to unwind ourselves from one another, as if to reassure ourselves that this was truly real.

Franck managed to throw his duffel bag in the luggage compartment under the bus while I bought us tickets from the driver. There was a sleek black limousine parked in front of us and as we climbed on together Franck nodded towards it. "I always thought limousines only existed in American movies. It never occurred to me that they were actually a real thing."

"They're real," I said as we found our seats. This was all real.

It was the last thing we said for a long time. We couldn't stop kissing and our hands roamed, rediscovering each other's familiar yet at the same time strangely unfamiliar terrain.

"I'm dying," Franck said, urgency in his voice. "It was torture when we were apart. You would come to me in my dreams, but it would never be enough."

"I know," I murmured, kissing that tender spot I loved behind his earlobe. I understood. The problem with dreams was that I would wake up, and Franck would be gone again. Now, he was here, and he wasn't going anywhere. I was desperate to be alone with him.

I had fretted that maybe my feelings wouldn't be as strong for Franck when we saw each other again, that maybe our chemistry had been as much a product of circumstance and geography as connection. I had been wrong. His presence filled every cell of me. All those doubts about James or limiting my possibilities were extinguished by this ... this visceral connection between us when we were together. Nothing could even come close.

The balloons stuck to the ceiling and I somehow managed to keep them from drifting to the front of the bus with my pinky finger, even though both my hands were thoroughly occupied.

Some time later we squealed to a stop on Sherbrooke Avenue. Thank God, because we were not far off crossing the line of public indecency.

"What do you think of Montréal so far?" I asked with a smile, as I took his hand and stood up.

"Better than I could ever imagine," he said. "And you know me. I can imagine a lot."

chapter eight

The bus left us at the bottom of rue Université and Sherbrooke. The air had a bite to it and taxis and cars honked and weaved their way around the four-lane thoroughfare.

Franck gazed around him. His eyes under the streetlight were disbelieving. "The cars really *are* bigger here. I feel like I'm in a rerun of *Starsky and Hutch*." He shook his head. "Sorry. I'm just having a hard time believing I'm truly here."

This was Franck's first time outside of France, I reminded myself. I wrapped my arms under his jacket and kissed his neck. "Me too. You must be freezing. I hope you brought some warmer clothes, although I promise to do everything I can to keep you warm."

"Funnily enough, I'm not cold." He grinned down at me. "But no way I'm saying no to that offer."

"It's a hike up to Molson House at the top," I said. "Sorry. There's no other way up but on foot."

"Is that where your bed is?" Franck asked, lifting his chin towards the top of the hill as we turned onto rue Robert-Bourassa.

I squeezed his hand and nodded.

"Then, just a warning, I might sprint."

He didn't run, exactly, but he walked with fast, strong strides with his gunny sack, which looked heavy, slung on his back. I held the balloons, and he hauled me along beside him with his free hand.

The background hum of the city was subsumed by the beat of my heart. All the things I had planned to do with Franck in the city receded, replaced with the things I wanted to do with him in my bedroom.

The shared need to be alone together thrummed between us. Thank God I didn't have a roommate.

We reached the top of the hill. Students were drifting in and out of Bishop Mountain Hall, the central cafeteria building—it was the last half hour of the dinner service. I was thankful it was quiet. I didn't have the patience to make small talk or introductions to anyone.

I ran my index finger across Franck's palm like a promise. "It's the building straight ahead of us," I said. "Molson Hose. Like I said in my letters, it's a dump."

Franck drank me in with his eyes. "It has everything it needs. Let's get up there. Fast, *s'il te plaît.*"

There were two bras hanging off the hedge at the front of the building, and we had to pick our way through a few crushed beer cans to get to the stairs. The lobby smelled vaguely of stale beer and vomit as usual. "Last night's party," I said. "It might be noisy tonight too." Mercifully, James and Anne were nowhere in sight.

Franck shook his head. "Doesn't matter." His voice was strained.

I picked up my pace until I was practically running up the stairs. With a fumbling hand I found my room key in my jacket pocket and drew it out without breaking my stride. "Almost there. Just one more floor."

Franck didn't say anything, but when I glanced at him keeping pace beside me his eyes were dark and intent.

Finally, I slid the key in my door. It swung open and we fell in the room, already locked together. Franck kicked the door shut and had me backed up against it in a millisecond. Without looking, I reached behind me and slid the deadbolt.

I heard the thump as Franck's gunny sack hit the ground. We were too busy to care where it landed.

Franck paused for a second and took my face in his hands. "We're alone," he murmured.

"*Oui.*"

Those were the last coherent words we said for a very, very long time.

Sometime in the wee hours of the morning, I woke up to a rustling beside the bed. I cracked an eye to see the shadow of Franck, completely naked, crouched on the floor beside me.

"What's going on?" I whispered. "Is anything wrong?"

He moved closer, sitting beside the bed on his knees, he covered me with the top half of his body, taking his time to kiss me. "God, no, everything is the rightest it's ever been. I just got hungry."

"Ah," I said, smiling sleepily. "That's the um ... exertion ... and the jetlag. It's breakfast time in Burgundy."

My eyes were adjusting to the dark, and there was always a bit of filtered light from the streetlamps outside. I could see his eyes widen. "Is that what jetlag is? I've heard people talk about it, but I never really understood."

"That's it," I said. "Your body is all confused. You feel awake when you should be asleep and sleepy when you should be awake and hungry when it isn't time to eat and then full when it is. It's bonkers, but it only lasts a few days." I reached my hand out from under the duvet and pinched his chin. "Besides, I would have been very surprised if you hadn't worked up an appetite over the last few hours."

Franck chuckled and gave me another kiss. "I think those past few hours will go down in history. You must be hungry too. You didn't eat dinner, did you?"

I hadn't even thought about it, but now that Franck mentioned it my stomach rumbled. "You're right, I am hungry."

"No surprise there," Franck said. "You did your fair share."

I certainly did. I smiled and stretched in the dark and mentally inventoried the food in my tiny mini fridge. There wasn't much. "I think I may have an apple we can share," I said. "And maybe some cereal, but I think I'm out of milk."

"Have no worries *mon amour*," he said. "I will feed you. Or rather, Mémé will feed you."

"What?"

"She was convinced that I was leaving to a savage land where I would have to forage in the forest for food, so she insisted on packing my bag full of things so I wouldn't starve."

I blinked away tears. My emotions felt so close to the surface anyway, and the thought of Mémé carefully providing Franck with enough sustenance to survive the Canadian frontier made me want to both laugh and cry.

"*Sacré Mémé*," I murmured. "It must have been so hard for her to see you leave."

Franck bit his lip. "She wept. They all did. I promised I would come back eventually and bring you with me, but I don't think any of them truly believed me."

"We'll just have to prove them all wrong," I promised Franck, reaching my hand out so it rested on his bare shoulder. My stomach rumbled again at the idea of Mémé's cooking. Any of Mémé's cooking. "What did she pack?"

Franck began to empty out the contents of his bag. "What *didn't* she pack? Most of it's at the bottom."

"How did you get that through customs?" I wondered.

Franck paused in his movements for a second. "I don't know. I never thought about it. You mean you're not allowed to bring food into Canada?"

"Not things like dairy products, which means cheese. No alcohol. All sorts of things, when I think about it. Usually dogs are around to pick up the scent."

"My guardian angels must have been smiling down on us then," Franck said, pulling several packages wrapped with aluminum foil from the bottom of his bag. "Because look what we have." He extracted a bottle, then another, then another.

I stated laughing at the surprise bounty. I'd so missed how Franck always managed to astonish me. I slid out of bed and dropped to the floor beside him, draping the duvet over both of us. His skin felt so warm beside mine. I nestled closer, amazed at how our bodies fit together like interlocking puzzle pieces. "So what do we have?"

"I'm not exactly sure," he said. "I was busy playing petits chevaux with Emmanuel-Marie one last time while Mémé was filling up my bag." He began unwrapping one of the lumpy, aluminum foil packages. Mémé, having lived through the Nazi occupation, always reused her aluminum foil several times over. My heart squeezed at the familiar sight of her packages.

The delicious scent of garlic and herbs and meat wafted up towards me. My stomach made a noise.

"Ah," Franck said. "*Pâté en croûte.* She knows me well."

"Did she make it?" I asked. I had learned enough in France to know that most people bought their *pâté en croûte* at the *charcutier* because making it was quite an involved process.

"Blasphemy, *mon amour*! *Bien sûr* she did."

Franck squinted at the bottles in front of us. Now that my pupils had dilated, I could make out the labels.

"I'll put this *crémant* in the fridge for later," Franck said, putting the different shaped bottle aside. "I know she put this one in because she wanted us to celebrate being together again."

"We *definitely* celebrated."

Franck pressed me back against the side of the bed with a kiss. "Tell me about it. I've never celebrated so hard in my life." He finally picked up the middle bottle. "Ah. The wine from Jayer in Magny-lès-Villers. That will go perfectly with the *pâté en croûte*, don't you think?"

"Perfect," I said. I left the warmth of the duvet and found us a corkscrew, a knife, and two plastic Tupperware glasses—hardly worthy vessels for the Burgundy wine, but better than not drinking it.

I settled back down beside Franck and pulled the duvet over us again like a tent. Meanwhile, he had assembled the perfect picnic of *pâté-en-croûte*, a ripe round of camembert, a saucisson sec and, for dessert, slices of Mémé's slightly squashed but still delicious *gâteau de savoie*. We dug in with gusto.

The earthiness of the pâté married perfectly with the leather and cherry notes in the wine, and the camembert was perfectly oozy around the edges while satisfyingly soft and solid in the middle. For dessert, the crunchy, lemon simplicity of Mémé's *gâteau de savoie* satisfied every taste bud.

We ate and drank and kissed. It was the best meal I'd ever had in my life.

chapter **nine**

It took us until Monday to emerge from my bedroom, apart from the occasional covert mission to the bathroom and the showers. I had unplugged my phone and neglected to do any of my homework. We didn't go to Bens or to get fresh bagels. We had plenty to keep us busy between my four walls, and enough to eat with the food that Mémé had sent. Besides our first picnic we'd also discovered homemade mini-quiches, a huge slab of *comté* and a metal tin of *tuile* biscuits. We shared the bottle of *crémant* on the second night in bed. Our own little celebration was perfect and didn't even require getting dressed.

An early English class at eight-thirty Monday morning forced me to face real life outside the bubble of my res room. Besides, I reasoned, reality, or the new version of it with Franck, would have to resume eventually.

I left Franck—all warm and snug in my tiny bed—with a long kiss, instructions on where to meet me after class, and a campus map I had picked up somewhere during frosh week.

I dressed haphazardly and slipped out, leaving the key inside with Franck for him to lock up. I looked around the familiar hallway and everything felt different. This residence, which for the past two months had felt like my home, no longer did. Franck and I couldn't live here long term, I realized. Also, had the carpet in the hallway always been this grungy, and had that bright blue stain always been there?

Re-entering my old life felt awkward, like it had become a pair of pants that had shrunk in the wash. I dreaded bumping into people I knew. This thing with Franck felt too new and too precious to talk about yet. I was still too much in the middle of living it to answer people's questions about it with any perspective.

I was pleased the day had dawned crisp and sunny with what promised to be a clear blue sky. Perfect for Franck's first real glimpse at what was now our city.

I passed the cafeteria building where I hadn't gone all weekend. I would have to start going there, not only to feed myself but to sneak food for Franck. From our late-night chats it sounded like, although he had done his best to work three jobs and save money before he boarded the plane, his budget was limited until his papers arrived and he was able to look for work.

I began to walk down the hill as I had so many other days. I took a lungful of chilly air. The leaves had mostly fallen, which was a shame for Franck, but a thin layer of frost made the world sparkle. My mind rotated in slow, indulgent circles. Franck was no longer just a memory. He was asleep in my bed, as solid and tangible as the concrete sidewalk underneath my Doc Marten boots.

The past two days had felt suspended in time but now it was up to me, or up to us—I still wasn't used to that—to create a life here for ourselves.

I had almost reached the intersection with Pine Street when I heard somebody calling my name. I turned quickly to see Anne half jogging, half sliding on the frost down University Street towards me.

"Thank God." She was out of breath by the time she got up to me. I grabbed her thin arm to keep her from toppling over into the busy intersection. "I can't even begin to explain the crazy speculation about you this weekend. Some people thought you were dead. I'm assuming Franck got here?"

I nodded. I couldn't find the words to express what the last forty-eight hours had been, nor did I want to. It had meant something completely different from the way Anne talked about sex.

She narrowed her eyes at me. "Wow. How many times did

you guys do it this weekend?"

I borrowed a trick from Franck and shrugged.

"Lost count?" she guessed.

"Can't remember."

"You can tell me!"

"Sorry. Private." The light turned green and I was happy to cross the street and keep walking.

Anne groaned. "You're such a prude."

I smiled a secret smile. The last forty-eight hours had proved I was definitely *not* a prude, but I did believe some things were best kept between Franck and me. "What did you do this weekend?"

She grimaced. "Nothing much. A bit of studying. We went out and grabbed some dinner on Saint-Laurent. Mainly I tried to distract James. He was misery incarnate."

I sighed. I knew I would have to confront this sooner or later. I hated to hurt James, but I would if it meant choosing Franck.

"So you know?" I asked Anne. "About James?" I had never mentioned it to her before. I hadn't been certain if she knew how James felt about me, and I worried telling her would only compound his hurt. I didn't believe in kicking people when they were down.

"He told me, but I suspected before that. I'm not a complete idiot, you know."

"I feel sorry for him," I said. "But I've always been crystal clear to James about Franck."

"Sorry for him?" She rolled her eyes. "You should feel sorry for me. I was the one who had the task of trying to cheer him up. I failed, by the way."

"Ugh. Sorry."

Anne stopped walking and turned to me. "Listen. You're not responsible for James's emotions. Nobody is except James. He's got to do the emotional work himself to get over you, and I think he's going to start now that Franck is here. The thing is I don't think he ever truly believed that Franck would find a way to immigrate. He wasn't giving up because he figured that if he just stayed patient, eventually you and Franck would break up because of the long distance and that maybe you might consider him then."

Anne was right about James's emotions not being my responsibility. I still had that nagging burden of feeling like it was up to me to make everyone happy, but that wasn't true. James was the only one who could make James happy.

Still, I was left with the uncomfortable truth that James hadn't been completely off the mark. If there wasn't Franck, I might have been open to James's interest. But there was Franck, so that was that.

"But now he knows there's no hope," she said. "It's just taking him time to assimilate this new reality, but I saw signs this weekend that he'll get there eventually."

"Thank God," I said. "I wonder if he and I could ever go back to being friends?"

She bit her lip. "Maybe, but not likely. Not for his own good, not for a long time anyway. Do you see what I mean?"

I nodded. We had started walking again and were almost at the crossing with Milton Street.

"Enough about James," she declared. "He took up enough of my weekend as it is. My question is, how long do you think you're going to get away with hiding a Frenchman in your room?"

"I think I'm about to find out."

"Sam is going to figure it out, you know." She was right. Sam kept a keen and over-enthusiastic eye on everything. "Everyone was talking about you this weekend."

"Shit." I didn't like the sound of that.

"You'll probably be safe for a week or two, but after that—"

"We'll have to find our own place." That idea thrilled me as much as it intimidated me. It would be incredible to be able to live together—just the two of us. At the same time, I would have to try to explain the situation to my parents, whom I depended on for my rent and I was dreading that.

I'd had a fairly standard WASP upbringing, meaning that puritanism was alive and well in our family values. My parents did not believe that couples should live together before they got married. It was not because of any deep religious faith, but rather because ... well, I didn't know exactly why they felt so strongly about it. I suspected it had more to do with what other people would think.

I paid for my own tuition and books, but my summer job didn't earn me enough to pay my rent and food as well without taking out student loans. I didn't want to do that, but I might have no other option if I wanted to stay at McGill and live with Franck.

It wasn't like me—an inveterate planner—to have left the plans for Franck's arrival and our living arrangements so vague. I guess I had not only felt terrified by the idea of bringing it up with my parents, but I had also felt superstitious, as if making plans for our shared future in Montréal would be jinxing him getting here. I wanted more than anything to run back up the hill and just hide away from all of this in my residence room with Franck.

At least, I realized, brightening, I didn't have to face all of this on my own. Franck and I were a team. We would face it together. I couldn't wait to meet him at the library so we could start to make some plans.

"When are you going to introduce him to us?" Anne demanded. "You're not embarrassed of him, are you? Is he a troll?"

I chuckled. "You'll see for yourselves. In a day or two. Promise."

"You're not planning on dumping me, are you?" she said.

"What do you mean?"

"Dumping me and the rest of your Molson Hose friends. I can see about how things are awkward with James, but don't chuck me along with him now that you've got a boyfriend."

"Of course not." But as soon as the words were out of my mouth it dawned on me just how insular life in residence was, and if I was no longer there, what would happen exactly? I wasn't sure.

I left Anne on this uncertain note as she branched off to her class and I hurried to my own in the Leacock Building.

chapter ten

Not surprisingly, I had a hard time concentrating in English class. Somehow Chaucer's *Canterbury Tales* wasn't quite as compelling as the idea of my boyfriend sleeping in my residence bed up the hill.

Nevertheless, I forced myself to knuckle down and continue taking notes on the complexity of *The Wife of Bath*. I was not going to drop out of university, no matter what. Just because my dream of Franck had come true didn't mean I was going to abandon my other goals.

I chewed my pen as my thoughts wandered to what Franck could possibly do for work once his papers arrived. He never had a problem finding work before, but it was usually short-term jobs to earn money for something specific. He'd gone right from university to his military service to meeting me. It would be nice for him to finally be able to use his communications degree from the Sorbonne and do something more interesting than packing boxes or bagging groceries like he had done in the past.

I wondered idly how long his immigration papers would take to come through. Hopefully not long. We had a lot to figure out. I checked my watch. Only an hour until I saw him again. For now, I had to listen about the contrasts between *The Prioress* and *The Wife of Bath*.

Franck was late meeting me in front of the McGill library, but I didn't waste my time. I'd grabbed a copy of the free university newspaper, the *McGill Daily*, perched myself on the wall outside and began circling "apartments offered" ads in the classifieds with a yellow highlighter. Not knowing our potential combined budget was going to make things difficult.

I shivered. Today the weather felt like it was getting colder as the day wore on instead of warmer. A gusty wind blew across the campus, cutting through my wool duffel coat.

I heard a familiar whistle and looked up. Franck was there, walking towards me wearing a puffy dark blue Millet jacket and his jeans. A smile lit up his face when he saw me. I felt shy all of a sudden, which was fairly ridiculous considering our past forty-eight hours together. I could feel heat kindle under my skin.

I stood up. "*Bonjour, toi.*"

He pulled me into a firm embrace and murmured, "*et bonjour toi, mon amour,*" against my lips before kissing them.

"Sorry I'm late," he said when we finally came up for air. "There was a line-up for the shower this morning, then I'm embarrassed to say I got kind of lost finding the library. I realized far too late that I was holding the campus map upside down."

I squeezed his hand. "You're forgiven. It's a lot to take in, this whole big city outside of my room." I sent him a cheeky smile.

"Ah, now you're teasing me. I've lived in Paris, remember?"

"Maybe, but that's different than a North American city."

"They speak French here. How different can it be?"

Different, but he would find that out for himself. "You hungry?" It was only eleven o'clock but I didn't imagine Franck had found much food left in the room. I'd skipped breakfast and my stomach was protesting.

"Starving," he said.

"How does a smoked meat sandwich sound?" I asked.

Franck raised his eyebrows. "I have no idea what that even means."

"Pastrami," I explained, but I could tell from his expression that this only added to his confusion. "It's a Montréal specialty and there's a place right near here. They have the best cheesecake for dessert too."

"Cake made out of cheese?" Franck grimaced. "Please tell me that's a joke."

"It's delicious," I said. "You'll see." The novelty of being able to show Franck around made my blood fizz. So far in our relationship, he'd been the one to introduce me to new things. I grabbed his hand, and our fingers intertwined like they had been doing that for centuries. "*On y va.*"

Bens restaurant was not that far away—just on the corner of De Maisonneuve and Metcalfe. I had happened upon it two years earlier when I had arrived in Montréal with my father to take a tour at McGill. It'd been early December and we hadn't gotten to our hotel until about eight o'clock at night. The blowing snow stung our faces and we were both starving. We stumbled outside into the frigid night and walked towards a light at the end of our street. As we drew closer, we realized we had hit the jackpot. Bens welcomed us in all of its 1950s diner glory. It had everything: fluorescent red letters outside reading "Restaurant–Deli," chrome panels on the walls, swivel stools, formica tables, a counter that wrapped around one whole side of the restaurant, and the scent of perfectly seasoned pastrami.

My dad and I didn't need to consult. We just headed inside. Once I'd caught our first breath of warm air, we looked around. Seated on a chair at the entrance by a cashier stand was a wizened man holding a cane. Above him was a sign that read "The people who walk under this door are the nicest people in the world – our customers."

We feasted on smoked meat sandwiches on rye bread served with fries and massive slices of New York cheesecake smothered in strawberries for dessert. My dad didn't drink coffee, but I had several mugs in a traditional white diner mug.

Since then, Bens was one of my favorite places in the city. It wasn't that the food was superb or the service wonderful, in fact, all the waiters were distinctly grumpy. For me, the restaurant just felt like Montréal—a fabulous mishmash of different cultures and influences. I particularly loved the faded photographs of famous people who had frequented Bens on their "Wall of Fame." There was everyone from Liberace to Leonard Cohen.

I ushered Franck in the door and was relieved to see that old Irving Kravitz was seated, as usual, by the cashier stand, ruling his domain. He looked like an ancient gnome as he held tightly to his cane, but he greeted us as he did with every single one of his customers who walked through the door. Franck, I could tell from the glint in his eye, was charmed.

We were ushered to a table by an unenthusiastic middle-aged waiter with fading ginger hair.

Franck gasped as he surveyed the visual glory of the interior. "What is this place?" he murmured, reverent.

"This," I said, sweeping my hand around us with ceremony. "Is Bens."

Franck sat down on his round chrome stool and gave it a swivel to try it. "It's like being inside the set of an American movie."

"I know. My dad and I stumbled on it the first time I came to Montréal. It's like a time capsule or something."

Our waiter, the same red-haired man, appeared beside us, tapping his pencil against his order pad. One thing they were not at Bens was leisurely.

"Two smoked meat sandwiches," I said, in English. "Lean. With pickles and coffees."

He scribbled it down, nodded curtly, and then left us.

"I ordered for us," I said to Franck, switching to French. "I hope that's OK." I was still high on being the tour guide for a change.

Franck tried to lean back, but almost fell off his stool and had to grab the formica edge of the table to yank himself upright again. "These need to come with a safety warning." He laughed at himself. "As for the ordering, I love a strong woman, you know that. What will I be eating, or is it a surprise?"

"We'll be having smoked-meat sandwiches. It's a Montréal and a Bens specialty. When it's cold outside like today nothing tastes quite as good."

The waiter returned and deposited two white ceramic mugs of coffee on our table.

Franck stared down at his, and then back up to me. "What is this?"

I laughed at him. "Coffee." I'd forgotten. He was used to espresso in tiny cups when he ordered *café*.

He took a tentative sip and grimaced. "I beg to differ. I have no idea what this is, but it's not coffee."

I thought back to all those bracing, smooth espressos we had sucked back in France together. "It's North American diner coffee," I said. "It's more or less what most coffee is like here."

"But ... how can I order a real coffee?" Franck's face looked pale, and I didn't think it was just from the jetlag.

I shrugged. "I guess you could order an espresso."

"Really?"

I snorted. "No! They don't do espressos here. Espressos are fancy, not to mention expensive. This is a diner. Diners serve only diner coffee like this so ..." I picked up my mug and took a sip. "Bottoms up."

Franck looked down at his mug. "Must I?"

"You must. I had to adjust to espressos in France."

Franck opened his mouth as if to say something, then shut it again. I knew what he was thinking: it was easier to adjust to *better* coffee. He wasn't wrong, but I was enjoying myself too much to admit that. "Try again."

He gritted his teeth but did take a sip and managed to swallow it. "It tastes like the river water from Saône. Same color too."

I clicked my tongue. "Suck it up *mon amour*. You wanted more than anything to travel and experience different cultures. This is it. Is there *nothing* you like about the coffee?"

Franck's brows drew together as he pondered this. "It's hot," he said, at last.

Luckily, the smoked meat sandwiches arrived, smelling of that heavenly spice mix that each smoked meat purveyor in Montréal guards with their life. The sandwiches were piled high with thin slices of smoky, piping hot pastrami.

Franck sniffed at his as though it could be poison. "It smells good."

"You don't need to sound so surprised. It is good," I said. I reached for the bottle of yellow mustard that stood atop every table and squeezed it on the side of my plate.

"That doesn't look like mustard," Franck said. "It's so … yellow."

"It's not Dijon mustard, if that's what you mean," I said, then I started chuckling. "Do you know what we call it?"

"What?"

"French's mustard, although I've never seen any of this in France. Ever."

"Does it taste the same?"

"No, but French's mustard goes well with smoked meat. You'll see."

Franck took the bottle and squeezed some on his plate and then picked up his knife and his fork. I, on the other hand, took the first half of my sandwich in my hands and took a big bite.

Meanwhile, Franck tried to cut his sandwich but it just toppled over and fell apart. He sighed. "I'm so confused. How does this work?"

"Definitely not with a knife and fork. You have to eat it with your hands."

Franck looked appalled. I laughed inwardly. Franck, like every French person I knew, had a hard time eating anything with their hands besides breakfast and baguette slices. The French even ate pizza slices with a knife and fork.

"Really?" he asked, with pleading eyes. "With my hands?"

"Yup. Pick up half your sandwich, dip it in your mustard." I demonstrated for him. "Then open your mouth as wide as you can and take a bite."

I chewed as I watched Franck try to do this. His movements were cautious at first, but as he chewed I could see as a light spring into his eyes. "*Dis-donc*, this is good," he said.

"I know," I nodded. "I'm thrilled you like it, as smoked meat sandwiches are cheap and plentiful in Montréal. It's the perfect meal out for a student, or a new immigrant." I winked at Franck.

We both polished off our sandwiches. The waiter came by and refilled my coffee. Franck didn't need his refilled, but he was taking the occasional distrustful sip. Progress. I had been munching on my dill pickle throughout the meal. Another thing they had perfected in Montréal was the dill pickle. Franck's, however, still sat on the Melmac plate between us, untouched.

"Aren't you going to eat your pickle?" I asked.

"Is that what that is?"

"Of course. They go with smoked meat sandwiches. Another Montréal specialty."

Franck picked it up gingerly. It was about one thousand times the size of the tiny cornichons eaten in France. He took a bite and tilted his head. "Hmmmm ... crunchy."

"They're made in-house," I added. "That's the case in most smoked-meat places in Montréal. The pastrami and the pickles are made with top-secret recipes."

He nodded but was intent on eating his pickle. After the waiter had wordlessly whisked our plates away, Franck asked. "Is that the only course?"

I nodded. "Multi-course meals aren't really a thing here. Lunch is something we do quickly and on-the-go during the week. Are you interested in dessert, though?"

"I know you're interested in dessert." Franck was well-aware of my sweet tooth. "What do they have?"

"Cheesecake," I said. "We can share a slice. It's delicious. Trust me."

Franck reached across the formica table and grasped my hand. "Cheesecake? Fine. I sense I am not going to get away with avoiding that travesty for much longer, but please note I am only doing this because I love you."

"Do you trust me?"

He narrowed his hazel eyes at me. "Not when it comes to cheesecake."

I reached across the table and squeezed his hand. "Noted. You're very brave."

I placed the order and Franck had his coffee refilled. "It's terrible, of course," he said, sheepishly after the waiter had left again. "But a person could drink gallons of this stuff."

"Oh. We do," I said, blowing on the top of mine. "Free refills."

The cheesecake was placed in front of us, in all its towering glory, smothered with strawberry sauce.

Franck glared at it like the enemy. "Looks revolting. Why is it so *big*?"

That was something I hadn't thought of until that second. It was true in North America we often associated a good dessert with a large dessert, whereas in France it was usually the opposite. There, something small and concentrated with flavor was preferred over the over-generous and messy.

"It's New York-style cheesecake. It's always big. That's the way they do things in New York, I guess."

Franck picked up his fork, but still didn't venture a bite. "I still can't understand what maniac would have the idea to make a cake with cheese."

"But it's not cheese in the sense of Camembert or Époisses," I explained. That would be disgusting. "It's made out of cream cheese which is more like … more like Saint-Moret. A soft cheese, except cream cheese is a bit sour as well as creamy."

Franck shook his head. "Doesn't matter. Cake and cheese just don't go together. It should be against the law."

I had been waiting with excitement to have Franck taste all my North American favorites, but now I was assailed with doubts about the cheesecake. I'd vaguely heard in the past that the French were notoriously critical of food from other places—anything that strayed beyond the realm of French food, basically. I had never expected Franck to be as closed-minded as his countrymen. A doubt snuck into my brain. *Was mixing cheese and cake a good idea?* Wait. Cheesecake was delicious. I had always loved it. I couldn't let Franck sway me.

I took a forkful. The strawberries on top were perhaps too sweet and I wasn't sure their vivid red color was entirely natural, but the cheesecake underneath was creamy with that unique sweet and salty mix I adored.

I motioned with my head to Franck. "Try."

Frowning, he picked up his fork and took some of the strawberries and the cake. He paused with the forkful hovering in front of his eyes, his usually mobile mouth fixed in a grim line.

"I ate a pig's foot in France," I reminded him. "Man up."

"A pig's foot is delicious."

"A pig's foot is revolting," I said. "I'll never eat one again if I can avoid it. It's all a matter of opinion, you see."

Franck looked ready to continue this debate, but I knew it was just another form of procrastination.

"Delaying will just make it worse." I laughed. "Bite the bullet. Or the cheesecake, in this instance."

Franck took a bite, his expression so fearful as to be ludicrous. He chewed and then made a gagging sound.

"Oh, come *on*."

He swallowed, but with apparent difficulty.

"*Mon Dieu.* What a song and dance over cheesecake."

"It's disgusting," he gasped, and took a swig of coffee.

"Ah ha! Coffee not so bad now, eh?"

"Only in comparison. How can you possibly like that? It's sort of ... salty. The tastes are completely unharmonious. Salty and sweet do *not* go together."

"Then you're in for a surprise. People love the combination of sweet and salty in North America." I took another bite. I liked it, no matter what Franck thought. "You're not going to have any more?" I asked. There was no way I could finish the entire cheesecake slice on my own. I was already stuffed.

He shook his head. "No. I think that's enough for one day."

"I never thought you'd be so ..."

"So what?"

"So *French*."

Franck's eyes flew open and he jerked back, again almost falling off his swivel stool. "I am not," he said. "It's just that certain things taste good, and other things don't."

"Like I said. *French*."

He gasped.

"It's true. The French have never been known for being adventurous eaters outside of French cuisine. They're notoriously closed-minded. I never thought you'd be one of them."

Franck's mouth clamped into a determined line and he defiantly stabbed another forkful of cheesecake and shoved it is his mouth. He swallowed. And repeated the motion. Again and again and again. At a certain point he gagged, and I briefly wondered if he was going to throw up. I had a few more bites, but he didn't give me much chance.

He threw his fork down. "There."

"Did you change your mind about the cheesecake?"

"No. It's still vile."

I smiled at him, highly entertained, but also a little concerned. If cheesecake was proving to be such a hurdle in adjusting to Montréal life, what else would be? "I think you may have a tougher time adapting to life here than you anticipated."

He shook his head. "Nope. I ate it."

I checked my watch. "As entertaining as this is, I have to get to my next class."

"Oh," Franck sipped at his coffee too, as it was the most natural thing in the world now. Maybe he could adapt after all. "Which class?"

"Philosophy of Feminism."

His eyes open wide. "You're a feminist?"

"Of course I am. You are too, right?"

He shook his head. "Definitely not."

This shocked me to my very core. How had we never discussed this before? "You mean you don't think women and men should get equal pay?"

"Of course I do, but that doesn't make me feminist."

"Sorry to disappoint you, but it does."

"No. Men and woman are fundamentally different and trying to make them the same just ruins everything."

"You should come to my class and make that statement. They would rip you to shreds."

Franck frowned at me. "This lunch has been … surprising."

It had, for me too, and I was reeling a bit at its implications.

"Second thoughts?" I asked.

He shook his head. "Never, but ..." He sighed. "I guess I need some time to wrap my head around everything."

Love for him melted my heart. He looked confused, not to mention lost. I was expecting too much, too fast. He was the fish out of water for the first time in his life.

"Of course you do." I caressed the front of his hand. "The shock of finding out your girlfriend is a feminist who loves cheesecake takes time to recover from."

He leaned over and gave me a kiss. "Unruly woman."

"Always."

chapter eleven

I had been smuggling apples and bananas and cheese and crackers into my room for Franck and we'd gone to the grocery store to pick up a few things—namely to make tuna melts.

We were in the tiny kitchenette at the far end of the residence hall. So far, I had been able to sneak Franck in and out of my room without attracting too much notice, but I lived in constant worry that we would be found out. Harboring a boyfriend who was not paying rent was a straight-up cloak and dagger business.

Franck's immigration papers still hadn't arrived in France, but his parents were under instructions to send them to us via express post as soon as they did. I had been perusing the classifieds for apartments as often as I could, but our situation was not ideal.

First of all, we had no idea until Franck found a job—and he couldn't even begin to look until his papers had arrived in France—what our rental budget would be. Secondly, I was dreading the conversation I would have to have with my parents when I informed them I was moving in with my French boyfriend. Not only was I fearful of the revelation itself, I was also scared of the consequences. Would they fly out to Montréal and try to stop me? Would they cut me off financially? What would we do then?

My rather carefree student life didn't feel so carefree anymore. Franck's arrival had catapulted me into a more adult life, and I didn't feel ready to cope. It was still lightyears better than a life without Franck, although I knew trying to explain that to my parents would sound like a young girl in a Hallmark TV special to their ears.

Franck was helping me make tuna melts for both of us for dinner. It was the same thing I had made us for the past three nights.

"Can I ask you something?" he said, eyeing me warily as he grated the cheese.

"Sure."

"Are tuna melts the only thing you know how to make?"

I thought about it. Tuna melts were certainly the only thing that came to mind. "I guess so. Why?"

"I thought maybe that was the case," he said. "It's just that … how about I cook dinner tomorrow?"

I nodded to the makeshift oven and toaster oven in front of us. It was far from a gourmet kitchen. "I have no cooking equipment," I reminded him.

"Not even a pan?"

I thought about it. "Not even a pan. Are you getting sick of eating tuna melts?"

Franck lifted one shoulder eloquently. "A little. They're very good, but we all tire of eating the same thing repeatedly, *n'est-ce pas?*"

I frowned. I was not a cook, but the issue hadn't come up in France because usually we ate meals out or at Franck's parents' house. If ever it was just the two of us, Franck cooked.

"Do you know how to cook?" Franck asked, finally.

I knew how to cook some basic things, but I had also been known at home for creating fires and a significant amount of mess in the kitchen, so my mom had banned me from cooking for most of high school. I didn't much mind, because I preferred reading anyway. "What does that mean, after all? Know how to cook?"

"You know, know how to make a variety of dishes."

I shook my head. "Then, I guess not."

"No-one ever taught you?"

I shook my head.

"But I don't understand. You like eating so much."

In North America that would come across as an insult but I knew in France it was a compliment. I was considered a *gourmande* in France, which meant I loved good food and wine, and other pleasures in life, including those in bed. I'd learned being *gourmande* was viewed as one of the most appealing, attractive qualities in a lover or a friend.

Franck kissed me at the nape of my neck, something which never failed to make me want to drag him back to my bed immediately. "Look, I don't care if you can't cook, it just surprises me given how you love all the good things in life. Anyway, I'm looking forward to teaching you when we get our own place. It's just that I have to admit, yes, I am getting a bit sick of tuna melts."

I thought back briefly to my philosophy of feminism class. "You don't think I should learn to cook because I'm a woman, do you?"

He burst out laughing. "Laura, almost all of the Michelin-starred chefs in France are men. I believe everybody who loves eating should know how to cook. It's got nothing to do with gender."

I exhaled. "I'm glad to hear that. Speaking of our apartment problem, we should look at spots this weekend, except I have a huge essay I'm supposed to write about *Canterbury Tales*. Damn Chaucer."

Franck bit his lip as I slid our two tuna melts into the toaster oven. "I wish my papers would arrive. That would make things so much easier."

"I know," I said. I shared Franck's impatience. The fact his papers hadn't arrived as scheduled meant that we were both in limbo.

"I also worry," he said. "You know, that there's been some problem."

I held up my hand. "Don't even mention that possibility. What would we do then?"

"Go on the lam."

"I have a university degree to finish," I reminded him.

He sighed and played with my ponytail. "True."

Just then Sam walked by. So far, thanks to extreme sneakiness, I had been able to avoid either Franck or me running into him.

Sam stopped at the kitchenette, staring at this cozy domestic scene. "Laura." He grinned wide, like he always did, but something lurked behind it this time—something accusatory. "Strange. I haven't seen much of you lately, although I've been hearing a lot."

"Oh … Hi Sam," I tried to answer breezily. "Yes, well, I've been busy, I guess. How's it going?"

He didn't answer that, but instead nodded at Franck. "So this is the Frenchman you've been hiding in your room?"

So he knew. *Shit.* I opened my mouth to say something, but he cut me off. "No need to deny it. People talk. You know I can't allow it for much longer."

Surprisingly, a part of me felt relief that finally things were out in the open—no more skulking around. At the same time, this put a timeline on our apartment search.

"How much longer?" I asked.

Sam thought about this as he rubbed his chin. "Two more weeks. Until the end of the month. After that, my hands are tied." He had not stopped smiling throughout the entire conversation, which made him appear slightly deranged.

I nodded. "OK. That's fair." It was more than fair, actually. For such a relentlessly cheery individual, he wasn't all bad.

"But please continue to be discreet," he added. "Because if you get found out between now and then it's my head on the chopping block."

"I will, and I appreciate it," I said. "Truly."

"Just make yourselves scarce," he said. "You seem to have a talent for doing that. Also, figure something out."

Sam marched off down the hall, and I turned back to Franck. He was looking at me with confusion writ on his features. He had his fingers on the small of my back during the entire conversation and I could sense he'd intuited it was an important one. Still, it had all been in English.

"That was Sam, the floor fellow," I translated into French. "We have until the end of the month until we have to move out."

Franck's brows snapped together. "Two weeks? That's not a lot of time."

I shook my head. "You see why cooking isn't high on my list of priorities."

Franck grinned and took a bite of his tuna melt, then he rolled his eyes back in his head and sighed in mock ecstasy. "Laura! This is the most delicious tuna melt I've ever tasted." He attempted the words "tuna melt" in English.

"Hey!" I dropped my tuna melt on the second plate. "Was that your first English word? Tuna melt?"

He laughed. "I guess so. How *à propos*."

The next day we treated ourselves to a smoked meat sandwich at Bens before going for a walk on the paths of Mont Royal to discuss our housing crisis and give me a break from thinking about all those pilgrims in *Canterbury Tales*.

We had puffed our way up to the lookout on the top, just in front of the old stone lodge. I dragged Franck over to the edge so he could get the best view. Usually there was a scattering of tourists up here, but today it just looked like fellow Montréalais, getting out despite the minus-three-degree weather.

I could see our mingled breath as we gazed out at the frigid city that lay out in front of us. The glass sides of the skyscrapers reflected the gray winter light and steady streams of smoke rose out from their tops. In the distance, I could make out the faint hum of traffic and the odd honked horn.

"What do you think?" I grabbed on to Franck's bicep through his puffy jacket and heavy wool sweater.

"It's so North American," he said, smiling down at me.

The Saint Lawrence River floated sluggishly in the distance. I wondered how long it would take for it to freeze over – I'd heard it did that every winter.

"Not a lot of stone buildings compared to France," I observed.

"It all looks so very, very new." Franck gathered me close with his arm. "It's strange, it's like European cities turned inside out. In France, the oldest parts are always in the center, and then the more modern buildings are in the outskirts, like La Défense in

Paris. Here, the most modern bits are in the center it seems. Or maybe it's just that all of it is so modern."

I was still thinking about this when a familiar voice said behind me, "Finally!"

I whipped around, knowing before I did that it was Anne. She sounded pissed, and she had every right to be. I had promised I was going to introduce her and James to Franck, but what I had done was abandon them completely. Franck still felt like part of another life, part of a more private life, and that whole business with James … I was being a coward, and putting off the uncomfortable, I realized. I should have been more courageous and a better friend.

"Anne!" I said and went over to give her a hug. "It's so great to see you." I was acutely aware that I was trying to make up for my errors with enthusiasm that was even more grating than Sam the floor fellow's.

"Yeah," she said. She didn't hug me back, and her shoulders were drawn up around her ears.

I dragged her in front of Franck. "Franck, this is my friend Anne. Anne, this is Franck."

Franck reached out his hand and shook it warmly. "*Enchanté*," he said.

Anne looked slightly less angry and even smiled, but when she turned back to me there was a scowl on her face. "So, Laura," she said. "Was that so hard?"

"No," I answered. "Look. I'm so sorry. It's just been really—"

She waved her hand. "Whatever. You've made it clear what your priorities are, and it's not us."

"Us?" I echoed. As far as I could tell Anne was alone, but I looked past her shoulder and saw James making his way towards us. He must have been inside the lodge. His mouth was twisted into a grim expression.

My stomach dropped. I knew it then—James was the reason why I'd been avoiding Anne. What had been muddled before was now crystal clear. She almost always came in a package deal with James.

I felt odd about those few weeks when James had been in love with me and I—at brief moments—entertained that as a possibility if there hadn't been Franck. But there was Franck, standing here in the cold beside me. I was caught between two worlds colliding.

I had no reason to believe that Franck was a jealous person, but I'd mentioned James on the phone to Franck—would Franck remember? I hadn't done anything wrong, not technically, unless entertaining doubts and thoughts about alternate futures was wrong.

It would be better if Franck never put two and two together that this James was the one who had wanted to get together with me. *Better for me or for him?* Franck was hot-blooded like most French people, and I wouldn't put it past him to throw a punch if provoked.

For a few moments I froze, unsure how to act. What I felt like doing most of all was grabbing Franck's hand and running away.

"Hi James!" I called over instead, as manically cheery as a cruise director. "I'd like you to meet Franck." I waved over to Franck.

Franck eyed me questioningly.

"Franck, this is another friend of mine, James," I explained in French.

Franck shook his head and nodded, but I noticed he did not say *enchanté* or offer his hand as he had with Anne. I could feel his body stiffen beside mine. *He remembered.*

James looked pale and frightened. It dawned on me that he probably had no idea just how much I had told Franck. No wonder he was scared. I smiled at him and gave him an infinitesimal shake of my head, to put him out of his misery. He took a deep breath and his shoulders dropped.

"Nice to meet you," he said to Franck in French. "We've heard so much about you from Laura."

"Ah," Franck said, and raised a brow at me.

Hanging out with the three of them was going to be emotionally exhausting, I realized. Still, I was willing to do it to make up for the sense of shame that reverberated in me. "It's freezing," I said. "Do you guys want to join us in the lodge and grab a coffee?"

James opened his mouth to say something, but Anne spoke before he got a chance. "We're just heading down now," she said. "We have plans to go to Foufounes tonight."

"Of course," I said. "Saturday night. Drag night, right?"

Anne nodded, making a point of not inviting me. I didn't blame her. They turned and began to leave, but not before James bid us a polite *au revoir*.

With Franck, I was no longer a student in the same way other students in residence were. One way or another I would be living off campus so soon anyway. An unsettled feeling roiled in my stomach. I no longer knew where I fit.

Franck's mitted hand stole around mine as I watched Anne and James leave and walk away. I leaned against him, a melancholy I didn't think I should be feeling winding around my heart.

"That was James?" Franck asked. "The James you told me about on the phone."

"*Oui*." Thank God I hadn't told Franck about the note James had left me in that English lecture. "I'm sure he's already on to someone else by now." I didn't know that, but I hoped.

"As long as he knows you're mine," Franck said. "And I'm yours."

"He does. I made that crystal clear." If James hadn't understood, after all that, it was his own fault.

Franck didn't say anything, but he did lean down and dropped a kiss on the top of my toque. He seemed to sense what I was feeling without me explaining anything, and I was grateful for it. It reminded me that even though I didn't belong in residence anymore, I fit with Franck. That was one true thing I could count on.

chapter twelve

By the end of the next week, we had visited four apartments that we would have taken gladly, but nobody wanted to rent to us.

Franck had no papers and no job, and I had very little to show for myself either. I was a student, just another poor student. I couldn't ask for any kind of financial guarantee from my parents because I knew they were going to disapprove of me moving in with Franck. Also, there was the small wrinkle that I still hadn't told them.

I knew I had to call them, but it was easier to keep putting it off. I should have learned from the situation with Anne and James—procrastination made nothing better, yet I found myself making the same mistake.

In the case of my parents the procrastination could not really make the situation worse. No matter what my timing was going to be, they were going to be seriously unhappy.

When I thought about it, I understood their objections. I was only nineteen. They had never met Franck. I already had a place to live for this year in Montréal. There was also the added issue of them not believing in living together before marriage. I didn't agree with that, of course, but the rest of it … I could see where they were coming from.

I'd taken Franck to a restaurant popular in the student ghetto, Le Santropol. It was characterized by the jungle atmosphere that reigned inside—the sheer number of plants growing in the window and the thick condensation that made it impossible to see the interior from the sidewalk. It was also famous for its peanut butter lettuce sandwich on the menu.

"There's some pretty crazy stuff on offer here," I warned Franck as we were seated by a cascading fern that kept tickling my forehead.

Franck, since my observation at Bens, had been determined not to act like a stereotypical French person abroad and to open himself up to the wider world of flavors. Still, I could tell it was a mighty struggle for him. He remained extremely French despite his best intentions.

"Like crazy good?" he asked hopefully.

"I suppose that's a matter of opinion." I shed my wool jacket. I wasn't sure what their heating bills must be at Le Santropol but they always managed to create a hothouse climate within the restaurant. It was a welcome change from the biting cold outside, yet once seated I found myself overdressed and sweating underneath my winter clothes.

"Ugh." I pulled the neck of my cobalt blue sweater. "I always forget that I need to dress in layers in here."

Franck had already stripped down to his T-shirt. My skin tone had lost any vestiges of its summer glow and had reverted to its natural Scottish pallor, but Franck's arms were still ruddy and tanned. How I longed for an olive complexion like that. Maybe if we had children one day … *wait*. I was getting ahead of myself. A lot of things had to happen before that, notably finding an apartment.

"Still no word on the papers?" I asked, hopefully. I knew I would be the first person to know, but so much hinged on them.

He shook his head and reached across to cover my hand with his. "They will arrive soon," he said. "I know it. That color looks stunning on you," he added with a squeeze. "*Tu es trop belle.* It makes me very eager to get our own place and find a slightly larger bed."

I blushed, not just from the steamy air. I was looking forward to that too. My tiny smaller-than-single residence bed meant that neither of us was doing much sleeping, although we managed to keep busy in other ways.

The waiter came and I ordered a peanut butter and lettuce

sandwich. I wasn't sure how much of my English Franck understood, because he said to the waiter in French. "I'll have the same."

"Do you realize what you just ordered?"

"The same as you. The peanut butter thing."

"Have you ever tried peanut butter before?"

Franck shook his head.

"Then that was brave of you."

"Nothing ventured, nothing gained," he said. "I have to become Canadian, right? It seems to me eating disgusting food is part of that."

I lifted my finger. "Ah-ah-ah, now that sounds like something a *French* person would say."

Franck cursed under his breath. "This being French thing is stronger than I realized."

I nodded. "Uh huh."

"Laura!" I heard someone call from the entry to the restaurant. I spun around to see my friend Samantha coming in, shedding off her layers as she went. I had only seen her once or twice since arriving in Montréal. She was a year ahead of me and no longer living in residence.

An old fear struck my heart. We'd grown up together and went to the same high school together although she was a year older and a grade above me. She was petite and beautiful—a renowned knock-out and a large majority of guys at our high school were in love with her.

I often suspected that my wealth of male friends during my last few years of high school was due to my position as one of Sam's closest friends. For a flash second, I wondered if I could sneak Franck and myself out the back but then I reminded myself I wasn't in high school anymore.

She came to our table and it was actually a relief to see her, despite that weird high school insecurity bubbling up. She was a familiar face in a world that had suddenly become exponentially as confusing as it was wonderful.

"Hi Sam." I stood up and gave her a huge hug. "It's so good to see you."

I gestured over at Franck, who was standing up. "This is Franck." I'd told Sam about him over the summer, and I knew that like so many of my friends she was curious to meet the man who had so comprehensively swept me off my feet.

"*Bonjour*," she said in French, revealing a beautiful smile with perfectly white, straight teeth. "*Je suis ravie de te rencontrer.*" She had gone to Belgium on the Ursus exchange the year before me, so her French was excellent and she was diligent with the language in a way I'd never been. My learning style for foreign languages seemed to be something akin to osmosis.

"*Bonjour.*" Franck smiled back and stood up and gave her the *bises*.

Despite a slight inner quaking that I tried to ignore, I said, "Can you grab a chair and sit with us for a while Sam? It'd be great to catch up."

She looked around the room. "I'm supposed to be meeting my roommate here for lunch but she's always late, so I'm sure I've got a bit of time. What's up with you—" Her blue eyes shifted to Franck. "Two."

I filled her in on our desperate need for an apartment in a mishmash of English and French.

Her eyes got rounder and she looked back and forth between me and Franck. "So you two are moving in together? I guess that makes sense but, Laura, your parents are going to … well, I don't know what they're going to do, but it's not going to be good."

Sam knew my parents well. At times she lived more at my house than hers during high school and my parents had taken her on vacation with us as well. She confirmed my worst fears.

I took a deep breath. "I know."

Franck's brows drew together. "I don't understand," he said. "Why would your parents mind? It's normal that we would live together."

We must have been speaking enough French for Franck to follow. I hadn't really broached this issue with him at any length yet. One more thing in my life that was well overdue.

Sam laughed out loud at Franck's question. "Laura, where should we even begin?" She rolled her eyes at me.

I thought back to how it had been in France. There had been no question that I would sleep anywhere but with Franck in his room, and everyone from Franck's grandmother to his elderly aunts saw this as completely normal. I searched for the right words. How could I begin to explain to Franck the puritan slant that penetrated so many aspects of North American society?

"I suppose it began with the pilgrims who emigrated to North America." I was going to take a stab at it. "They were protestants who believed in hard work and pure living."

Franck's upper lip curled in distaste at such a mindset. I couldn't blame him. After experiencing the hedonistic devotion to pleasure that infiltrated every layer of daily life in France, puritanism did not feel like a sensible way to live.

"Anyway, that's the way people are in English Canada," I said. "They generally believe that good people work hard, don't wear their emotions on their sleeve, and don't live together before they get married."

Franck cocked an eyebrow. "Sounds tedious."

"It is," I agreed. "Why do you think Sam and I were so eager to leave after high school?"

Sam was nodding in vigorous agreement.

"But people are people everywhere," Franck insisted. "I'm sure people in Victoria have affairs and drink in the afternoon and slack off their work …"

"They do," Sam confirmed. "It's just that they have to *appear* like they don't."

I nodded. "That's it exactly. Appearances. Image. That's what counts."

Franck shook his head. "That is the most bizarre thing I've ever heard."

I sighed. "I know it's almost impossible for a French person to comprehend, but it's why my parents are not going to be happy about us moving in together."

I could always stay in residence while Franck got an apartment, but that felt unthinkable. First of all, we'd always dreamed about moving in together. Secondly, I wanted to live with him. Thirdly, I would feel like I was abandoning him if he came all this way and I still stayed in my own place. We were in this together.

"Jesus," Sam said under her breath. "I do not envy you Laura. Are you going to do it over the phone?"

I snorted. "I'm certainly not flying back home to do it in person." The weight of that upcoming conversation pressed down on me like a block of cement, so I gave myself a shake. "Anyway, there's no point in breaking it to my parents before we find an apartment, and we've had no luck so far with that."

Sam got a familiar look in her eye—a look I knew well from our childhood when she was concocting some sort of plan.

"What?" I said.

"I may be able to help you."

"Really?"

She nodded. Franck too, I saw, was listening intently.

"The people in the apartment underneath us moved out suddenly three days ago. They've left our landlord, Denis, in the lurch. They didn't even pay last month's rent.

I decided to lay it all out on the table. "The issue is Franck's papers haven't arrived yet, so we can't show any form of steady income."

Sam shrugged. "I've heard rumors that Denis is somehow involved in the mafia—which mafia I'm not sure, as there seems to be several different branches in Montréal. Anyway, I don't think he's necessarily a stickler for doing things above board, as long as you pay your rent."

"The mafia?" I said. "You mean like in the *Godfather* films?" That was my extent of exposure to the mafia, and up until that moment I hadn't considered that the mafia might actually exist outside of TV and movies.

Sam shook her head. "No, he's not Italian. Like I said, every nationality here seems to have its own mafia. I'm sure there's an English Protestant one too." Amazing, even in its criminal underworld, Montréal was a diverse and equal-opportunity place.

I paused for a moment and exchanged wary glances with Franck. If what Sam was saying was true, was it worth the risk of a mafia landlord to secure an apartment? "Is he dangerous?" I asked.

Sam laughed. "Denis? No, he's harmless. He loves me and would do anything for me. So, interested?"

I knew from past experience with Sam that just because Denis loved her didn't mean he would love Franck and me. Sam was a good friend, but she had the obliviousness of a gorgeous woman. Her beauty paved her way in the world, so she just assumed that things flowed as easily for everyone. As I'd experienced with waiters, club bouncers, and teachers when hanging out with Sam in high school, it was not.

I looked over at Franck and he sent me a questioning glance back. I nodded, then he began nodding too. "We're definitely interested," I said. "Maybe a mafia connection wouldn't hurt."

chapter thirteen

Sam called later on that afternoon to tell me that Denis was willing to meet with us at the apartment just underneath hers, near the corner of Saint-Laurent and Prince Arthur streets, the next day at noon. This was excellent timing, as I had a fifteen-page English essay on the Elizabethan poets to write and hand in at eleven o'clock, just an hour before.

Despite my best intentions, I was doing an inconsistent job of keeping up with my schoolwork. The constant distraction of Franck in my residence room was proving to be, well, a distraction. He wasn't on a student schedule like me, and even though he encouraged me to get my work done while he lay on the bed reading *Le Guide Routard* for Québec that his aunt bought him as a going-away gift, I always succumbed to snuggling up close to him and doing things that were not at all conducive to the analytic thought required for essay writing.

It was wonderful of course, but at the same time I had promised myself to let nothing get in the way of my university degree, and here I was, doing just that.

I told Franck I was going to have to go to the library to write my essay, far away from him and any horizontal surface.

He put his *Guide Routard* down beside him on the bed and sat up. "I'll come with you."

"You'll be bored," I protested.

"Are you joking? Bored in a library?" He pulled on his sweater. "I could be locked in a library for days in a row and never be bored."

"But this is a university library," I explained. "It's mainly full of obscure academic works."

He grinned. "Even better. I can catch up on the theory of nihilism."

"Most of the books will be in English."

Franck stood up and put his hands on my shoulders. "Laura, what is it that's worrying you? Do you not want me to come?"

I sighed. "I'm just stressed about getting this essay done. It's going to be a huge amount of work, and I worry about what you're going to do in the meantime. I'm feeling badly that you'll be bored."

"Laura, you don't have to keep me entertained," he said. "I would never expect that or want it. That's not what couples do."

I sighed. "I'm trying to figure out how to be both a student and a girlfriend right now. It's not as simple as I thought it would be."

He leaned down and gave me a kiss. "If you have to study even for the next few days, that's OK. Your intelligence is one of the main things I fell in love with. I love that you're smart and ambitious. I wouldn't change that for the world."

That was exactly what I needed to hear. "I'm glad, because I'm not quitting school."

Franck jerked back. "I hope to God you'd never think I would want that."

I know," I kissed him back. "I worry too much about keeping people happy, especially people I love."

"Don't worry about me," Franck said. "I am happier than I've ever been, but I won't be if my being here makes your marks go down."

I nodded. "OK then. *On y va.* To the library!"

"To the library!" Franck cheered, and we headed out my door.

I worked in the library until one o'clock in the morning. Franck was amazed it was open twenty-four hours a day, unlike the libraries at the Sorbonne that kept strict office hours.

Franck was true to his word and found a teetering pile of philosophy books in French and a cozy corner. He was perfectly happy there until I could no longer keep my eyes open and we headed back up the hill.

I was glad for his company as we hiked up through the snow softly falling in the dark.

"Our first Montréal snow!" I said. Even though everyone warned me that I would soon be heartily sick of the white stuff, for right now I was charmed. It buffered us and the city around us in a cushion of serenity.

"And we're together." Franck lifted me up and swung me around, backpack and all. "Sometimes I feel like I need to keep pinching myself."

"I know." We started walking again.

"How much more do you have to do on your essay?" Franck asked. He kept his arm wrapped around my shoulders.

"I think I've done enough research now, but it's going to be an all-nighter."

"What's an all-nighter?" I had used the English expression in the middle of a sentence in French.

"It means that I'll need to work all night through."

"And not sleep?"

I nodded. "You'll get the bed to yourself for once, but I will have to leave the light on."

"Is there anything I can do for you?"

I thought about this. "You could make me a Bodum full of coffee when we get back to res. I'll need it."

"Consider it done." Franck looked up at the sky. The stars were obscured with snow clouds but they were up there, somewhere.

"I'm looking forward to being in our own place so I can take care of you when you have to work hard like that."

I was intrigued by this. "And how exactly would you take care of me?"

He shrugged. "You know. Cook you good things. Massage

your shoulders. Sharpen your pencils."

That sounded like heaven. "You seduced me by describing how you would make me a hot toddy for my cold and wrap me up in a warm blanket." The caring thing, the idea of caring for each other was one of the headiest love potions for me.

Franck clicked his tongue. "That was a good move, but didn't we fall in love as soon as we set eyes on each other?"

I thought about this. "I was definitely intrigued," I said. "But it was the hot toddy thing that really clinched it for me."

Franck chuckled. "In that case, expect there to be a lot more of that once we get our own place."

"I'm looking forward to it," I said.

I stuck out my tongue and could feel the refreshing chill of the fat, fluffy snowflakes melting on it. Maybe the next day we would solve our apartment problem. Or part of it anyway, I reminded myself as I thought back to my parents. Over the past ten days, my mom had left several messages on my answering machine I hadn't returned. When we did talk, she unfailingly launched into questions about Franck's plans, and whether he had found an apartment to live in yet. I didn't know what to answer. I was avoiding things again and it made me feel squirmy and gross.

As I predicted, I had to work straight through while Franck slept on my bed. I handed the essay in on time the next morning and dozed on and off during the lecture. Franck met me outside the lecture hall, and we headed off in the bracingly, cold, clear, snow-covered day to meet with Denis.

Sam had shown me the door to the apartment. It was inset in a brick, three-story building in an enviable location almost on the corner of Saint-Laurent—the street the locals often referred to as "The Main." It was the historic artery of the city—the place of summer festivals and the restaurants spilling onto the sidewalk like I had gone to my first night here with Anne and James.

A pang cut through my general wooziness of sleep deprivation. I hadn't seen James and Anne since that day on Mont Royal, and I was pretty certain they were actively avoiding me. Relief and shame over this warred inside me.

The cross street was Prince Arthur, where one of my favorite restaurants—a Polish joint where one could buy a meal of steaming borscht and homemade perogies for a few dollars—was located. I buzzed Sam's apartment, as she'd instructed me to do. The door itself, which had once been painted blue but was now washed out and flaking off, didn't speak of a particularly meticulous landlord, but we couldn't be picky.

A few minutes later I heard her clatter down the staircase.

She flung the door open. "Hi! Denis isn't here yet but he gave me a spare key so I can show you around while we're waiting for him to arrive."

"Perfect." I squeezed Franck's hand. Was this place going to be our new home? Was this the place where we—truly, officially—would begin our life as a couple together?

"You know, I haven't actually seen the apartment myself." She talked to us over her shoulder as she led the way up the steep staircase that smelled of cabbage and cigarettes. "But we'll be neighbors! We're the apartment directly above."

"That's definitely a selling point," I said. Part of me did fret that because Sam was an old friend, I might be reverting somehow to my old life by moving into the same building as her, but that was ridiculous. I was in a new relationship. I was in a new city. Sam being here too changed none of that.

"Obviously," she said, turning the key in the door that looked, like the door to the building, as though it had seen better days. "The location is fabulous. Tons of restaurants and coffee shops right on your doorstep."

We entered. It was bright, as there were no curtains or shades on the windows, but it was also so cold we could see our own breath in the air. The heat had probably been turned off when the tenants had taken off, I told myself. What landlord would throw money out the window by heating an unoccupied apartment?

Franck and I went into the kitchen. It was extremely bare

bones and looked onto a tiny patch of snow. The cupboards were made out of some sort of cheap wood composite and the counter was a linoleum that looked more like flooring than counter materials. It did boast, however, an oven with three elements and a banged-up fridge with a deep indent on its front that reminded me of the shape of Han Solo encased in carbon at the end of *The Empire Strikes Back*. I sniffed. The freezing air seemed to annihilate any smells. Nothing was making me gag, in any case.

Next came the bathroom, which housed a stained ceramic bathtub, a porcelain sink with a long hairline crack down it, and rusty rod without the shower curtain.

"Huh," I observed looking up at it. "I guess the previous tenants even took the shower curtain rings. That seems petty."

Sam shrugged. "I only passed them a handful of times on the stairs, so I have no idea why they took off in such a hurry. Denis is maybe a bit, well, edgy, but he's actually a pussycat."

I would wait to see that for myself, and not through Gorgeous Girl goggles.

"What kind of heat is it?" Franck asked.

Right. Those were proper adult questions. I hadn't learned to ask those yet.

Sam shrugged. "I don't know. There's a thermostat on the wall and we just turn it up. I guess I never paid attention to where it comes out."

Franck paused for a second, his eyes wide. He'd rented apartments in Paris while he was at university, but I doubted he'd been quite as clueless as Sam and me even the first time he'd arrived in Paris from Villers-la-Faye. He turned and examined the wooden floorboards where in the corner of the entrance there was a metal grate roughly cut into the wooden floor. "Electric," he said, turning to me with a grimace. "That means it'll be expensive to heat."

Truth be told, I'd never really thought of different kinds of heat before, but I did know my family home in Victoria was heated electrically. I was six years old when my parents built that house, and I had been buddies with the guy who did the wiring. "We have electric heat in Victoria. I don't think it's nearly as expensive as electricity in France. We have so many rivers and dams and stuff in Canada. It's all hydro-electric." I was impressed with myself. I remembered seeing the nuclear power plants in the countryside in northern Burgundy. It sounded as if I sort of knew what I was talking about.

"Still, my guide-book says it gets really cold here in Québec," Franck continued, crouching to inspect the heat grate.

I reached over and caressed his palm with my thumb. "*Chéri*," I said. "Should we be picky about the heat? Are we in a position to be picky about, well, anything?"

He looked at me and bit his lip.

"I don't think so," I answered my own question.

"Right," he said.

We went into the bedrooms—there were two and both rooms were a decent size with single paned windows looking out onto Prince Arthur. The walls were an extremely dirty shade of greige with remnants of old tape stuck on them here and there. The second bedroom was kind of a waste for us, but, wait, I *could tell my parents Franck and I were sharing an apartment but sleeping in separate bedrooms.*

I was still contemplating the feasibility of this when I heard someone call out "I'm here! I'm here, Samantha!"

We returned to the front hall which was now occupied by a short and extremely rotund man who looked to be an extremely neglected fifty-ish. I had pictured him younger and skinnier and in a beautifully cut suit for some reason. His gut hung over a worn pair of jeans and his hair looked far too solidly black to be natural. I could now smell one thing in this icebox of an apartment: Denis reeked of cigars.

Franck and I exchanged a look that spoke volumes. First impressions weren't good, but if Franck couldn't be choosy about the heat, I couldn't get fastidious about the landlord.

Denis barely glanced at Franck and me. His black eyes were fixated on Sam, particularly her boobs in her fitted sweater. I felt gross for my friend. Didn't she see how slimy he was? Or maybe she was just used to all men treating her this way, which made me feel sorry for her—a novel experience.

"So, you are friends of Sam?" Denis grunted in our direction. His accent was heavy, but I couldn't place it, except that I knew it wasn't French. In any case, he still spoke better English than my boyfriend currently did.

I tried for a charming smile. "Yes."

"Huh. You need an apartment?"

"Yes."

"This is great apartment." He waved his hands around to encompass the whole space. It wasn't a terrible apartment, but "great" was stretching it. "You would be lucky to live in such an apartment. I even think of moving here myself."

Then why were we here? "It's very nice," I agreed, trying to maintain my smile.

His chin jerked towards Franck. "And your man? Cat got his tongue? Why he not speak?"

"He only speaks French," I explained and then translated the gist of the exchange to Franck. "Do you speak French?" I asked Denis.

Denis spat on the ground and took a step back as though Franck's Frenchness was contagious. "No English? He is not one of these radical separatist Québécois, is he?"

"No," I answered, bewildered. *What Québécois radicals?* "He's from France. He just arrived."

This appeared to be marginally preferable than being Québécois in Denis's mind. "How do I know you two will stay together and pay the rent, unlike the last tenants who—"

"We'll pay the rent," I promised. "And we'll stay together."

I was making promises I couldn't necessarily keep. Everything was in flux. I *wanted* to be able to pay the rent and stay together with Franck. Still, the reality of life as a new immigrant to Montréal might not be easy—the cold, being uprooted from his family, the fact that his girlfriend had to study all the time, not to mention the worst of all: cheesecake.

"Why should I trust you?" Denis demanded, his chin raised defiantly at us.

I dug in my pocket and came up with five hundred dollars in cash that I'd saved while working over the summer in Victoria. I handed it over to him. "There's our damage deposit."

His eyes widened. He counted it with a licked index finger, then carefully wedged it deep into the back pocket of his jeans.

"All right." He handed me over a key. "I do this for Sam only." He sent her an oily smile and she fluttered her eyelashes back at him. "You'll have to get a copy made of that. This is my key and I want it back."

I nodded. The old tenants must have taken their keys with them. Then from his other back pocket, he removed a dirty piece of crumpled-up paper.

"This is the lease," he said. "Four hundred dollars a month, OK?"

I nodded. Maybe I should have done more research about going lease rates in Montréal, but it was too late for that. We had to be out of residence in a matter of days.

"Sign here." Denis pointed to a line at the bottom of the paper. "No point in your man signing if he doesn't even speak English."

"Thank you so much, Denis!" Sam said, smiling at him in a way that left him bereft of speech while I scribbled my name on the bottom of the lease.

I handed it back to him, waking him up out of his reverie. "When can we move in?"

He shrugged. "You have the key to copy. Leave my original key in the mailbox and I will drop by and get it. Leave your rent checks in there too, fifteenth of the month. I must go. I am tracking down those tenants who left me in the middle of the night." His face tightened into a snarl that sent ice down my spine. "They will pay for that." He slammed the door behind him, leaving us there.

It took me a minute to calm my gut instincts that were yelling at me that Denis was a scary dude.

I gave Sam a hug. "My God, Sam, thank you so much. Er, are you sure Denis is harmless?"

She hugged me back. "Yes. Trust me."

I decided that there was no point fretting over a done deal. We had an apartment of our own now. The lease was signed. "You've solved all our problems, and we're going to be neighbors!"

She grinned, then her smile disappeared, like a water draining out of a bathtub. "I haven't solved all your problems," she said. "You have to tell your parents now."

chapter fourteen

Franck and I whooped once Sam went back up to her apartment and we made our way down the steep stairs and into the street. We hugged and kissed each other, barely noticing that it had started to snow again.

"Our new home!" I said.

"Our first *chez nous*!" He spun me around.

But as we walked back to residence hand in hand, I fell silent. There was no more putting it off. I would have to call my parents. My heart squeezed with apprehension, but I reasoned it was better to bite the bullet than stay in this limbo of waiting to call them.

"Stressed about phoning your parents?" Franck reached over to brush off the snowflakes that had been collecting on the crown of my head.

I nodded.

"I'm sure it will go much better than you think it will." His hand slid down my temple and brushed my cheek. "Surely they will understand that we want to live together because we love each other."

I laughed at Franck's naïveté, and it came out more bitter than I had intended.

"They let you travel to France for a year alone when you were only seventeen," he continued. "Most French parents wouldn't trust their children to do that. I'm twenty-three and my parents could barely let me leave. Moving in with me by comparison is nothing."

How could I even begin to explain? As much as travel and

independence and winning things such as the Ursus scholarship were prized in my family culture, indulging in things like a passionate love affair was seen as self-indulgent and, worse, illogical.

Objectively, I could hardly blame my parents. I had just turned nineteen, and here I was embarking on my undergrad degree and moving in with a guy I had met in France the year before? If someone else told me they were doing that, I would probably jump to the conclusion they were crazy too. It took a deeper knowledge of that connection Franck and I had together for it to begin to make any sense at all. The problem was that nobody but Franck or I could possibly have that understanding.

I looked down at my Doc Marten boots kicking up the snow as I walked. "It's just so different here than in France about these things."

Franck nodded. "Perhaps, but I am quite sure your parents love you. They will come around."

I was sure they loved me, but as for them coming around … I had my doubts.

When we got back to my room at Molson Hose I was tempted to go make some coffee first or have a snack, but instead I forced myself to sit on the bed and pull the phone sitting on my desk towards me. Truth time.

Franck hung his jacket up in the wooden built-in cupboard and sat beside me. He slid his arm around my waist. "What can I do to help?"

I shook my head. "I have to do this."

He dropped his head into his hand. "I hate that me being here has put you in this position. I never imagined living together would be an issue."

Having lived in France, I believed him.

"Do you want me to stay or leave?"

I thought about this. "Stay, but give me a bit of space." Just having him nearby would make me feel more supported.

Franck shuffled up to the top of the bed and lay down, interlacing his fingers over his torso. Maybe I could join him and I could make this call tonight ... No.

I dialed with shaking fingers and swallowed hard just before my Mom picked up. As usual, there was five minutes of breezy conversation. The pond in my grandmother's back yard on Salt Spring Island had sprung a mysterious leak and my little sister won a math contest.

I was just about to cut off the chit-chat when she gave me an opening. "So," she began, her voice airy. "Has Franck found an apartment yet?"

I cleared my throat. "As a matter of fact, yes. That's actually what I was calling about."

"That's good news." She sounded relieved, which compounded the ball of dread in my stomach. "I've seen the size of your residence room."

"The apartment is in the same building as Sam's apartment. In fact, Sam just lives upstairs."

"How nice."

"I'll be moving in there too."

"What do you mean? Into the building?"

"Yes."

"Into Sam's apartment?"

It was the moment of truth. "No. Franck and I will be living in the apartment below Sam ... together."

She gasped. "But Laura, you can't ... you have your residence room!" I then heard some muffled noise as she must have put her hand over the phone receiver. "Here's your father."

My father? My heart sank. He must have come home early from work. I had planned to break it to my mother first without him being there.

My father came on the phone line and cleared his throat. "Laura. Please tell me your mother misunderstood just now."

I braced for a fight. "No. She didn't. Franck and I have found an apartment. It has two bedrooms so we can each take one." I regretted those words as soon as they were out of my mouth. They were not only a blatant lie but smacked of desperation. It was beneath me, and it was beneath my parents.

"Laura, do you think I was born yesterday?" My father's voice was quiet. Ominously so.

"No." I understood why he felt insulted. Of course he wasn't that naïve. "I don't see why you guys have a problem with it. Franck moved here so we could be together and I'm nineteen. What does it make a difference if I live in residence or in an apartment?"

"It makes all the difference. You know how we feel about living together before marriage. Mark my words, the next step is that you are going to drop out of university."

"I would never do that," I said, and meant it. "I can live with my boyfriend and go to university, you know. It's the 1990s."

"Are you going to get married?"

"I'm nineteen. Why would I get married?"

"Laura, why would a man buy the cow when he can get the milk—"

"Don't you dare finish that sentence." All those theories and lectures in the philosophy of feminism class that I was almost failing came to the rescue. Part of me actually felt sorry for my dad at the righteous fury igniting inside of me. "Are you actually comparing me to a cow? What do you think I am, chattel?"

"No ... I don't think that but—" My father and I didn't butt heads often, but when we did it was epic. We were both stubborn as mules.

"Then why would you ever say something like that?" I didn't let him finish. "Do you think that just because I'm female I have no intrinsic value beyond my virginity? That my only value comes from catching a husband?"

He paused for a moment, regrouping at the unexpected swerve of the conversation. "Laura, I don't want to debate the issue." He was using his authoritative tone again, but I was feeling too much indignation to be cowed. "You are not allowed to do this," he said. "I won't pay for it."

"You're saying you're cutting me off?"

"If you do this. Yes. If you're going to live with a man, that man can support you."

I made an exasperated sound. "It's no longer the 1950s, Dad."

"That's my final word."

"I'm sorry to hear that Dad, but I'm going to do this anyway."

I thought I had the final word with that, but in fact my Dad did by hanging up the phone without so much as saying good-bye.

I held the receiver in my hand for a while, my shock reverberating to the soundtrack of the dial tone. Slowly, I hung it up. It was only then I realized how much my hand was shaking. I hadn't paid attention to Franck during the call, but now I saw he had moved. He was perched on the narrow window ledge, his hands knotted together, staring at me.

"I didn't understand all of it, but it sounds like you gave him hell," Franck said.

I nodded slowly. "As it turns out, that Philosophy of Feminism class came in handy."

"Still—"

My face must have look as stricken as I felt. "I'm cut off financially," I said. "What are we going to do?"

Franck rushed over to me and took my hand. "I have some money saved."

"But that is to tide you over until your papers arrive and you can look for a job. I just cleaned out my bank account with that cash I gave Denis for the down payment."

"My papers will be arriving any day now. I'm sure of it."

"If they don't, we are screwed," I said. "I don't like the idea of being late paying rent to Denis. I should look for a job."

Franck's face was lined with worry. "I never intended to come between you and your family. Like I said I—"

"I know, you never imagined this would be an issue. Trust me, I believe you. Also, this isn't you coming between me and my family. It's between me and my parents. I think it's been a long time coming."

"We'll figure it out," Franck assured me.

"So we're moving anyway and just taking a leap of faith?" I asked, almost disbelieving at the situation I was finding myself in.

Me, the inveterate planner and strategizer.

Franck reached out and took my hand in his. "I don't see any other way. Besides, leaps of faith have held us in good stead so far, haven't they?

That was true. Franck wouldn't be here right now if we hadn't taken one. "In that case," I said. "We'd better start packing."

chapter **fifteen**

By the end of the weekend two things had changed. I had packed my worldly possessions into two massive suitcases and an extremely heavy metal trunk, and Montréal had been hit with the first blizzard of the winter—a bad one, according to the news.

Several feet of snow had fallen in a few short hours on Sunday night, and we woke up on Monday, our moving day, to a freezing winterscape outside of howling, glacial wind, stinging ice crystals in the air, snow drifts everywhere, and warnings of more snow.

Sam the floor fellow had come by the night before to tell us that we needed to be out by the end of the next day and to say a gushing good-bye. I had gone to the administrative office of the residences and cancelled my lease as of December 1st and arranged for the refunded money to go not to me, but to be reimbursed back to my parents via a check in the mail. We were poor now, but I had my principles.

Franck and I stared out my residence window one last time. It was practically a white out.

"*Merde*," I said. "Maybe we should splurge for a taxi to move the stuff." Even as I said this, I knew we didn't have the money for it, not even a single cent. We didn't even have enough money to buy a bed yet, and taxis were expensive, especially as this would take two or maybe three trips. Still …

"No need for a taxi," Franck said, his hand resting on my lower back. "I can do it."

I looked down, where I could just barely make out deep-looking drifts of snow on the ground below.

Franck smiled and straightened up. "I'm strong, remember? Maybe I can't make things right with your parents, yet, anyway, but I can move our things."

The apartment was a good twenty-minute walk away from the residence, plus up that flight of extremely steep stairs in our apartment building. It looked and I was sure, felt, like the North Pole outside. All Franck had for warmth was his old ski jacket his Mémé had bought him when he was invited on a ski trip to the Alps when he was a teenager.

"All right." I turned to him, still doubtful. "Maybe for the trunk it can work if I carry one end and you carry the other?"

"No." He shook his head. "I'll manage with the large items. We should probably make our first trip now."

We bundled up in our coats on and equipped ourselves with toques and mitts.

Franck lifted up one of my suitcases, and I regretted yet again that I wasn't more of a minimalist. I had tried to lift it the night before and it weighed a ton.

I looked around for something useful to take and I grabbed two potted plants and a light triangular IKEA plastic corner table that hadn't fit anywhere else.

"Do you have the key for the apartment?" Franck asked.

I'd made a copy of the key the day before and slid the original into our mailbox at the apartment as per Denis's instructions. "Check."

"*On y va.*" Let's go. Moving in a blizzard didn't feel like the most auspicious start to our life together as a couple, but then again, we were fighting together against the odds. That counted for something, didn't it?

Half an hour later I unlocked the front door of our new building and we plunged inside the small entryway, desperate to get out of the cold.

The weather reports had been right. It was without a doubt a blizzard. Franck carried the suitcase on his shoulder the entire way.

It took us both a few seconds to catch our breath. "*Putain de bordel de merde*," I gasped at last.

I had never experienced cold like that. It had to be minus twenty with the wind chill. The wind cut through everything I wore like one of those Japanese chef's knives. The snow wasn't coming down in those lovely fluffy flakes like it did when the temperatures were milder. No. What fell from the sky now was tiny but deadly: equal parts snow and ice that the wind whipped like needles against any bare skin. We had staggered along, hunched over, sinking in snow drifts that appeared out of nowhere. If Hell did freeze over, it would be exactly like the current situation outside.

"I concur." Franck ran his hand through his hair, but because it was frozen it stood straight up on end. "Let's get upstairs to our place and turn on the heat."

At the top of the stairs I opened the door with my new key. The apartment looked far too big and empty. Besides my little plastic table we owned no furniture and didn't have the money to buy any. It was a good thing I had grown up camping like many Canadian kids.

I dropped the table in the front hall and it echoed in the vast emptiness. I looked down at the plants I carried in my other hand. They had gone from bright green and healthy to two black shriveled balls in the pots.

"Shit," I muttered. There went my attempt at decorative touches. When I breathed out, I could see my breath. I went into the kitchen and put the dead plants on the counter. I'd deal with those later. The priority was heat. I ran from thermostat to thermostat, cranking them all up as high as they could go. I'd worry about how we were going to pay our heating bill another day.

I was in the bigger bedroom when Franck finally came in, breathing hard under the load of the suitcase he had slung over his right shoulder. He dropped it on the floor with a thump and leaned against the wall to catch his breath.

"Welcome home, honey," I said in the cheery tone of a 1950s housewife, then cackled with laughter. "Isn't it cozy?"

"Hey," he gasped. "You didn't give me a chance to carry you through the threshold."

"You carried that huge suitcase of mine," I said. "That's good enough. Anyway, I think your shoulders are already sore enough." I plastered myself against him and sighed in relief as his body heat seeped into mine. "It's almost as cold in here as it is outside. I've turned up all the heat as high as it can go."

A gust of wind rattled the window near where we stood. I could feel a blast of cold come through the single pane. I squinted at the glass. "Hey," I said. "Is that?—"

I scratched at the glass with my fingernail. My eyes hadn't deceived me. There was a layer of ice on the inside of our apartment windows. "Huh," I said. "That's the first time I've ever seen that."

Franck reached out and pulled me back against him. "Don't worry about that," he said. "It'll start to heat up now and the ice will melt. Besides, we'll keep each other warm."

We stood like that for several minutes, neither of us tempted to take things further because not only was the move far from over, it would require removing clothes. Eventually, Franck sighed. "*Ce n'est pas le tout.* I have to go back and get the next load."

I sighed. "I guess you're right. Let's go."

"No, no." Franck put his hands on my shoulders and shook his head. "You stay here and unpack."

I stared down at my suitcase. It was the only sort of container I had. I had no dresser or drawers. "I don't have anywhere to unpack to."

"Is your duvet in that suitcase?" Franck asked.

"Yes."

"Then you can work at making us some kind of makeshift bed, then maybe you can go upstairs and drink a mug of warm tea at Sam's."

"But I can't let you do a trip on your own."

He leaned over and gave me a kiss. "You certainly can. You had to brave the storm with your parents. Now it's my turn."

"But the trunk," I said. "It's too heavy for one person."

Franck gave me a parting kiss. "We'll see about that. Stay warm!"

He clattered back down the stairs and I was left alone in our new apartment. I kept my jacket on—the radiators didn't seem to be heating the place up very quickly, but then to be fair, it had been a veritable ice box for the past several days.

I was thirsty after the exertions of the walk, but it dawned on me that I owned only two glasses and I had no idea where I'd packed them.

I unzipped my suitcase and there was my duvet on top. Luckily I had been using a double bed sized duvet on my single bed, but as I considered the hard and cold wooden floor underneath my feet I wondered how I was going to make a comfortable bed with only a duvet, pillows, and sheets?

I set to it, determined to make the best possible makeshift bed.

In about an hour Franck came back with the second suitcase. He dumped it in the bedroom where I was just finishing up the bed.

"How is it out there?" I asked, not really wanting his answer. The window rattles from the wind were coming more and more frequently, some so violent that I began to worry the glass might shatter.

Franck couldn't answer, because his teeth were chattering too hard. Luckily, I had anticipated this and had run upstairs to beg a cup of tea from Sam and her roommate Alison. They had outdone themselves in their welcome, because once I explained the moving situation, they lent me a kettle, a teapot, several teabags and two big mugs to use.

I handed Franck a steaming mug of tea. "Here. Drink this." I couldn't invite him to sit down anywhere as we didn't own chairs.

"Did you see our bed?" I took him by the hand as he took his first sip.

"Ahhh," he said, as he followed me into the bedroom. "Do you know the only thing that is missing from this tea?"

"What?"

"Half a bottle of rum."

I laughed. "When we get some money, we'll buy you a bottle."

I waved down to the bed with a flourish. Truth be told, I was rather proud of my creation. I had taken the fitted mattress sheet and stuffed it full of clothes that I didn't think I'd need right away, creating a mattress. I had laid my duvet and my other blanket on top and topped with two pillows. Being an overpacker had some silver linings. It almost looked like a regular bed, although I couldn't be sure how comfortable it would be. Probably not very.

Franck raved over my ingenuity and finished his tea as I rubbed his arms and shoulders and legs, trying to warm him up. I wasn't seeing our breath in the air anymore, which I supposed was progress, but it still hadn't warmed up enough for me to want to take my jacket off.

He finished off the last dregs of his mug and smiled at me. "Only one more trip left."

I left his side for a second and peered out the window again. Whereas before I could make out the buildings and the little grocery store across the street, now I could just see white. The wind had picked up and it was snowing harder. "I think it's what they call an official white-out out there now," I said. "Maybe the trunk could wait until tomorrow?"

Franck shook his head. "No. I'd rather get it all done."

"But you can easily get lost in that kind of weather." I jerked my head towards the window. "Or fall in a ditch and get covered up by snow and die of hypothermia."

Franck stood up. "Don't worry about me, I'm tough."

"I know," I said, reaching up through his jacket to give his bicep a squeeze. "But can't you take a little break first? Maybe it'll clear a bit. I can make you another tea." I really didn't like the idea of him going outside again.

Franck shook his head. "I think it's going to get worse rather than better as the evening wears on. I'll go now. I'll be back soon, you'll see."

I didn't know what to say, so I just gave him a kiss on his cold cheek.

He left with his mouth in a determined line.

I sighed and went back into the bedroom to unpack my second suitcase and to wait. Because I had nowhere to unpack to, I just made little piles of my clothes along the wall—one for sweaters, one for jeans.

Walking together in the soft summer air through the vineyards around Villers-la-Faye only five months before, I could never have imagined that our romance would bring us here. That had been idyllic, but now we were facing harder stuff. Real life.

After about fifty minutes I started to fret. I parked myself by the window with a fresh mug of tea and peered out. I could barely see anything—from time to time I got a brief peek through the gusting snow but then it would be obscured again. I had a sense that Montréal was either going to be the making of us, or the end of us. Gazing out that window, I understood this city was not a place of half-measures, and it had every intention of testing our strength.

I started to picture Franck keeling over into a ditch or just passing out from the hypothermia. I thought back to my metal trunk. It was an old metal steamer trunk that I had bought second hand. It was plenty heavy on its own, even without all the stuff I had frantically stuffed inside it. It had to be impossible for one person to carry. What had I even been thinking when I let him try and go get it himself, especially when he was already frozen to the bone from the previous two trips? I paced back and forth in front of the window. I could go upstairs and use Sam and Alison's phone, but to phone where? My residence phone line had already been disconnected, and chances were Franck had left there already. He had to be out there somewhere in this city he had come to for me, in the middle of that blizzard.

The world felt stacked against us. Our utter lack of money. The fact his papers still hadn't materialized. My parents not talking to me. This storm outside.

I chewed my thumbnail, then made a decision. I had to go out and look for him. It was my fault I had so much stuff. I already had my jacket and my shoes on so I took a last sip of my hot tea. I saw something in a small break between white gusts out the window that made me pause. I leaned closer and peered out.

I could make out a dark figure. I rubbed the condensation from my breath off the glass so I could see better. Was it him?

It was. I recognized the way he moved. I made an incoherent noise of relief. Emerging from the storm was Franck, slogging down Prince Arthur with my heavy metal trunk carried on his shoulder.

My heart contracted. He'd done the impossible. I ran down the stairs and flung open the door of the building for him. His hair was covered in white and the sweat on his face had frozen. He wore a mask of ice. He thumped the trunk on the end on the lower stair and wrapped me up in his arms, kicking the door shut behind him.

"We are officially moved," he said, giving me the wintriest kiss I'd ever had.

chapter sixteen

"Anything?" Franck asked as I dug through the pockets of every pair of pants I owned. I had even dismantled the "bed" to check through the clothes that made up the stuffing of our de facto mattress.

I counted the change I had put in a little pile on the wooden floorboards.

"Fourteen dollars," I said, then counted the coins I still held in my palm. "No, make that fourteen dollars and thirty-four cents."

I sighed, then looked up to meet Franck's eyes. His face looked as grim as I felt. Our gazes both travelled to the phone sitting on my plastic triangular table in the corner of our bedroom. We had found a table at the salvation army and three odd chairs left on the curb of Aylmer Street two days before, so our kitchen was coming along, even though I had thrown out the dead plants. They had showed no signs of reviving and the black stumps had started to grow mold.

But in the bedroom the table and phone were the only items in the room besides our bags, and our makeshift bed.

Anyway, right now the phone was the biggest problem, or rather the fact that it hadn't rung. Franck's parents still hadn't called to say that they had received his permanent residency papers from the Canadian consulate.

"Explain to me again," I said. "Why you can only look for work once we know your papers have arrived in France? If we know they're on the way, surely that's good enough, isn't it?"

Franck sighed. "I know. It seems ridiculous to me too, but the woman at the Québec delegation emphasized that I should under no circumstances look for work until I knew from my parents that my papers had been received. She said if I was caught doing that, I could lose my permanent residence status and be flown back to France."

He was right. That was too big a risk to take. This was one of those administrative hoops we would just have to jump through. Also, I was too grateful to that woman to do anything contrary to what she recommended.

"Let's sum up the situation," I said. "Without news your papers have arrived, you can't begin to look for work. You've run out of savings. I've run out of savings. My parents have now officially cut me off."

Franck nodded.

"And we're cold all the time," I added. Since the move-in blizzard, the weather's artic grip on the city hadn't loosened. We'd quickly come to the realization that even with the heat completely cranked up to its maximum in our new apartment the walls were still poorly insulated, or maybe not even insulated at all. Nevertheless, a heating bill would arrive, and when it did, it would be a doozy.

"Not *all* the time." A mischievous quirk of his lips made it clear what Franck was referring to.

"I stand corrected. *Most* of the time. And as of today, all we have to last us until your papers arrive and you can look for work is—"

"Fourteen dollars and thirty-four cents?" Franck nodded down at the rather pathetic looking pile of change on the floor.

"What are we going to do?" I asked as much to myself as to him. "I'm going to have to look for a job starting tomorrow."

Franck shook his head. "You have to concentrate on school. I'll have to go and find work under the table."

"Absolutely not." Yes, Franck getting a job would help us … eat … But what if he lost the ability to immigrate that we had fought so hard for? No. Even now, with $14.34 to our names, it still wasn't worth it.

I indicated the pile of coins with my finger. "So, I suppose the question is, how are we going to live on this?"

Franck chewed his lip. "We can make quite a few tuna melts with that."

I snorted. "You're sick of my tuna melts, remember?"

"They're actually starting to appeal to me again," Franck said. "I must be getting very hungry."

"Ha ha." I tucked my legs up to my chest and wrapped my arms around them. "It's true that cans of tuna are cheap, so is a loaf of rye bread and a jar of mayonnaise. I guess we could forgo the cheese." I never thought I would hear myself utter such blasphemous words.

"Let's go shopping," Franck suggested.

I glanced outside the window, where snowflakes were being whipped around by the gusts of wind. It didn't exactly look welcoming. "God, look at it out there. You must hate me for luring you to this icy hellhole."

Franck lowered himself to the floor beside me and gathered me in his arms. "No place can be a hellhole with you in it," he murmured in the whorl of my ear. I shivered, but not from the cold. "At least we'll be warmer in the grocery store than we are in this apartment." Franck's words were as seductive as his breath against my ear.

"At times like this I really wish the grocery store across the street sold, you know, edible food."

The day after we moved, I tried to go into the grocery store across the street, the one we looked on to from our bedroom window, to pick up some milk. Everything I picked up from the shelves was covered with a thick layer of dust. The man sitting behind the cash register with a cigarette behind each ear looked daggers at me. I didn't linger.

Later, I asked Sam about the oddly threatening experience and she was clearly amused. "I should have warned you. That place isn't really a grocery store at all."

"What is it then?"

"It's for money laundering, and who knows what goes on in those back rooms. It's owned by Denis too. If you watch out your window you will see some shifty characters go in and out of there.

Oh, but maybe make sure they don't see you watching them."

"So, it's a mafia place?"

She nodded.

"And like Denis you don't know which mafia?"

She shrugged. "I'm never really sure. From what I hear there seem to be so many of them in Montréal. Italian. Greek. Portuguese, Eastern European, Protestants, Québécois. There's more than that, I just don't know them all."

"So it's equal opportunity criminality in Montréal?"

She nodded. "I guess you could say that. Don't go in there again though. I don't think it's safe."

That was not a problem. I had zero desire to go and tango with the dodgy types and buy their expired food.

"Yes, but it's not a grocery store, remember?" Franck reminded me now. "The thing is you just have to stop thinking of it like one. Let's go to La Vieille Europe."

That was a store further up Saint-Laurent, so a few minutes' walk in the bracing cold, but I knew it would be worth it. The store was a haven that smelled like cured sausages and strong espresso and was filled with the chatter of countless different languages. It was always warm too, as Franck reminded me.

"OK," I said. "La Vieille Europe and tuna melts it is." I collected our change from the floor and stood up. I grabbed my jacket from over the electric heater in the front hall. One of the previous tenants, or maybe it was Denis—though I had a difficult time crediting him with such thoughtfulness—had cleverly installed two hooks over the heater, so our jackets were cozy when we put them on. The warmth dissipated quickly, but it was still a welcome respite from the outside.

"Your papers better arrive soon though," I said as we headed out the door.

"They will," Franck said. "Have faith."

I knew from experience that faith was more Franck's department than mine.

The chill outside made me feel like all the air was being choked out of my lungs. I grabbed Franck's mitt-covered hand in mine. We bowed our heads against the wind and made our way trudging up the icy sidewalk on Saint-Laurent to buy our cooking supplies.

Whatever daydreams I'd had about my first year of university, none of them covered how logistically tough it would be to start a life here with Franck or how a Montréal winter seemed to make us walk with a permanent hunch in our backs.

After what felt like a long time, Franck opened the door to La Vieille Europe. I tumbled inside and my glasses fogged up immediately. I rubbed them on my scarf and inhaled deeply. The curing sausages hanging from the ceiling and the brine from the olive vats and the intense bitter whiff from the massive Italian espresso machine that sat on the counter at the coffee bar smelled like heaven.

I looked over to Franck as we both knocked as much snow as we could off our boots on the plastic mat in the entrance. He'd removed his toque and was taking off his gloves and looking longingly over at the espresso machine. I could also kill for a proper espresso to warm me up, but they were expensive—far more expensive in Montréal than they ever were in the cafés of France. With fourteen dollars and thirty-four cents, we had to forgo such luxuries. Still, it didn't mean we would stop wanting them.

I reached over and brushed my finger over his chilled cheekbone. "When your papers come and you get a job, we can celebrate with an espresso, *d'accord*?"

"Do you think we'll have enough money for espresso left over after we pay the next month's rent and the heating bill?" Franck asked, but with a smile. If we lost our sense of humor about our situation, then we truly would have nothing.

"We could always stiff Denis on the rent?" I said, chuckling over the preposterousness of this. I would never even entertain the thought of doing such a thing, even if Denis wasn't some sort of dodgy mafia guy.

Franck laughed. "Somehow I get the feeling that Denis isn't the type of person you ever want to be indebted to."

Indeed, in the past couple of weeks I saw Denis from time to time disappear in the "grocery store" across the street and once lingering in front of the storefront, having a heated conversation with a shaggy-haired man with huge muscles. There had been pushing.

"You're right about that. So, tuna …"

We took our time finding the canned tuna section, enjoying the warmth and the noisy bustle of the store. The tuna choice was impressive. Maybe we weren't the only ones surviving on tuna melts.

While we dreamed of the white albacore, in the end we grabbed four of the least expensive tins and struck out towards the sauces in search of mayonnaise.

As it turned out, mayonnaise was expensive—especially the good stuff. We settled on the least expensive jar. It was made in Hungary, *not* a country that as far as I knew was reputed for its mayonnaise. It was a slightly toxic shade of yellow, but we grabbed it, hoping for the best.

We threw our frugality to the wind when we got to the cheese aisle. We debated for a long time whether or not we should splurge on one of the little plastic wrapped packages of odd-shaped cheeses to grate on top of our tuna melts. It felt like a luxury, but I argued that even a tiny bit of cheese would help our mental health immensely. We ended up picking the smallest piece out of the basket. It felt like the biggest indulgence I had ever made.

I was reluctant to leave the store and I could tell from Franck's slow walk and lazy smile that he was in no rush to leave either. It was lightyears more hospitable than our empty and freezing apartment.

Our total came to $10.54. I clenched my teeth. That left us with less than three dollars, which was all we had until I didn't know when. I briefly considered calling my parents and begging them for help but immediately squashed that idea. I had made this decision. Now it was up to me to figure out a way to make it work.

"Bread next?" I asked Franck.

He nodded and looped his arm in mine. Conveniently, our favorite bakery was located just across the street from La Vieille Europe. Its windows were always completely steamed up from the heat generated inside from all those delicious things inside and the chitchat of its loyal customers.

I thought we could dash across the street without having to pull my mittens and toque back on, but I was wrong. By the time Franck opened the door of the bakery I felt as though I'd been flash frozen. Luckily, it was even warmer in here than it was in La Vieille Europe.

The bakery was always staffed by women who dressed in white aprons with white handkerchiefs tied over their hair. They were uniformly unfriendly as though they would rather spend time with the bread they so expertly baked than the customers who bought it.

Their specialty was rye bread, and initially Franck and I hung at the back of the crowd of people at the counter, simply breathing in the delicious tang of freshly baked rye.

"Do you think we should get one loaf or two?" I said.

"I think only one," Franck said, his nostrils flaring. "Their loaves here are long."

"But we have enough money left over for two."

"Yes, but won't it be better to think that we still have enough money in a few days to buy another fresh loaf? Mentally, I think that would be better. If we have to live on a loaf of bread, wouldn't it be better if it was fresh?"

"True." He'd convinced me.

We reached the front of the line and bought our loaf, which steamed up the inside of the plastic sleeve immediately. Franck tucked it under his ski jacket like a newborn baby while I held the paper bag from La Vieille Europe. We put our mitts and toques back on—the constant dressing and undressing required by Montréal winters was almost a part-time job—and shuffled home as fast as we could along the icy sidewalk.

Half an hour later we were sitting at our kitchen table, poised to devour our dinner of a slice of rye bread with the tuna and mayo mix, parsimoniously sprinkled with grated cheese. It felt like a meal fit for royalty.

"There's nothing better for the appetite than hunger," Franck said.

I nodded agreement but couldn't actually say anything as I had already taken a huge bite of mine. Neither of us had taken off our jackets. Even if the ice on the inside of our windows had melted, it was still glacial inside.

The Hungarian mayonnaise had turned watery with the heat of the oven, but I was too ravenous to care. I sank my teeth in again and my hunger plus the earthy flavor of the rye and the brine of the ocean in the tuna and the unctuousness of the cheese made it one of the most delicious things ever to pass my lips.

"So good," I moaned. We made short work of our melts and then used the last of the coffee grounds I had brought over from residence in my Bodum to make two strong coffees. I was just pressing down the plunger when the phone rang.

Franck and I looked at each other for a second, then he dashed into the bedroom faster than I'd ever seen him move. I could hear him skidding across the floor and crashing into the wall as he picked up the phone.

"*Allô?*" he gasped.

My heart stopped during the next few moments of silence. Then Franck's triumphant shout rang through the empty apartment. I left the coffee half-plunged and ran into the bedroom to see if it was true.

From the pain in my foot, I knew I had given myself a decent splinter from the worn floorboards, but whatever. "Your papers?" I demanded, out of breath from excitement. "They've arrived?" My eyebrows felt like they were somewhere up around my hairline.

Franck grinned at me and gave a thumbs up, then punched the air above him in triumph. I sagged down against the wall beside his legs, listening intently as he went over things with his parents back in Villers-la-Faye—explaining what method of postage they needed to put on the papers so they were tracked as well as arrived as quickly as possible, and also double and triple confirming our mailing address here on Prince Arthur.

When he finally hung up, he dropped down beside me on the floor and we hugged and kissed each other for a long while, then stood up and did a little jig around the room like Mémé did whenever she was celebrating something.

"Does this mean you can start looking for a job?" I confirmed, gasping from our dancing.

Franck squeezed me tight against him then let me go so he could do a ninja air kick. "Yes! That was what they told me in Paris. As soon as my papers arrived in France I could start looking for work here, and tell my employer that my paperwork is arriving, which is now *true*."

He lifted me up and swung me around while I yelped with joy.

We finally exhausted ourselves with all the dancing and collapsed on our makeshift bed.

"Hey," I said. "Maybe we can buy a real bed soon! Or a futon, at least."

Franck patted my creation underneath us. "I don't know. I'm kind of becoming fond of this one."

I laughed. No matter how we arranged the clothes under the fitted sheet, we both ended up sleeping more or less on the cold, bare floorboards. As a result, we had developed sore backs and hobbled around the apartment like two old people when we got up in the morning.

"Think of what we could do in a proper bed," I said, then gave him a long kiss.

"I'm sold," he whispered in my ear.

I lifted my head after a while. "The timing of it all is so miraculous. Just when we were running out of money for real."

"I know," Franck said. "But it's no random miracle. It's the magic of your tuna melts. I'm sure of it. Now we can be crazy and go have another one."

chapter seventeen

Franck began looking for work the next day. He set out that morning full of enthusiasm, but when he slammed the door on his return in the evening, after I had come home from classes, his smile had disappeared, and his eyes were heavy.

"Not good?" I guessed. We didn't have any money yet to buy him a transit pass, so he had to choose his job interviews based on whether they were within walking distance. I had heard the job market was fairly dire, and the no-transit-pass thing would cut his possibilities right off the bat.

He shook his head and hung up his jacket. I shifted my notebook aside where I was outlining an essay on Shakespeare's obscure play *Troilus and Cressida*.

He collapsed in the only other chair. "You know what?"

"What?"

"The Québécois don't like the French very much."

"Really?" I had a hard time wrapping my head around that. The French loved the Québécois and French Canadian singers and actors like Roch Voisine and Céline Dion were all the rage in France. I had always assumed the affection went both ways.

Franck examined his fingers, glum. "Everywhere I went they called me *maudit français*."

"Maybe it's affectionate?" I said, but meanwhile I was thinking that the direct translation of "damned French" did not sound particularly friendly.

"Afraid not. Apparently, they see us French as interlopers trying to steal their jobs."

I had never anticipated Franck would encounter any sort of prejudice during his job search. That innocence, I wryly realized, came from being white. The world could really suck.

"Am I right that there's not many jobs out there?" I said.

Franck nodded. "Everyone at the employment center is talking about how desperate the employment situation has become."

I never paid much attention to job statistics in the past, but since Franck's arrival I had begun scanning newspapers in coffee shops, and I realized unemployment was a big problem in Montréal. Some people blamed it on the constant political instability of the separatist movement, others on industries moving to cheaper markets such as Asia. The more I thought about it the more I realized I shouldn't be so surprised that Franck's reception hadn't been as welcoming as we'd naïvely expected.

"The Québécois see the French as *colonists*." Franck expelled the word like a bad shrimp. "Me?" He tapped his chest. "My ancestors were revolutionaries. We cut off the king's head! A colonist? *Jamais*."

I was certain that if we were outside, he would have spat to underline his point.

I rubbed my chin. "Well, it's true though, isn't it? Technically the French did colonize Québec, at least initially."

"Us French are anarchists. Fighters of freedom. We're not like the English. They were the true colonists."

"Yes, the English have plenty to answer for," I said. "But so do the French."

"But it was our very own Charles de Gaulle who shouted '*Vive le Québec Libre*!' Franck shook his head in disbelief. "Surely that should count for something."

I decided Franck mainly needed a bit of time to adjust to this new reality. "Tell me what happened," I said.

He shrugged, looking more defeated than he had when faced with my disapproving parents or moving a full metal trunk in a blizzard. "There may be something. It's completely the bottom of the barrel, but I don't think I can be choosy."

I hadn't even been expecting this much given his slumped shoulders, so I grabbed his hand in excitement. "Really? What is it?"

He averted his gaze from my eyes. "I'm not entirely sure and I'm not sure how I feel about it from a moral perspective."

"You haven't joined the mafia too, have you?" I squeezed his hand.

That at least got a crooked grin out of him. "No, though I would definitely be earning more money if I did."

"Don't keep me in suspense," I said. "Are we going to be able to buy any food besides a loaf of rye bread?"

His lips quirked up a smidgen. "If I have anything to do with it, yes. I'm still not sure if I understood the explanation of the recruiter. It was all very convoluted. I have to make random phone calls to people and try to convince them to go to this free weekend up somewhere near Mont Tremblant. It's a ski resort."

There was a strange intonation when he said the word "free."

"It's not really a *free* weekend, is it?"

He shook his head. "No. The people do get to stay for free. That part is true. But in exchange they have to attend these obligatory sales pitches from developers trying to convince them to buying a condominium in this new complex being built near the mountain."

"Do the people know what they are getting into?"

He shrugged. "I'll get a clearer idea tomorrow. Still … I can't imagine the sales tactics once they've got the potential buyers in person are subtle."

"How are you paid?"

"Minimum wage, then by commission. I get a certain amount for every person I can get to show up at the mountain."

Phone sales. I would be terrible at that, and I knew that if Franck felt he was deceiving innocent people, he would be terrible at it too.

"Maybe you can do it, but, more honestly than the employers want. In your own way."

"I'm counting on it." Franck traced a line in the soft pine tabletop with his thumbnail. "Because I can't say no to this, not until I earn some money and my papers arrive, in any case. I do have some good news though."

"Let's hear it."

"I met this other French guy at the employment office and we hit it off. He's waiting for his papers to be sent from France too. We ended up going to our interviews together and he was hired at the same place. The job sounds terrible, but at least I have a new friend there."

"That's amazing!" I was shocked to feel a stab of jealousy. Our lives had been solitary since Franck's arrival. It wasn't like we had any money for entertaining, or for going out for that matter. Sam and Alison were fabulous neighbors, but our schedules didn't match up very well, and they both had new boyfriends to boot.

Anne and James and the people I knew from residence had drifted away, and I couldn't blame them. I had made a choice, even though I hadn't felt aware of it at the time. I hadn't chosen them.

"What's his name?" I asked.

"Pascal," Franck said. "He's from Alsace."

"Did you mainly talk about all the food you miss back from France?" I guessed.

"Of course. What else would we talk about?"

"On that note," I said. "What should we eat for dinner until we wait for your first paycheck? A tuna melt or a tuna melt?"

Franck pretended to give it serious thought.

"How about a tuna melt?" he said with a real smile.

He set off to work the next morning well before I left for my first class. I helped him get his jacket on and wrapped a scarf around his neck.

I gave him a kiss on his right cheekbone—one of the few bits of exposed skin left on his face. "Stay warm," I said. "And *bonne chance*."

After I shut the door behind him, I went to the bedroom window and watched him walk away, hunched over against the blowing snow.

Even though we were still very much camping at our apartment, and it was pretty much as cold and uncomfortable as one could get without actually living outside, it was starting to feel like home, or home base, in any case. I still hadn't let my parents know my new address and phone number. Guilt washed over me. They had probably heard I was all right from my sister Suzanne, but that wasn't the same as hearing from me.

I still didn't agree with the things my dad had said, especially not the cow and milk analogy, but I could understand they were worried about me moving in with a boyfriend they had never met, especially considering I was only nineteen. There were times when I would get a flash of what my relationship with Franck sounded like to them, and I could understand their objections.

I felt capable of making important decisions like moving in with Franck, but it was natural they still saw me as their child rather than an adult. This stalemate between us was hurting me. I already felt detached from the few friends I had made here in Montréal, and all I really had left was Franck and Sam. I moved slowly over to the phone in the corner of the room and dialed my home number in Victoria—the same one I had memorized in Grade One.

The relief in my mom's voice when she answered made me feel even better about my attempt to reach out. The conversation was stilted. I had expected that, but I gave her our new phone number and street address and I said Franck's papers had arrived in France and he had already gotten a first job.

I was vague when my mother asked exactly what his job was. If Franck had qualms about its morality I didn't want to test it out on my parents at this point.

We were winding up the conversation when she said, "Just a second Laura. I'm going to see if I can find your father."

I didn't feel ready to talk to my dad yet. I still hadn't figured how to manage my guilt (having disappointed him) with the fury (that moving in with my boyfriend was something that *did* disappoint him). Those old-fashioned attitudes had no place in the world anymore.

She was holding the phone receiver against her chest and she was talking to someone. I could tell because of how her voice was muffled and coming out as vibrations. I debated hanging up, but that would put me back to square one with them. Was my mother urging my father to talk to me and he was refusing? Despite my resentment that thought made my heart ache.

She finally came back on the phone. "I'm passing the phone to your father."

My father took the receiver and cleared his throat. "Hello Laura. Thank you for passing on your new phone number and address. What are Franck's plans for Christmas?"

Of all the questions I had been anticipating, this was not one of them. I didn't know what to answer. Probably the truth was best.

"I don't know," I said.

Franck and I had been so busy dealing with the day to day that we hadn't even thought that far yet, yet it was already December 1st. I had a plane ticket home for Christmas that my parents had bought back in August, but now I thought about it I couldn't abandon Franck in Montréal and he definitely didn't have the money to fly back to France.

"What if we fly him out here to have Christmas with us?" my dad said.

"What?" I asked, stunned. I had no idea if Franck meeting my family was a good or disastrous idea. Still, it meant that our Christmas plans were solved.

"I think we should meet him," my dad said, in a tone that wasn't entirely friendly, but I would worry about that later.

"Well, thank you," I said. "This is wonderful. It will be so nice for him to see the West Coast."

"Yes," he agreed. "It is the most beautiful part of Canada, after all." I knew one thing my father could never resist was boasting about how wonderful the lifestyle was on our island. He was ever so slightly biased.

I gave my dad dates to start looking for tickets and then he passed me back to my mother.

"I'd better go now, Mom," I said. "I've got to walk to class. We can talk tomorrow, OK?"

She said good-bye but I could hear the smile in her voice, and that warmed me up better than the warmest toque.

As I walked along Milton to get to my Philosophy of Feminism class, I wondered at the reception Franck would get from my father. I knew my mother would be warm and friendly, but all the boys I went to high school with had been terrified of my dad, and not without reason.

Any male who entered our house was promptly given a personal tour by my father of his gun room. That, combined with a stern glance underneath his military-style crew cut was all the dissuasion most boys needed. How would my Dad act given that Franck and I were already living together? I was hoping this didn't mean Franck would get a tour of the ammunition locker in the basement, or worse.

chapter **eighteen**

Franck and I had arranged to meet after his shift was over in a coffee shop just off Saint-Catherine on McGill College Avenue. Franck was sure he would have earned enough commission, which was paid out daily, to buy us at least a drip coffee each.

I got there first, of course, because I was always on time and Franck was always late. I climbed to the second floor and saw that nobody was sitting at the best table—the one right in front of the half-moon window that looked directly onto Saint Catherine Street.

The coffee shop was called Van Houtte. I'd heard it was a chain of some sort, but I'd never seen it before moving to Montréal. It smelled of coffee grinds and pencil erasers. Lots of students came to set up camp here to work and avoid the no-food-and-drink rule in the McGill library.

Besides my classes, I had been working hard in the library and at the apartment trying to catch up. It was amazing how fast one could fall behind in university. The terms were short but unbelievably intense. In the next week I had a huge test as well as three essays due. I was relieved Franck had started working so I could devote myself completely to my studies during the day.

I jiggled my right leg as I waited, unable to contain my need to tell him about the Christmas invitation from my parents. Would he be thrilled or horrified at the prospect?

I had little doubt that once I got him to the West Coast we would be expected to run the gauntlet of friends and relatives. Everyone would be curious to meet this mysterious Frenchman who had turned my life upside down.

I tapped my fingers on the table, waiting for that mysterious—although he no longer felt that way to me—Frenchman to arrive. I peered out the half-moon window at the sky outside. The clouds were dark gray and hung heavy in the sky.

I wondered if it was going to start snowing again. Really though, I had few points of reference. It snowed very little in Victoria. I could predict rain and ocean storms fairly accurately, but snow was largely outside my purview. Or at least it had been until moving to Montréal.

There was already a thick layer of it on the ground, but it had turned a greyish black from the cars and the exhaust and being tramped on by hundreds of pairs of boots. I still had a difficult time envisioning this winter weather lasting through March or April as everyone warned me it did. In Victoria we had cherry blossoms in February, and sometimes even January. Six months of winter … why would anyone choose to live here? Then again, many people would probably think the same thing about our winters of leaden skies and never-ending sogginess on the West Coast.

I pulled out the outline of my English essay on John Donne's poem "The Flea" and began making notes in the margins. I became absorbed in my thoughts and the scratch of my pencil on the paper of my notebook, so when I felt the weight of a hand on my shoulder, I jumped about a foot in my seat.

I looked up to see Franck looking down at me with an expression so filled with tenderness that my heart clenched. "*Désolé, mon amour*," he said. "I never meant to scare you."

I laughed and indicated my outline with my pencil. "I was lost in the metaphysical poets. So? How was your first day at work?"

He leaned down and kissed me gently. As much as I enjoyed the kiss I did wonder about his lack of an answer.

He pulled out the opposite chair and sat down across from me. "I came in here fed up with my new job," he said. "Then I saw you. You looked so studious against the window with your glasses on and your hair clipped up and your pencil poised over your notebook. Did I interrupt important thoughts?"

I closed my notebook. "You did, but never fear. Important thoughts always come back."

"I love having a brainy girlfriend," he mused, reaching across the table and taking my hand.

"It's nice having a boyfriend who thinks I'm brilliant. It's also nice that I finally feel like I'm starting to catch up in my courses."

He nodded, solemn. "That's important."

I gave a flick of my pencil. "Speaking of important ... the job? How did it go? Do we have enough to get coffees?"

Franck frowned and took out his wallet. "I can't help but feel this is tainted money, but I actually have enough for two hot chocolates ..."

I squealed. Hot chocolate was about three times the price of a drip coffee. "You sold some condos?"

He shook his head. "No, we don't do that part, but I booked three couples today for their 'free' ski weekend. I was extremely clear to them about the sales seminar requirement, but they didn't seem to care. I have a sneaking suspicion they were all rather old and not exactly in the market for ski condos."

He tapped his wallet. "How about I go and get our hot chocolates and then I can fill you in on all the morally questionable details?"

"Excellent idea," I said, and watched him make his way back downstairs. It never stopped being miraculous to me how I could look at Franck in a place full of strangers and just *know* it was him. He was my person. I couldn't believe I was lucky enough to have found him, an ocean and a continent away.

I gazed out the window as I waited for him to come back, thinking how much progress we'd made in little more than a month since he'd arrived. The move, his papers, now a job. We weren't settled yet, but it felt like we were on our way.

I squinted at the tiny objects that had begun to fall from the clouds. Was that snow or hail? Before I could decide, Franck was back upstairs, a huge mug of hot chocolate in each hand, topped with Matterhorns of whipped cream and chocolate shavings.

I made an inarticulate sound of pleasure. "I want to drag out this hot chocolate but I'm not sure if I have the restraint. How many more bookings do you think you'll be able to take tomorrow?! I meant, as I was sure Franck knew, how regular a feature could these hot chocolates become in our lives?

He sighed. "I thought I was doing quite well, but apparently three bookings is pathetic. Some guys are getting thirty or forty a day. I have a confession to make."

"What?"

"I think I'm terrible at telephone sales."

"But it was your first day," I said. "You're still learning."

"I am, but I think my policy of warning them about the sales trap is not exactly helping."

"Ah." I couldn't argue against his morals, because I happened to agree with them.

"The fact is, while I will keep doing it for the money because we need to eat," he said. "My heart isn't in it. Those people on the phone today—they sounded so *thrilled*, like they really believed they had won a contest even when I explained that *everyone* wins."

"Maybe a weekend in the mountains would be nice for them?"

Franck shook his head. "Victim to a bunch of smarmy sales sharks? I doubt it. I worry they're going to get swindled out of their life savings. That doesn't sit well with me."

It didn't sit well with me either. Suddenly my hot chocolate didn't taste quite so exquisite anymore.

"Also, I called a bunch of people up in Northern Québec. Laura, even though we were both speaking French—or, at least, I think we were—I couldn't understand them at all, and they couldn't understand me."

I frowned. "I guess nothing is stopping you from looking for another job as soon as your papers arrive."

Franck nodded. "That's what I plan to do. I asked my parents to send them by the most express of express posts. Besides, I may not have a choice about looking for a new job. I think the supervisors must listen in on our calls periodically and at the end of the day Pascal and I—that's my friend and he's just as bad at the job as I am or maybe even worse—got a bit stir crazy and started to make each other laugh by impersonating famous French actors."

I had a string of truly crappy jobs all through high school, but I never would have had the nerve to goof off like that. I was shocked and secretly thrilled. "Which ones?"

"Jean Reno. Jean Rochefort. Gérard Depardieu ... Can you believe so many people here in Québec don't even know who they are?"

I sighed. Franck and I had been over this many times before. "I've told you *chéri*, pretty much nobody outside of France knows French musicians and actors."

I knew Franck and all the other people I knew in France had a hard time believing that the fame of such national icons as Johnny Hallyday and Vanessa Paradis didn't transcend international borders. France often felt like its own little self-contained world.

I had to ask. "So people truly thought it was Gérard Depardieu on the phone trying to flog a weekend on Mont Tremblant?"

Franck's lips quirked. "*Absolument*. Pascal can do amazing accents. I was laughing so hard I couldn't breathe. For the last forty minutes I just sat there and listened to him."

"I have to meet this Pascal," I said.

Franck nodded. "You do."

I took a fortifying spoonful of whipped cream and sighed as it melted on my tongue. "I have news too."

"Tell me." Franck wiped off an errant bit of whipped cream off my nose with his thumb.

"I phoned my parents this morning."

His face lit up. "I'm so glad. I hated that I was causing problems between you and them. How did it go?"

I lifted a shoulder. "A bit awkward at first, but I suppose that was to be expected. My mom saw my call for what it was though: a peace offering. Then, my Dad surprised me by getting on the phone and giving me his own peace offering. At least I hope it's a peace offering."

"You don't sound sure."

I waved my hand. "It's fine. I'm sure it will be fine. He wants to buy you a ticket to come out to the West Coast with me for Christmas and meet everyone."

I watched his face carefully, but his smile seemed sincere. There was no hesitation in his eyes whatsoever. Oh dear. He was so naïve. "That's amazing, Laura. It's so generous of him. I wish I was in a position to pay for my own ticket though."

I waved that away. "We need your pay to cover the rent and the heating for both of us. They want to meet you. If it goes well, even though they might not love our living situation, they may grow to accept it over time. They may not understand me ... or us ... but they are good people."

Franck squeezed my hand. "I never doubted that for a second. I'll charm them."

"It might be harder than you think. With my dad, in any case. Just be yourself."

Franck winked. "Isn't that the same thing?"

I squeezed his hand back.

His brows drew together. "Will it be a problem that I don't speak any English?"

I lifted a finger to put a pause on his question, then leaned over in my backpack and took out a Harrap's French to English dictionary. "I checked this out of the library for you. I don't know exactly how the language thing is going to play out, to be honest."

I imagined I'd be doing a lot of translation. I had a devious thought. Seeing as I would be the only go-between with Franck and my family, I could translate things in the most advantageous way possible.

Franck was already flipping through the pages of the dictionary. "I'm going to start learning tonight. Oh look! There's a special page for all the phrases we say around the table."

"Of course you would find that first." I sipped my hot chocolate as Franck mouthed new English words in an endearing fashion. I hoped my parents would find it endearing too, but I knew it could go either way. I glanced out the window again. Huge fluffy flakes floated down from the sky.

I jostled Franck's forearm and pointed. "Look."

Franck looked up from his Harrap's. "Incredible," he murmured. "When I dreamed about Canada when I was a young boy up in my bedroom in Villers-la-Faye, it was like this."

"Really?" I said, still gazing out the window. The snow was hypnotic in the same way as the flames of a bonfire. "What else was in your dreams?"

"Dog sleds," he said, considering. "A log cabin deep in the woods."

"I can't do much about the lack of dog sleds," I said. "Or the cabin in the woods, but we do have our apartment and it's certainly as *cold* as a cabin in the woods."

"How about we buy some potatoes and eggs on the way home and I make you a nice potato omelet for dinner?"

I was discovering that just as tuna melts were my comfort food, potato omelets were Franck's. How had I never realized that in France? The relationship we'd had then felt more like a dream whereas who Franck and I were in Montréal was rooted in a new, tangible reality.

"Sounds perfect," I said, "But first, let's just sit here and enjoy this for a while."

We drew out finishing our drinks, staring dreamily out the window at the gently falling snow. It was a welcome parenthesis of peace. Franck's papers were in the mail on the way to us. It looked as though there was a possible reconciliation with my parents in the cards. Franck had a job, and even though it was one that he despised it brought in some money for eggs and potatoes, and most importantly, the rare hot chocolate.

We cut through the McGill campus on our way home and walked down Prince Arthur holding hands and marveling at the huge snowflakes that made everything seem fresh and hopeful.

"Let's check our mail," I said to Franck as soon as we stepped into the vestibule. "You never know."

Franck reached in the pocket for his key to our mailbox and opened it. "I doubt—" he was saying over his shoulder when I yelped.

The end of what looked like a large manilla envelope poked out of the long metal rectangle.

Franck slid it out. "My papers," he breathed, reverent. "They're finally here."

I looked at the envelope in his hands. It was amazing to think that his papers were finally here, after he had worked so hard and been so tortured over them.

I whooped in triumph and Franck spun me around in the tiny vestibule until my lower back collided with the bannister and I yelped in pain.

We raced upstairs and shed our jackets and gloves and toques carelessly on the floor as we made our way into the kitchen. Franck put the eggs and potatoes and salad we had bought en route on the counter and took our sharpest knife from the utensil drawer and slid its tip into the corner of the envelope.

"Careful!" I warned, my mind conjuring up terrible visions of immigration documents sliced in two.

Franck went slowly, so slowly that it was almost torture, but finally slipped out the documents on our pine kitchen table. We each carefully inspected them. Everything looked in order. The only thing that confused me was the paragraph about Franck having to exit Canada and re-enter to have his permanent residency visa activated.

"What is this about exiting Canada?" I said.

"Oh, right. The woman at the Délégation du Québec in Paris explained that to me. She called it 'walking around the flag-poles.'"

"What does that mean?"

"What I understood was that I have to go to the nearest American-Canadian border and literally walk around the flagpoles."

"How bizarre." I shook my head. "But I've heard people talk about a border crossing that's about an hour away. It's called Champlain or something like that. I'd bet there are buses that go there."

"Perfect," Franck said. "We'll have to do that as soon as we can."

"Saturday morning?" I suggested. "I can't miss any classes this week."

"Excellent. The timing is perfect. They were putting pressure on me at work today to show them my papers."

"I'll look into bus tickets tomorrow," I said. The whole process made me uneasy, but I didn't want to spoil Franck's hard-won relief. What if once Franck left Canada, they wouldn't let him into the United States? Or what if they wouldn't let him back into Canada and he was forever stranded in no-man's land? I bit my lip. I couldn't think like that. The woman at the Québec delegation had been our savior – I had to trust she knew what she was about.

Franck was already up and slicing the potatoes with the same knife he'd used to open the envelope. My stomach grumbled its approval. I was looking forward to a potato omelet for a change.

"Where are you going to keep your papers?" I asked, panicked at the idea of them being lost or stolen. "We have to safeguard them." I shivered. No matter how high we jacked up the heat in our apartment, we were pretty much always freezing.

"Don't worry," Franck said, dropping the diced potatoes onto the frying pan. "I've got it all under control."

Famous last words.

chapter nineteen

That Friday night before we left for the border Franck and I decided a celebration was in order. There was a lot to celebrate. Franck was being paid. It was not much, but it felt like a lottery win compared to what we had been existing on before—and his papers had arrived. Plus, he was coming out West with me for Christmas, although whether that was something to celebrate or lament remained to be seen.

"Somebody in one of my English classes was talking about this cool bar with live music in Old Montréal," I said. "It's called Les Deux Perroquets. Let's go."

Franck and I were in bed. We had hopped right in as soon as he had gotten home from work. It was the warmest place in the apartment and besides, there was more than one way to celebrate a successful week. He drew his knuckle down my jawbone, then kissed my chin. "Sounds great," he said. "I haven't even been to Old Montréal yet. Although it's going to be difficult to get out of this bed."

I pulled his ear. "Don't get too excited about the name 'Old Montréal.' Remember 'old' here doesn't mean the same thing as it does in Europe."

Franck's kisses were getting higher, one by one. His lips finally reached mine. "Right," he murmured. "Old basically means new."

"We're never going to get there," I sighed, kissing him back. "Are we?"

But miraculously we did manage to bundle up and hop on the

metro to the Champs de Mars station. We generally walked everywhere, but the temperatures kept plummeting, even when I thought it could not possibly get any colder. Walking to Old Montréal was just too far with the arctic conditions. Taking the metro to Les Deux Perroquets was a splurge but it was one I thought we'd earned.

The bar wasn't too long a walk from the metro station, but at minus thirty degrees even a few meters would have been too far. By the time we burst through the first of the double doors, I couldn't feel my toes, fingers, or nose anymore.

"At what temperature do we start to get frostbite?" I asked Franck, shivering as we unwrapped ourselves after the first set of doors. We had learned this was the polite thing to do in wintertime in Montréal, so as to leave most of the snow on our clothes in the vestibule and not actually inside.

"I'm not sure," he said. "But I'm feeling like it's not far off whatever it must be outside. Can you feel your nose?"

"Nope."

"Toes?"

"Nope."

"Fingers?"

"Definitely not." My numb fingers were numb and awkward. "I'm having a hell of a time trying to undo my zipper."

"Here. Let me help you." Franck managed to unzip my jacket for me, but I could tell his hands were clumsier than usual too. Far clumsier than they'd been in our bed two hours earlier.

"I wonder if anyone else is crazy enough to go out tonight," I said, wondering why we were doing this in the first place. "The bar is probably deserted."

Just then Franck cracked the second set of doors open, and the sound of singing, laughter, shouting, and the banjo surrounded us. Franck cast me a glance over his shoulder. "We shouldn't have doubted the Montréalais," he said. "Not for a second."

He was right. Inside, the ambiance was raucous. As far as we could tell it was free seating, and from the smell of spilled beer and freshly popped popcorn it seemed like the sort of place where everybody was having too much fun to care, so we grabbed a wooden table near the middle of the room. The three guys on the stage wore plaid lumberjack shirts, suspenders, and heavy-duty boots. They were playing the banjo and the drums and a trumpet and singing in such a strong Québecois accent that I couldn't make out most of the lyrics. They were phenomenal.

"I have no idea what they're singing," I shouted across the table to Franck. "But I love it!"

"They sound just like the people from Northern Québec I talked to on the phone!"

Franck sat back in his chair and grinned. He set down an attaché case he must have had inside his jacket beside the leg of his chair.

I pointed down at it. "Are those your papers?"

Franck put a finger over his lips to silence me as though it was a state secret.

"Why did you bring them?" I yelled, because that was the only way to make myself heard over the band.

"I was worried they would be stolen if I left them at the apartment. I don't trust Denis."

I didn't trust Denis either—no sane person would—but there was no way that his papers were safer here at a bar than at home. I'd already seen a pitcher of beer spilled two tables away. This was the sort of the place where that, or worse, was likely to happen.

I shook my head. "That's crazy," I shouted back. "They're way safer back at the apartment."

But Franck was either ignoring me or truly caught up in the music. Anyway, this argument was going to have to wait for later. It was impossible to make ourselves heard and my throat was already getting sore from the yelling. A waiter swung by and delivered a pitcher of beer on the table and a huge bowl of popcorn.

"Been here before?" he asked in French.

I shook my head, hesitant to say anything and reveal my Anglo accent.

"Popcorn's free," he said. "Beer is five bucks for the pitcher." He slid two glasses on the table as I gave him the thumbs-up to show I'd understood.

Franck poured us each a glass and grinned at me, tapping his foot to the irrepressible beat. I took a sigh and leaned back, deciding to soak up this rare opportunity to let off steam. Franck's papers were Franck's responsibility, not mine. I was so relieved that things were stable enough in our lives again to be able to go out and do things like this.

Having Franck with me in Montréal was a dream come true, of course, but at the same time we had met with more obstacles than I ever could have imagined. Back in the summer when I pictured the two of us living in this new city, I had never considered the mafioso landlord and my parents cutting me off financially and almost as many tuna melts as there were blizzards.

A man on the stage who had been playing the trumpet now exchanged it for a kazoo he had pulled from his jeans pocket. The energy from the music filled me up and took me elsewhere. By the time we had moved on to our second pitcher of beer and our third basket of popcorn, I was feeling in love with not only Franck (even though he had made the bizarre decision to bring his paperwork to the bar), but also Montréal.

The spirit of this city was awe-inspiring. The weather was wretched outside, but inside there was so much energy and celebration and music. The determination of the Québécois to live fully in the face of their winters had a life force all its own, and I was swept away in its vigor.

By the time Franck and I stumbled back to the metro station many hours later, our ears still ringing from the kazoo and the banjo, the cold somehow didn't seem as bad, even though the thermometer had dipped yet again. We laughed and agreed to go back there and to new places as well. If our future in Montréal held more evenings like the one we'd just had, things looked bright.

Once we walked Franck around the flagpoles and got his papers legalized, things were going to become so much easier. I was sure of it.

It felt like a refrigerator back in the apartment, so we undressed and leapt into bed as quickly as possible. We wrapped ourselves as tight around each other to try and get warm until I felt Franck's body go completely still in a way I instinctively knew wasn't sleep.

"What?" I whispered.

There was silence, and then, "I left my paperwork at the bar."

Expletives raced through my head. I'd been right about it being riskier to take the paperwork to the bar with us than leave it at the apartment. Of course I was. Franck was the victim of his own paranoia. Well, that and his forgetfulness. *Vindication.*

"You're not going to say anything?" Franck asked, letting go of me and flipping on his back to stare at the ceiling. I could see the outline of his profile backlit by the streetlights outside.

Blood rushed in my ears. How could he possibly be so careless with something as important as his immigration paperwork? He wasn't just jeopardizing his future, but mine too—everything we had worked so hard to achieve. The desire to reiterate how I'd been right was almost overwhelming, but something stopped me.

From the tone of his voice I knew Franck was mortified, not to mention in the throes of complete panic and self-recrimination.

Franck was my first real relationship and I had never felt so angry with him, but still … I knew deep within me that, as much as I was tempted, it was not right to kick someone I loved when they were already on the ground.

It might be satisfying in the moment—hugely satisfying—but I knew I would regret it.

"I don't know what to say." I turned so I was facing him. That wasn't entirely honest. To distract myself from all the things I *wanted* to say, I started ruminating solutions.

Franck sat up. "I'm going to go there now."

Again, with the complete lack of common sense. "It'll be closed."

"Yes, but there might be people there cleaning up still," Franck said. "That floor was a sticky mess."

"Don't forget it's only open at night," I said. "They have all day to mop the floors. Besides, remember those double doors? Even if there was someone inside and you were banging against them, they probably still wouldn't hear you from inside the bar."

"I have to try—"

"The metros have also stopped running by now," I said. "Which would mean the only way you could get there is walk."

"I could do it," Franck said. It was true. If anyone could do it, it was Franck. Still, that didn't change the fact that it was a bad idea.

"I know you could," I said. "But it would be an hour's walk and it's dangerously cold out there."

"But—"

"The best thing to do is go there on the metro first thing tomorrow morning and get them then."

"Do you think so?" Franck turned his head towards me.

"I do," I said. "There's nothing you can do now except sleep."

Franck lay back on his pillow. "I don't think I'll be able. What about our bus tickets for tomorrow? I'm supposed to be walking around the flagpoles. I can't do that without papers. *Mon Dieu*. We'll have to cancel the bus tickets."

I shook my head in the dark. "I'm not going to cancel them. Not yet. Try going to the bar tomorrow morning, then we'll decide."

"I'm sorry Laura," he said, putting his hands over his face with a groan. "How hard is it for you not to say *I told you so* right now?"

"You have *no* idea."

"Well, I appreciate it."

"I'm glad."

"But I'm never going to sleep." He sighed, still staring at the ceiling.

"We've got to try," I said.

In five minutes, Franck was snoring, and it was me who was left wide awake for hours. Finally, I crept to the bathroom and muttered all the things that I hadn't said to Franck to my reflection in the chipped bathroom mirror. This couple thing was not for the faint of heart.

I had the John Donne essay still to work on the next morning before our mid-afternoon bus departure, so I got up with Franck before the sun rose, and began working as soon as he left, wishing him Godspeed for finding his papers. When the door shut behind him I let loose a stream of expletives to vent some of my spleen before turning to how "The Flea" contrasted with "Ode to a Grecian Urn."

Two hours later, Franck came swinging back in the door, holding his black satchel triumphantly in front of him. He had to unwrap the scarf from around his face before he could talk.

"*Victoire!*" he declared, when his mouth was finally revealed.

My legs felt weak all of a sudden. I staggered back into the kitchen where all my library research books were spread over the table and collapsed on one of the chairs. I dropped my head in my hands. "You are soooooooo lucky." No wonder Franck lacked common sense for certain things. He always seemed to emerge unscathed.

"I know," he said, grinning.

"I think my heart stopped about one hundred times today thinking of it, and what would happen if someone stole your satchel from the bar last night, or if it had just been thrown out, or—"

"I know." Franck reached over and covered my hand with his.

"So, what happened?" My curiosity needed to be satisfied.

"You were right about having to bang on the outer doors for a long time. My fists are still sore, but I figured someone had to be in there, and I was right. They never did hear me though. A guy eventually came out to throw two huge bags of garbage in the dumpster.

"Lucky," I muttered.

Franck continued, unperturbed. "At first, the guy—I recognized him as the bartender from last night—said he had no memory of my satchel, or of anyone bringing it to his attention. He was not optimistic about finding it, but I insisted he let me in to look around."

"How did he react to that?"

"He called me *maudit français* of course, but you know something? I might be getting used to that. I'm choosing to hear a bit of affection in that epithet."

Whatever worked.

"You'll be happy to learn that the bartender, like you, thought I was completely deranged to bring my immigration papers to the bar with me, and he certainly didn't express it as diplomatically as you did. I thought perhaps that might take away some of the sting of your restraint last night?"

I pressed my lips in a tight, straight line, willing myself not to show the satisfaction I felt.

Franck twisted my ponytail around his finger. "C'mon Laura," he cajoled. "Not even a tiny bit better?"

I lifted up my other hand and measured half a centimeter of empty air between my thumb and my forefinger. "Maybe teeny tiny."

Franck laughed. "I thought so. I'm getting to know you well."

This was true, but I wasn't so sure how I felt about Franck getting up close and personal with my spiteful side—one I usually managed to keep firmly under wraps. "Enough about my compulsion to get even," I said. "Where did you find the paperwork?"

"In a cabinet under the bar sink, right beside a garbage can."

I sucked in air. "Good God, do you realize how easily it could have been thrown out? You are so lucky."

Franck twitched a shoulder. "Luck, or guardian angels?"

I had forgotten about Franck's belief he was protected by various guardian angels, notably his grandfather, Pépé Georges.

"Pedantics," I declared. "Does it really make a difference to the outcome? You found your satchel after leaving it in a random bar. That's all I need to know."

Franck patted the satchel, which lay on the table between us. "Yup, and before you ask, I checked. All my papers are in here, and still in order."

I shut my mouth. I *was* just about to ask that.

"So Laura, do you want to come to America with me this afternoon and validate my permanent residency before I screw up again?"

"Don't even joke about it."

"Not when you look at me like that. You're terrifying."

My shoulders dropped. "Too soon Franck, too soon. My restraint has limits, you know."

"*D'accord, d'accord.* So, wanna cross an international border with me?"

I pulled out the bus tickets from the back pocket of my jeans. "I'll be watching you, and your papers, like a hawk."

Franck leaned over and gave me a kiss. "You may think I don't like the sound of that, but I do."

chapter twenty

We caught the bus to Champlain, New York State, at the bus depot downtown. The wind had calmed, and the world outside resembled an ice palace. The snow on the sidewalk had morphed into random, pillowy drifts of sparkling white snow. Huge icicles hung off the roofs, some of them over a foot long.

We got to the bus depot in plenty of time, thanks to my military planning, and also the fact that I lied to Franck about the bus's departure time by twenty minutes to make sure we weren't late. Maybe I was truly getting to know him too.

The trip took about an hour, and while I enjoyed the landscape whipping past the bus window, I fidgeted in my seat. I tried to imagine how this whole walking around the flagpoles procedure would play out, and whether such an odd-sounding thing could truly be legal.

Franck wasn't exactly relaxed either, which the basest part of me was pleased to see. He gripped the handle of the satchel so tightly that his knuckles were white.

Before I knew it, the bus squealed to a stop in front of a low glass building with several Canadian flags waving out front.

We got off the bus and eyed the building. "I guess this is where you need to start," I said, sounding more certain than I felt.

We went inside and I was relieved to find a kind Québécois customs, lanky with one of the thinnest faces I'd ever seen, officer who took Franck's papers and listened patiently as Franck explained what the woman at the Québec delegation had said about walking around the flagpoles.

"I'm not sure if it's a euphemism for something else," Franck admitted to the officer. "It sounds odd."

The officer clicked his tongue. "Ah no. It's not really that unusual. Somebody comes here and does it every few days. Far cheaper than taking a flight back to Paris."

We nodded in agreement. That was so beyond our budget as to be laughable.

He picked up his pen and wrote things on Franck's paper and entered some information on his clunky-looking computer. He gave the papers back to Franck and gestured out the door. "Go outside, cross the border on foot, and then come back."

Franck took the papers back, but neither of us made a move to leave the desk. "Are you sure the American officers won't, like … shoot me or something? I've seen movies, you know."

The customs officer shrugged. "They are armed. All us Canadian officers get as weapons is our stamps. I can't exactly guarantee the Americans won't shoot you, but I think it unlikely."

A quiver of his mouth made me hope he was just joking. *Please let him be joking.* Us Canadians as a rule were deeply suspicious of the American love for firearms, and I couldn't quite shake my anxiety.

He pointed out the door. "You'll see the American flag out there, just across from the No Man's Land. It's huge, you can't miss it. *Bien sûr* they made certain to make theirs bigger than ours."

We were almost out the door when he called out one last piece of advice. "Oh! Don't forget to go into their customs building to get your documents verified, then make sure you bring them back to me for processing."

"Just out of curiosity," I said. "What would the Americans do to us if we forgot any of that?"

He shrugged. "Not sure, but good thing to remember about the guns, I guess. Have a nice walk!" He waved us out the door.

Outside, we saw that the customs officer was telling the truth. The American flag that hung limply—there was still no wind— was massive and sat atop an equally impressive flagpole. It was about one hundred feet away from where we stood, across a stretch of empty asphalt cleared of snow.

Franck and I looked at each other. "*On y va?*" I said. We grabbed each other's hand.

Franck took one last look at the American flag and nodded with a determined gleam in his hazel eyes. "Our first international trip together! Let's go."

It was eerie. I had entered the U.S. via airports, by car, and even by boat a few times around Vancouver Island, but I had never considered walking across the border. I felt exposed in the blank space between two countries, like a solider caught between the trenches in a war.

"Do you know the words to the American National anthem?" Franck asked.

I searched my memory. "I don't think so. I can sing 'Oh Canada' though."

Franck glanced over his shoulder. "Nope. We're over halfway across. I don't think 'O Canada' would help us now."

We both began to giggle. The situation was absurdly outlandish. Because of our nervousness, the giggling spiraled.

I dug a nail into Franck's palm. "We have to stop it," I hissed. "I think the Americans take this sort of thing seriously."

"What sort of thing?"

"You know, borders. I don't think laughing would be a good start."

"Then stop laughing." Franck nudged me and made an odd smothered noise.

"I'm trying." My voice sounding high and strangled.

We veered towards the United States Customs and Immigration building, but as we approached a bull of a man in a uniform of a white shirt and navy pants stepped out of the door. "You have to *actually* walk around the flag!" he said.

I wasn't sure if he was messing with us, but a handgun hung from a holster on his side and *it* sure as heck wasn't joking. We changed direction towards the flagpole and walked a complete circle around the base of the American flag. It was larger than it looked from a distance.

When we'd finished, Franck glanced back to the door of the

American building, where the armed officer was still watching us, his hands on his hips. "Do you think we should go around a second time just to be sure?" he whispered to me.

"Um, yes. Let's." I realized belatedly that I probably didn't need to be walking around the flagpole at all. I wasn't immigrating to Canada. In fact, my Canadian passport was in my backpack.

We looked back at the officer watching us. He was grinning now and beckoning us over into the building with a crooked finger. I couldn't believe he wasn't freezing with only his uniform shirt on, but maybe Americans from New York State were almost as impervious to the cold as the Québécois.

He ushered us into the building, cheerful now, but with one hand still resting on the butt of his gun. I grew up with a father who hunted, but beyond shotguns used for procuring our moose roasts and stew meat for dinner, guns were not part of my life. Like most Canadians, I found handguns used in daily life disconcerting.

The American office had a different feel than the Canadian side. It was shinier somehow and less run down, and everyone seemed to take themselves more seriously. I concluded the guns probably had something to do with that.

I glanced over at Franck. His face had an expression that I had never seen before: a mix of wide-eyed fascination and wariness. There was no French being spoken, and the English here had a different accent than mine. A bit twangier and more drawn out on the vowels.

The officer buffeted Franck with a slap on his back so hearty that he stumbled forwards. I stuck out my arm to stop him from falling.

"Welcome to America!" the officer said. He then slid, with some difficulty, behind his desk.

Everyone was talking several decibels louder than I was used to, and the officer asked for Franck's papers in the same quasi-shout.

I'd forgotten to warn Franck about that. Canadians generally spoke louder than the French, but the Americans were even louder than us Canadians. I remembered how in Beaune I could always detect the Americans in the crowd—it always sounded like they were bellowing compared to the soft-spoken Europeans.

"Passport," the man said to me. I slid over my navy blue Canadian passport with the royal insignia of the commonwealth emblazoned on the front. He gave it a cursory glance, but as he passed it back to me he said, "Can you explain to me why the Queen of England is on your money in Canada? I've never been able to figure that one out."

"She's the Queen in Canada too," I said, thinking of my Grandma Agnes back on Salt Spring and her faded portraits of the Queen. She very much considered herself a subject of the Queen as a Canadian. So did I, although not as enthusiastically. However, I doubted most Québécois I had met so far in Montréal would feel the same way as me. I got the distinct impression that many of them didn't even feel they belonged in English Canada, let alone the British Commonwealth.

"But how can that be? She lives in her castle in London. It makes no sense."

It made perfect sense to me. The Queen was something, like the sun rising in the morning, I never questioned. At the same time, I didn't think I could go into the complexities of the Canadian parliamentary system and our ties to the British monarchy and actually get Franck's paperwork completed by the end of the day. Such an explanation might take years.

I waved my hand. "It's to do with the Commonwealth. But mainly it's because we didn't have a revolution in Canada, unlike the U.S and France," I nodded at Franck, silently congratulating myself on such a masterful segue.

It worked too.

"Just as I thought," the officer nodded his massive head repeatedly. "You should have had a revolution up in Canada too." He winked at Franck.

"I imagine everyone was too busy trying to keep warm," I said.

He guffawed. "Good one."

He opened Franck's passport and flipped through the pages

several times. *Was there something wrong?* Alarm fluttered in my throat.

"Where's your visa?" The officer rose a pair of steely gray eyes to Franck.

"Visa?" I echoed. Americans and Canadians flowed smoothly across the border in both directions. Did the French need a visa to come to the United States? I cursed myself that I hadn't even considered that possibility. From the way Franck was nervously clearing his throat, I could tell it had never crossed his mind either.

"I'm sorry," Franck began in stilted English. "I did not think—"

"Does he need a visa to cross into the US as a French citizen?" I asked. "I'm so sorry, but we didn't know that. If we did, we would have—"

I was cut off by the officer breaking into a grin. He waved his hand. "I was just having a little fun with you, like I did about the flagpole."

What? So that had been a joke?

"I can issue your guy an I-95 right here," he said. "That's what the tourist visa for countries like France is called. Anyway, it's not like either of you look like you're planning for a long stay in our fair country."

I shook my head with a smile. All we had for luggage was Franck's satchel and my school backpack.

The officer winked at me. "You'd better explain to your guy there. He still looks confused."

"Oh, right." I turned to Franck and explained that the officer had just been joking and that he could issue Franck the visa in his passport right away. I gestured at the officer who was scribbling stuff on a little green piece of paper that he stapled onto the pages of Franck's still-virgin passport.

"I need you to pay twenty dollars though." The officer looked up at me. "And that's not a joke."

I took my wallet out of my backpack and passed over a crisp twenty-dollar bill.

He didn't take it but stared at my hand.

"What in the name of God's good earth is that?"

"Twenty dollars."

"I meant twenty dollars in *real* money. I don't want any of your Canadian monopoly money."

Merde. I hadn't thought to bring any American money with me. "Do you take credit cards?"

"Please," the officer shrugged. "You are now in the United States of America. Of course we take credit cards, including American Express and Diner's Club."

I passed him over my student Mastercard. He took it with a grin and processed it through one of those carbon copy machines.

He then looked through Franck's immigration paperwork as both of us held our breath. He signed and noted a few things on the paperwork, then handed it back to Franck.

"There you go," he said. "You're all set to go back to the Canucks and have them finish that up."

"Thank you, Officer," I said and nudged Franck, who was still looking awed.

"Yes, *merci,*" he said. "Thank you."

The officer lumbered around from behind his desk and accompanied us to the door of the building. "I'd better keep an eye on you two as you cross back. Try anything fishy and I might have to shoot you."

He said this with a smirk, but, as he ushered us back out onto the concrete he asked, "Have you enjoyed your stay in our fair country?"

"Of course," I said.

"All righty then. Hurry back to the Great White North. God bless."

Hurry back we did. The more distance I could put between us and the creepy no-man's-land and the armed officer, the happier I was. We were almost running by the time we burst through the door of the Canadian building.

I took a deep gulp of air and sighed in relief. The desks were a bit bashed up on the edges, and the customs officers were mostly joking around. Tim Horton's takeaway cups littered the desks. The officers wore only stamps on their belt buckles and there wasn't a gun to be seen. A mix of French and English created a familiar background hum. Ah, Canada.

The customs officer we'd been dealing with before smiled at Franck. "Welcome to Canada," he said. "Your new home."

Franck and I looked at each other. Franck was entering into Canada legally for the first time, and not just as a tourist, but as a permanent resident who could work, be covered by the medical system, and do basically everything a Canadian could do except vote in Federal elections.

"Is Canada starting to feel like home?" I asked Franck in a low voice.

He leaned down and dropped a kiss on my forehead. "You're my home."

We walked to the desk, where Franck presented the officer with sheath of now signed documents and his passport. Processing it took the better part of an hour, but it ended with the officer putting a large page-sized permanent resident sticker in Franck's French passport.

"*Voilà*! So what made you come to Canada?" The officer asked, passing Franck's passport back with a lazy smile.

Franck looked over at me. "Love."

The officer looked back and forth between us. "I guess that's an excellent reason. Best wishes to both of you. By the way, my name is Jacques. You can name one of your children after me if you like."

I blushed. We weren't quite there yet. We had the Christmas in Victoria with my parents to get through first.

"Sure thing," Franck shocked me by saying. "I always liked the name Jacques anyway."

"Want to see something funny?" the officer said, just before passing Franck's passport back to us.

"Always," I answered promptly.

He pointed to a little box he had filled in at the bottom of Franck's permanent residency visa in his passport. It said "entered by:" and the officer had written in pen "by foot."

"You entered by foot." He winked at us. "You can show this to people and tell them you swam across the Atlantic Ocean and then climbed ashore in Newfoundland."

We all burst into laughter. It was an absurd end to a nonsensical, but triumphant, day. Franck took his passport back and put it carefully into his satchel.

"Thank you," he said. "I think I'm going to like it here in Québec."

"Snow for six months of the year." The customs officer shrugged and took a sip from his insulated Tim Horton's travel mug. "What's not to like?"

chapter twenty-one

Shortly after our cross-border stroll, my exams hit with a vengeance. I was completely absorbed with studying and revising.

Franck was busy at work and also busy trying to find another job while he wasn't at work. In between, he made me lots of cups of coffee and food as I worked like a fiend. He didn't resent me being completely pre-occupied. In fact, he seemed just as invested in me getting good marks as I was.

With a bit more money trickling in we bought a second-hand double futon bed and some sheets. We bought it off a buffed engineering student who said he was selling it because he was buying a bed with "better suspension." I tried very hard not to think about what had transpired on the bed before it came to us and doubled up on the fitted mattress sheets.

We also discovered stacks of empty milk crates behind the mafia "grocery store" across the street.

At first we questioned the wisdom of taking any of the milk crates even though they seemed abandoned. We didn't want some mafia vendetta on our heads. Franck finally worked up the guts to go in and ask politely if we could take some (an approach that had never crossed my mind) to just ask.

The burly specimen man at the cash register, patently eager to get us out of his store as quickly as possible, waved his hands and told us to help ourselves to as many as we wanted.

We were thrilled. It turned out that empty plastic milk crates were a seriously underrated item of furniture. They served as a telephone stand, drawers, and bedside tables. Our apartment still looked empty, but not quite as empty as it had been.

We also managed to find Franck a flight to Victoria. Mine had been booked up weeks before, but we found a flight leaving two days later on a budget airline. It had the advantage of flying direct from Montréal to Vancouver, but the disadvantage of arriving in Vancouver at two o'clock in the morning.

I decided I would go over on the bus and the ferry to meet Franck at the Vancouver airport, then we'd have to grab the first ferry in the morning over to the island.

My stomach was constantly in a knot between the stress of my first university exams and apprehension about the upcoming confrontation between my life with Franck and my life back home, especially given my parents' disapproval over the last two months. I was entirely unsure about what kind of reception Franck, or I, for that matter, was going to get.

The exam week passed in a blur and my hand cramped up into a claw-like appendage from writing as much as I physically could in the three-hour exam blocks. I didn't think I'd done brilliantly, but considering the upheaval of the past few months, I thought I had acquitted myself rather well. Besides, this was still only my first term at university. I was still learning the ropes, and I knew many fellow students in my classes who were on the fast track to flunking out already.

Franck was still at work when I grabbed the bus to the Dorval airport for my flight home. It was hard leaving him alone in Québec knowing that he would be rattling around our apartment by himself for a couple of days. But before he left for work that morning, he kissed me and assured me that he felt absolutely confident about meeting my parents and that he was sure that everything was going to go brilliantly. I wasn't certain if I was reassured or terrified by his confidence.

My mom and my younger sister Jayne came to pick me up at the airport in Victoria. Luckily my mother had a gift for jollying us through awkward moments, and Jayne had so much she wanted to tell me about her newfound obsession with New Kids on the Block and her friends and school and her violin lessons that there were zero lulls in the conversation. I'd never sufficiently appreciated her non-stop talking before.

Also, Suzanne, my older sister by two years, had already arrived back from university in Ottawa. I knew for a fact that her and her boyfriend from high school were pretty much living together in Ottawa, but she hadn't told my parents yet and was still continuing with the pretext of paying rent on two separate apartments. She would be on my side.

Once back at my parents' house, I settled into my old life immediately, shifting effortlessly into an earlier version of myself. This included sleeping in, drinking a lot of coffee from the ever-full pot in the kitchen, and enjoying long walks in the ocean air. I helped my mom decorate the tree and prepare the house for Christmas. It was surreal, yet I knew I couldn't let myself completely sink into the familiar comfort.

My father assiduously avoided any conversation about Franck with the exception of confirming my plans to go and pick him up the day before Christmas Eve. The capacity of us WASPs to avoid vexing topics of conversation is staggering.

When Suzanne drove me down to the bus depot to catch the bus to the ferry to Vancouver, I found it strange to be leaving home—my inner sanctum—for what felt like the final time. I had never brought a serious boyfriend to my family home before, and I couldn't shake the feeling that as soon as Franck and I walked in that door, home for me would no longer ever be the same.

On the ferry over to Vancouver I sipped my coffee and watched as the gulf islands slipped by outside the window. Tomorrow would be Christmas Eve. I'd never experienced such a short lead-up to Christmas.

I tried to imagine what it would be like to have Franck around my family for two whole weeks. Suzanne had always brought boyfriends home, but first of all, I hadn't had very many, and secondly, I'd always preferred to keep my relationships separate from my home life. At least, until now.

Before I knew it, the muffled announcement came over the loudspeaker for those of us boarding buses to return to the lower vehicle deck as the ferry was about to dock. I gathered my bag and my trashy magazines I'd bought at the gift shop on the promenade deck and headed downstairs to the bowels of the ship.

The plan was for Franck and me to wait at the airport until we could hop on the first bus to the Vancouver ferry terminal for the seven o'clock sailing the next morning. Neither of us would be sleeping much that night, and I was brewing a doozy of a cold. My throat ached and every breath I took created an unnerving whistle in my bronchial tubes. A night spent in the international terminal wouldn't exactly help matters, but at least I would be with Franck for most of it.

Once at the airport, I almost drifted off to sleep several times in the seats just across from the arrivals gates where I had parked myself, comforted by the familiar travel smells of carpet cleaner and spilled Coke. I jerked out of sleep each time, panicked that I would miss Franck's arrival.

Yet each time I squinted at the screens bolted on the wall above the seats I would see Franck's plane had been delayed and then delayed again. I started wondering if we would be able to make that first ferry across to Vancouver Island, or whether we would have to wait for the nine o'clock one, which would have us arriving at my house around noon. I started to shiver even in my warm jacket and sweater. *Oh lovely, so this cold came with a fever, did it?*

I thought back to the awkward conversation I'd had with my mother just five minutes before I was due to leave the house to the bus depot. She'd found me in the bathroom, where I was brushing my teeth.

"We need to discuss sleeping arrangements." She fiddled with a tube of toothpaste she'd plucked off the counter.

"OK," I said, bracing myself for the inevitable.

"Jayne sleeps upstairs, so I want you and Franck to have separate bedrooms."

"All right," I said. "But … why? We live together in Montréal."

She grimaced. "I'm aware of that. But what would Jayne think about you and Franck sleeping in the same bed?"

I shrugged. "I doubt she would think much about it to be honest, if it was presented as something normal."

I thought back to Franck's little brother In France, who was even younger than Jayne. Nobody considered for one second that he would be perturbed by his older siblings having their company in their beds. The whole sex thing was accepted as a natural part of life.

My mother shook her head. "No. Your father and I have discussed it. Franck will be sleeping in the guest bedroom."

From a French perspective this sounded like a completely contrived set-up. In Villers-la-Faye it would be exceedingly odd if Franck and I slept separately, and indeed if we did his family would fret about the state of our relationship. The cultural divide between Villers-la-Faye and Victoria felt uncrossable in that moment. How were Franck and my parents going to see eye to eye on *anything*?

"That's fine," I said, rinsing my toothbrush. "Your house, your rules. We'll sleep in separate bedrooms while we're here. Just, please turn off the intercom system in my bedroom and the guest room and don't come bursting in on us."

When my parents had built our family home in the late 1970s they installed a central intercom system so they could listen in and talk to me and my sisters no matter where we were in the house. It was all the rage in modern technology at the time.

"It's for your own good," I added, seeing my mother's frozen expression. "Otherwise, you may hear something you don't want to hear."

My mother nodded. "Fine."

It seemed we had struck a deal, but as my fever waxed and waned and my thoughts became frantic and warped, I wondered how I would begin to explain this separate bed thing to Franck.

Finally, over three hours late, Franck came walking through the arrivals door. His familiar hazel eyes were heavy with fatigue, but he grinned at me, dropped his duffel bag, and held out his arms.

I walked into his embrace and rested my head against his chest. His familiar scent of apples and bonfires seemed to do for me what two extra strength Tylenol had not. "Welcome to British Columbia," I said. "You must be exhausted."

He gave me a thorough hug and a kiss, then held me at arm's length and examined my face with an intent look. "It's you who looks exhausted *mon amour*. Beautiful, of course, but you're sick."

I waved my hand. "A bad cold. I feel like crap, but I'll be all right."

He sighed. "Ugh, and you've been up all night waiting for me. The plane was delayed before it even took off. The runways at Dorval were all gummed up with the snow and ice. There was a huge backlog of planes waiting to land and take off. There was another storm the day after you left."

"You'll be happy to hear there's no snow here on the West Coast," I said. "Just rain. Lots of rain." I checked my watch. "We should start walking over to where we can buy a ticket to catch the bus to the ferry. We don't want to miss it."

"It's funny," Franck said, swinging his military gunny sack over his shoulder once again. "I still have a hard time believing there's a corner of Canada that's not covered with snow all winter. In France, when people think of Canada, they think of snow."

"It's a relatively small corner," I said. "But I think Vancouver Island is almost the same length as all of France, so, you know, 'small' is a relative term in Canada."

Franck laughed down at me as we walked. "I think that's finally sinking in after that flight. To think I've been flying for six hours and I'm still in the same country. It's hard to wrap my mind around."

I laughed, which unfortunately morphed into a coughing fit. "And Montréal isn't even the *end* of Canada," I said. "It's still a plane trip of several hours from Montréal to get to the East Coast."

Franck stopped in front of a beautiful totem that overlooked the international terminal. "What's that?

"It's a totem," I said. "First Nations artists carve them. This one is Haida."

"Haida?" Franck echoed.

"That's one of the tribes, but they're centered further north, more around the Queen Charlotte Islands, which is called Haida Gwaii these days. That's the rightful name for their land."

"So much for me to learn," Franck murmured, his eyes sparkling with wonder.

"The First Nations have been here so much longer than the rest of us. We're all, no matter what our ethnicity or nationality, immigrants to *their* country."

"So you're an immigrant too?"

"Definitely. My grandparents or great-grandparents—depending on what branch of the family tree—came from Scotland, Ireland, and England."

Franck was staring at me. "It's so different than for me. My family goes back in France, well, as far as I know we've always been in France."

As much as I was enjoying myself, I checked my watch again. "I know, it's fascinating, but we'd better keep walking towards the bus ticket desk or we'll miss our ferry – that's the reality of island life. We're not the true masters of our time. The ferry schedule is."

Franck must have picked up my tone of voice. "You don't like the boat?"

I thought about that as we hurried along past the gift shop with the giant stuffed moose out front and the vending machines. I neither liked nor disliked the boats that transported us islanders to the mainland and back. They were just a fact of life.

I shrugged. "Honestly, I've never thought about it in those terms. I can't remember my first time taking a ferry. I've always taken them, to Vancouver, to Salt Spring to visit my grandma … They're a pain in the ass, but a necessity. There are worse ways to commute, I guess. But I know one thing I definitely don't like."

"What's that?"

"Missing a sailing. C'mon." I sneezed. "Let's pick up the pace."

We reached the bus booth just in time. I bought us our tickets and we didn't have to wait long. When our bus drew up in the airport bay Franck and I went over to the luggage compartment panel that was open low down on the side of the bus to throw in

Franck's gunny sack.

"Can you ask the bus driver to be careful with my bag?" Franck asked. "I'm noticing nobody is speaking French."

I chuckled. "I warned you most people only speak English. You're about to get a crash course, but why do you need the driver to be careful with your bag?"

"I packed a present for your parents in the middle of my bag so it's as protected as possible, but they're fragile—"

"What did you get?" I had no idea Franck was planning on bringing a present for my parents.

"As soon as I found out I was coming to your house for Christmas, I phoned my parents and got them to mail me twelve kir glasses. They arrived in two boxes the day after you left, thank God. I was beginning to think they wouldn't arrive before I left. I remembered you telling me how much your parents enjoyed kir when they were on that bike trip in Burgundy. I also bought a bottle of Vedrenne cassis and a bottle of aligoté at the liquor store up on Peel Street."

"You're brilliant." I stood on my toes and gave Franck a quick kiss on the corner of his mouth. He couldn't have hit on a better gift for my parents. They had traveled to Burgundy the first time the year before on a biking tour when I was staying at the Beauprés, my first host family with the Beaune Ursus Club. Just like me, they'd fallen in love with the area even though their exposure had been brief. They were enthralled with the local food, wine, and most of all, the kir – that garnet *apéritif* of blackcurrant liquor and local white wine that was an emblematic drink of Burgundy.

"I was rather proud of myself," Franck admitted.

I explained about Franck's bag in quick English to the bus driver and we watched as he tucked it away in a protected little alcove of the baggage compartment, shielded by the wheel well.

With that done, I gave Franck a more lingering kiss.

When we came up for air, he murmured, "Not that I'm complaining, but what was that for?"

I smacked my hand across my mouth. "Oh no," I said. "My cold. I'm probably contagious. I wasn't thinking. I'm just so amazed at your genius present idea."

He shrugged. "It's not like I would arrive with my hands empty. What do you take me for? Besides, I am determined to make a good impression on them. The glasses are all part one of my charm offensive."

"An excellent start," I said.

"Just keep your fingers and toes crossed that they arrive intact."

"Understood. Everything is crossed. Now, let's get on the bus and catch our ferry."

chapter twenty-two

Snuggled against Franck's chest, I struggled not to fall into a deep sleep as the bus pulled away from the airport. I knew that the ride to the ferry terminal at Tsawwassen—a word Franck asked me how to pronounce for him several times—wouldn't take long, maybe half an hour at the most.

Franck had his arm around me, but he was gazing out the window with wide eyes. "We're not going to go through downtown," I told him. "Basically fields and stuff until we get to Tsawwassen."

After a while, he jolted me out of a light doze by sitting up straight in his seat and pointing out the window. "Look!"

I peered out to see the beaten silver expanse of the ocean in the distance. "Yup. There it is. The Pacific."

"I can't believe it," Franck said. "I don't think anyone from my family has ever made it as far as the Pacific Ocean, not even centuries back. Growing up in Villers I dreamed of seeing it one day but I wasn't sure that I would ever have the opportunity."

It was a gift to be seeing my home through Franck's eyes, it was just a bummer that I was feeling so crappy.

"We'll be sailing on the Pacific in about twenty minutes' time." I squeezed his arm. "You made it happen."

Franck interlaced his fingers in mine. "No, *we* made it happen."

Within minutes our bus had driven on to the bottom deck of the ferry boat and parked. They always timed the bus and ferry connections seamlessly. I wondered when Franck would notice that things here on the West Coast were generally more organized than they were in France, or even in Québec.

"C'mon." I nudged Franck who was still gazing around at the bottom deck of the boat where the bus parked as though it was Xanadu. "We need to go to the upper decks. I desperately need some coffee."

"How often do these boats come and go?" Franck asked.

"From Swartz Bay to Tsawwassen every hour on the hour during the summer, every odd hour during the winter." I rattled off, just like any islander.

"Wow," Franck said. "That's precise."

"The ferry schedule is a precise business. They don't wait around for anyone, but if one of the boats breaks down or there are wind cancellations, trust me, it's a complete mess."

As I led Franck up the stairs I was sucking in air through the tightness in my chest. God, I was tired. I needed coffee, even BC Ferries coffee, which was not known for its exquisite taste.

Once we got to the first passenger deck, Franck stood still in the mass of people going in different directions, taking it all in. "C'mon." I tugged his arm. "We need to get to the cafeteria. The line-ups get long."

"But—" Franck lifted his arm to point at the ocean and the dock outside. "We need to sit outside so we can see."

"Outside? Nobody sits outside except tourists. Well, except maybe on an extremely warm day, but there aren't many of those on the ocean. It's December, Franck. Even though there's no snow, this is still Canada."

"You mean to say you stay inside during the ride?" He was staring at me in disbelief.

"Yes. Once the boat gets going it gets cold out there."

"But the *view*."

I could tell every cell in Franck's body was yearning to go outside and fully enjoy this novel experience. Funny, I'd never considered ferry rides an "experience," more like a necessary evil.

I strategized for a second. "OK, how about this? I'll go and get us coffees and then I'll bring them out, but I probably won't stay outside with you for very long. I'm feeling pretty terrible."

"Oh, if you're feeling sick then—"

"Find one of those to sit on." I pointed to one of the white painted life vest containers that lined the windows on the outer deck. "They're the best place." I didn't want my virus to stand in the way of his wonder.

"*Merci*." He swooped down to kiss my forehead and then pushed open the heavy metal door that led outside. I made my way to the cafeteria, chuckling to myself. *Outside?* He was crazy.

As I waited in line the ferry pulled away from the berth with its usual shakes and rattles. Maybe I should have warned him about that. It turned around and headed out over the Strait of Juan de Fuca towards Active Pass, which wound its way through the Gulf Islands on the way to Vancouver Island.

I could see out the windows that lined the sides of the boat that the day outside was typical for the Pacific Northwest in December with a steel sky and low clouds.

After about twenty minutes it was finally my turn. I filled up two of the largest size of takeaway coffee cups and snapped the lids on them. One of the good things—perhaps the *only* good thing—about ferry coffee was that it was always scalding hot.

It didn't take me long to find Franck. He was perched on the edge of one of the life vest containers. Thankfully he'd chosen the side of the ship that was sheltered from the wind. I passed him his coffee and leaned against the container, looking out. We were entering Active Pass and another large ferry, heading from Swartz Bay, passed close to us going in the opposite direction.

"It's more beautiful than I ever could have imagined," Franck said. The reverence in his words touched my heart. I hadn't been sure what he was going to think of my remote little corner of the world.

I hopped up on the container beside him and zipped my jacket up as far as it would go. Thankfully, my Montréal gloves were still in my pocket, so I slipped those on as well.

I breathed in a lungful of the ocean air. "You know what?" I asked Franck. One of the best parts of being with him was feeling free to share my odd, random thoughts.

"What?"

"No matter where I am in the world, I miss this air. It has the ocean in it." My nose started to unplug. I would never have considered sitting outside as a prescription for my cold if it weren't for Franck's eagerness but now that I was out here, it was proving to be more effective than any cold medication I'd tried.

Franck drew the air into his nostrils. "It *does* have the ocean in it!"

"Right?"

"Absolutely."

"We'll be going by Salt Spring Island soon. My grandma lives there and it's where my mom grew up."

"Salt Spring. Is it named that for any particular reason?"

"It was because the island has tons of natural springs underground. That's one of the things my grandfather used to do to earn money. He was a water diviner."

Franck tore his eyes off the scenery for a moment to look at me.

"A water diviner?" he tried out the English word. "What's that?"

"He would have special branches of wood. I think it was willow. If someone wanted to locate a spring on their property to say, build a well, he would go and find it for them with his willow branch.

"How?"

"The wood responds to the underground water, it … quivers, but only certain people can feel it."

Just then the hulking form of Mount Maxwell came into view. "There it is." I pointed. "There's Mount Maxwell. It's the highest point on Salt Spring. My dad hunts there every fall."

"Amazing."

"We'll go there for a day after Christmas to visit my grand-ma."

"Please," Franck said simply.

The announcement I was expecting came on the ship's speakers saying the whistle was going to blow. The passage between Galiano and Mayne islands was narrow and plagued with blind spots, so the boats had to warn each other of their presence. When the whistle blasted out, Franck jumped up nearly a foot from his cross-legged position. "What was that?"

"The ship's whistle. It always blows in Active Pass to warn other boats."

"It does that every time?" Franck asked.

I nodded. "Never misses. Although it isn't quite as ear-splitting inside."

The sun broke out from behind a hole in the clouds and lit up the cliffs of Pender Island and the bright green moss which hung from the red bark of the twisted arbutus trees. The lighthouse on the corner of Mayne gleamed a brilliant white and red. The isolated coves, littered with bleached driftwood, went from bright blue to a deeper, more mysterious teal as the water got deeper.

"*Mon Dieu*," Franck murmured. "I don't have words for it. Back in France, I could never have imagined in my wildest dreams such a place existed. It's like something out of a fairy tale."

Just then another announcement on the speaker, and it was one I hadn't expected. Orcas on the starboard side of the boat: our side. I beckoned Franck over to the white painted metal rail and pointed at their black fins sliding in and out of the water directly in front of us.

"Orcas," I shouted.

Franck peered over the side. "Those black things?"

I nodded. "What do you call them again in France? Ah! *Les orques*. That's it."

"They're hard to see if you don't know what you're looking for."

"My dad trained my sisters and me to spot them when we were out fishing. They would eat any salmon we had on the line, so we had to move or bring the lines up when we saw them."

We watched as the pod became more playful, spy-hopping and hitting the water with their tails. They blew air from their blowholes with that recognizable whoosh. The droplets of mist caught in the elusive winter sun and created a rainbow sparkling in the air.

"It's considered a good omen to see whales," I said, sliding my arm around Franck's waist underneath his jacket.

He smiled down at me. "How could it not be?"

They played and swam alongside the boat for at least fifteen minutes, until we exited Active Pass. I sent up a silent thanks to Nature—she was pulling out all the stops to welcome Franck.

Once the whales had swum on, we went back to sit on the container. Franck eyed the bags we'd left there. "We shouldn't have just left our luggage there. I got carried away and I didn't think—"

I waved my hand. "It's fine. I wasn't worried about them. There's not a lot of petty crime here."

Franck hopped up and pulled me against his chest with both arms wrapped around my torso.

"Oh *merde*," he said. "Maybe you should go back inside the boat. You're cold—"

"It's weirdly helping," I said. "I think." Besides, this was more fun than I ever could have imagined, seeing my West Coast through Franck's eyes.

A fishing boat passed the ferry with a tangle of bright orange fishing floats pulled up like a bustle on its stern.

"It's magic here," Franck said, tightening the hold of his arms.

I nodded, relieved he felt it too—that intangible alchemy that hung over the land here. Even as a child I'd sensed it: this place was somehow otherworldly. Maybe it was its remoteness, maybe it was the ocean. Whatever it was, I always carried a bit of that inside me, no matter where I went.

"It's fascinating seeing it through you," I said. "This is as close as I'll get to seeing my home for the first time, I guess, because it's impossible for me to remember a first time. I've been doing these ferry trips since before my earliest memory."

"It's like the villages and vineyards around Villers for me, I guess." He rested his chin on my shoulder. "I barely even noticed them until you came along."

"We're so lucky," I said, fully realizing it in a way I couldn't have before Franck came here.

It was a much-needed respite from worrying about how my father would react to meeting my new boyfriend for the first time—the one who didn't speak English, and who was living in sin with his nineteen-year-old daughter.

I could briefly forget about that until the ferry docked, at least.

chapter twenty-three

I was relieved to see it was my mom, accompanied by Jayne again, who were waiting to pick us up at the Swartz Bay Ferry Terminal. My mom was the perfect person to smooth over this awkward situation with her cheery ebullience.

I made the introductions and translated for Franck. He gave them both *les bises* which was, of course, the polite thing to do in France. Jayne and my mother were flustered but reacted with confused smiles. I hoped they were charmed, but I wasn't entirely sure.

I'd forgotten to warn Franck that *les bises* wasn't a thing in Canada, especially not on the West Coast. When we slid into the back seat of the family Subaru I whispered to Franck. "That was lovely, but *les bises* isn't done here."

I was terrified that he would try it with my dad. After all, Franck gave the *bises* every morning and evening to his little brother and his father, as well as all his male relatives and his close male friends. I knew my father would definitely be disconcerted rather than charmed. Men rarely hugged in my life, so *les bises* was too much of a stretch.

"How am I supposed to greet people then?" he whispered back.

"Just say 'hello' and 'nice to meet you'. Maybe shake their hand if they offer it."

"That seems so rude."

"It's not. Trust me."

During the ride into town, everyone was smiling and on their best behavior, though I started to feel sick again as soon as we got back out onto the highway. The fresh air and the coffee had sustained me for a while on the boat, but now my sore throat and aching chest and hacking cough came back with a vengeance.

"You sound worse, Laura," my mom said. "Maybe you shouldn't go with us to the midnight mass at Greg and Suzanne's church tonight."

I had forgotten I'd committed Franck and myself to doing that. Greg and Suzanne were planning on getting married that summer at Greg's family's Anglican church. They needed to show to the minister that they were churchgoing people from a churchgoing family, so they had recruited our entire squad to go to Christmas Eve midnight mass that night.

I was feeling wretched but had given my word. I was counting on Suzanne's support in regard to Franck and my parents over the vacation, and in this instance she needed me.

"I'll be fine," I said. "I promised her. They asked for all of us to go."

I quickly told Franck in French what I had committed us to that night. He seemed completely game, even intrigued.

"Is it a Catholic church?" he asked.

"No," I said. "It's protestant. Anglican."

"Fascinating," he said. "I don't think I've ever been to an Anglican church before."

In Burgundy, a church generally referred to a Catholic church. I had never come across a single Protestant.

Franck stared out the window for the whole drive from Swartz Bay to my family home in Victoria. He participated enthusiastically in any of the conversation I translated for him, but mostly I responded to Jayne and my mother's constant stream of chatter about innocuous nothings. Inwardly I wondered where my father was. I knew he was back from Kelowna. Was he still at the office or had he come home early for lunch to meet Franck?

When we pulled in our driveway my dad's car wasn't there. Still at the office. My heartbeat sped up and nausea made me swallow. I didn't know how to feel. I was dreading his first meeting with Franck as much as I wanted to get it over with.

Once inside the house, I showed Franck up to the guest bedroom. We'd been together for hours, yet somehow I'd neglected to inform him that we wouldn't be sharing a room. I opened the door and showed him the two twin beds—one pushed up against each wall.

Franck's eyes went from surveying the sleeping situation to me. "I don't get it."

I bit the inside of my cheek. "This is going to be your bedroom. Sorry."

"We're sleeping in separate beds?" he asked, his eyebrows drawn together in confusion.

"Actually, we'll be sleeping in separate *bedrooms*. I'll be sleeping in my bedroom."

"Are you mad at me?" he asked, frowning. "If I did something that—"

"No, no. It doesn't have anything to do with me, or you. It's ridiculous, but it's what my parents want, so I think we'd better respect that."

"They want us to sleep in separate bedrooms?" he asked again, his face a study in incomprehension.

"Yes."

"Even though we're living together in Montréal?"

"Uh huh."

"Oh … wait. Is this the puritan thing you were telling me about?"

"*Exactly*," I said, relieved.

"How fascinating." Franck's eyes lit up again, making me wonder if he wasn't going to embark on sociological research about the strange customs of WASPs. "I knew they didn't approve of us living together, of course, but I figured that seeing as we do—"

"Here's a piece of advice." I squeezed his arm. "Don't expect any of it to make sense."

"Interesting."

"Not interesting. Aggravating."

Franck reached over and tugged my ear. "It's going to be hard knowing you're just down the hall, but of course we have to respect your parents' wishes, Laura."

"We can visit at night," I said. "Quietly."

He gave me a wolfish smile. "This could be fun."

"It would be more fun if we could just sleep in the same bed."

Franck turned pensive again. "What do they think they're preventing from happening that hasn't already happened between us?"

"I have no idea."

"Also, what's wrong with sex? I just find this all so puzzling."

"It's a cultural thing." I waved my hand to sum up the generational weight of puritanism in North American Anglo-Saxon society. "To be honest, I don't think it's as much a matter of *preventing* us from sleeping together as it is preventing it *looking* like we're sleeping together."

"Huh." Despite this, I could tell Franck was still a mix of baffled and intrigued. "Intriguing."

He dropped his gunny sack down on the bed and began to empty its contents until he extracted the two boxes with the glasses inside. He opened one of the boxes, and then the other and sighed with relief.

"Nothing broken," he said. "*Parfait.*"

I stood there near the door jamb, taking in the incongruous sight of Franck—my Franck—standing in the lime green and butter yellow wallpapered bedroom that used to be Jayne's bedroom. My parents hadn't known her gender when they decorated it, so they decided yellow and green was suitable for either a baby boy or a baby girl. With two daughters already, I imagined they'd been hoping for a boy, but the estrogen was strong in my family. Franck was definitely the thing in this room I would point to if this was one of those "Which one of these things doesn't belong?" exercises from elementary school.

As he extracted the bottles of aligoté and cassis from his bag, he burst into sudden laughter.

"What?" I smiled as I waited to hear what stuck him as so funny.

"It's not like I'm going to leap on you every minute of every day, although it is tempting."

I thought about what I must look like at that instant—pale-faced and snotty nosed. I chuckled. "You must really love me if you want to jump on me right now." I broke into a rattling coughing jag.

He dropped the bottles on the bed and came over and wrapped me in his arms. "What I want to do with you right now is wrap you up in a warm blanket and make you a hot toddy. I still want to jump on you, but I think in your present state you would appreciate me taking care of you instead."

I was about to give him a kiss but then thought the better of it. I didn't want to give him this plague of mine, so I gave his derrière a little squeeze instead. "You're such a romantic," I said. "Waiting to jump on me until my snot has gone."

"I know," Franck said, a familiar muscle twitching in his jaw. "I have amazing self-control. Now, can you direct me to where I can find some wrapping paper and some tape to wrap these up for your parents?"

"Better still," I said. "I'll help you."

I led Franck to the sewing room where we wrapped the two boxes of glasses and the bottles of cassis and aligoté as a team effort.

"Do you think I should give them these now or tomorrow for Christmas?" Franck asked once we were finished.

"Now," I said. "One should never wait to give a peace offering."

That, and my father was due to arrive home any minute.

When we made our way back downstairs, my mom was cutting up bread to use in the stuffing the next day. "Did Franck get settled in OK?" My mom cast me a loaded look.

I gave her a reassuring smile. "Yes," I said. "He's settled in the guest room."

"Wonderful. I made a fresh pot of coffee." Coffee was a potent peace offering in my house. "And I put those two mugs on the counter for you."

I filled up the two Christmas mugs and was going to give Franck a tour of the house, but I couldn't get him further than the double-doored fridge a few feet away from the coffee maker.

"I've never seen such a big fridge," he said, rooted in front of it.

"It's quite standard, actually. That's what most people have."

"I'd heard people talk about how large the fridges were in North America, but I thought they were exaggerating."

"Do you want to see the inside?" I asked.

Franck nodded, eager.

I opened it up, and my mom turned around. "Oh! You two must be hungry. There's some fresh smoked salmon in there and some cream cheese."

"Thanks," I said, opening up the different compartments for Franck, who merely stared. "I'm just looking for right now." I knew that I wouldn't be able to eat a speck of food until the introductions between my father and Franck had happened.

"Incredible," Franck murmured. "How can you ever keep it full?"

When all five of us were home the problem was usually that we ran out of room, but I didn't want to blow Franck's mind too early in the game. Besides, I was distracted, listening for my dad's car.

It looked as though he could have spent more time standing in front of the fridge, marveling, but I grabbed his arm and gave him a tour of the rooms inside and then out to the garden and the back patio outside.

Just as we were on the back patio, I heard a car pull in the driveway. I recognized it as my father's station wagon.

I must have gone rigid, because Franck gave me a sharp look. "What?"

"My father," I said in a strangled voice. Franck's eyes flew wide and he straightened his spine.

Within seconds, my dad came marching around the back of the house. His hair was cut, as it always was, in a short, square crew cut. His face was strained, but he had a smile plastered on it. This had to be incredibly hard for him, and I appreciated the effort he was making. That smile told me that he had already made up his mind to take the high road with Franck. I went weak with relief.

He reached us and, before he said anything to me, he stuck out his hand. "Hi Franck, I'm Bryan. Nice to meet you."

Franck didn't need nudging. He took my dad's hand and shook it. Thank God I had warned him about *les bises*.

I had never been so appreciative of my father's kind heart until that moment. It said a lot for his character that even though he hated the situation, he was doing his best to make this easy for Franck and for me.

They let go. "Thank you Bryan," Franck said in stilted English. "Your home is beautiful."

Franck's accent was heavy, but he had said the right thing there too. My parents had built this house from the ground up when I was six years old and my father took great pride in it.

"Dad," I said, after he had greeted me. "Franck's brought you and Mom a present from France that I think you should open now that you're home."

His eyes widened. *Ah-hah*. So my dad had been planning on saying his polite hello and then making a getaway. "Sure," he said, his eyes darting back and forth. "Great."

We made our way back into the house.

"Did that sound OK?" Franck whispered in my ear as we walked behind my father. "I've been rehearsing it."

"Perfect," I whispered back, my heart squeezing with love.

In the kitchen, we beckoned my mother over to the table and Franck presented his wrapped boxes and bottles to my parents.

My dad's eyes lit up as he saw the glasses; he knew exactly what they were. "Kir glasses!" he exclaimed, holding them up. "Like we drank from in Burgundy! Remember Lynda?"

I pointed out how each one was emblazoned with the crest of a different winemaking village of La Côte and also dropped the fact that Franck had gotten his parents to send them to him and had hauled them all the way here from Montréal.

Quickly, my father unwrapped the bottles and put the aligoté in the fridge to chill so we could enjoy a kir together when he got home from work that evening. My dad and mom began reminiscing about the villages they had biked through and stopped at on their trip. We realized that they had even biked through Franck's village of Villers-la-Faye and stopped in front of the tiny boulangerie just up the street from his parents' front gate—the one that Mémé—Franck's grandmother, had owned and run as the village *boulangère* for decades.

My dad asked my mom to get out the photo album from their trip and we all looked through it together. They peppered Franck with questions which he patiently and thoroughly answered and I translated.

I could see that it was dawning on both my parents that maybe, just maybe, there might not just be disadvantages to their daughter having a French boyfriend.

I made smoked salmon bagels for Franck and myself and we ate lunch with my dad. After he returned to the office, looking far more relaxed than he had a mere hour before, I took Franck for a walk to the ocean three blocks away.

"Your dad was so nice," Franck said. "You hadn't prepared me for *that*."

"In my defense, you were the first live-in boyfriend I've ever introduced to him. I had no idea how he was going to react. This is all new for me too."

"So many new things for both of us." We reached the ocean— Cattle Point—a special place for my family. This is where we launched my dad's boat to go fishing and crabbing. This is where we came if we were ever upset or happy or needed to think something over. A small fishing boat was being pulled up onto a trailer at the boat ramp and the Olympic Mountains in the distance were covered with snow. The familiar smell of seaweed and ocean brine wafted over us.

"I guess I underestimated him," I admitted. "I won't make that mistake again."

Franck sat down on a bench beside us and began to take off his right shoe.

"What are you doing?"

"I'm going to dip my feet in the Pacific Ocean for the first time in my life."

"It's going to be freezing," I warned.

He winked at me. "Sometimes the hardest things are the most rewarding."

chapter twenty-four

It was stupid on my part to have gone for the walk instead of going for a nap, I realized after dinner. So far, the day was going incredibly, unbelievably well.

My parents were thrilled with Franck's gift and increasingly, I suspected, with Franck himself. He had waded into the ocean and would have gone swimming if I hadn't caught his arm when he'd slipped on the seaweed at the bottom of the boat ramp.

After our walk, he came to the kitchen freshly showered and dressed and immediately began helping my mother set the places and bring the food to the table. He praised the baked salmon my mother served (and my father had caught) and took it upon himself to serve kirs until everyone was rosy and laughing. Everyone except me, that was. I was spiking a fever again and both my nostrils were completely blocked. My chest ached from coughing and my eyes were drifting shut.

"You don't have to go, Laura," my mom said, smiling at me serenely now that Franck was already up and clearing the table. "It looks like you need to go to sleep."

"I promised Suzanne," I said. "I'll make it. I'm sure I'll get my second wind."

Suzanne and Greg were having dinner at Greg's parents' house and we were all meeting at the church.

"Stay home, Laura." My father was exceedingly magnanimous under the effects of three kirs. "If I had the excuse of being sick, I wouldn't hesitate to use it."

"Bryan!" My mom pretended to be scandalized, but the effect

was ruined when she started laughing.

My father had never been a churchgoer. In fact, he actively distrusted anyone who was too religious, declaring them sanctimonious and judgmental, and most likely a little brainwashed as well. He professed he found God in the depths of the West Coast rainforest or bobbing on the ocean in his fishing boat rather than between the walls of a church.

"It's important for Suzanne and Greg," my mother said, collecting herself. "So none of that talk tonight please, Bryan."

My father grimaced, then turned to me. "You know what you need, Laura?"

"A jumbo box of Kleenex?" I guessed.

"A hot toddy."

Franck recognized these magic words, and he said in bad English. "Yes! That is what I have telling Laura! She need hot toddy."

Franck's grammar was lamentable, but my father somehow understood. "Excellent. I'm going to make you one, Laura."

I wasn't going to argue when my father and boyfriend were bonding. Besides, I was tempted. A warm soothing drink ... it couldn't hurt.

We all moved into the kitchen where my dad busied himself at the bar.

"Would you like to go fishing sometime after Christmas, Franck?" my dad asked him as he poured rum—what looked like quite a generous quantity of rum—into a mug and then put it in the microwave to heat.

I translated for Franck, and he nodded fervently.

I told my father that he would love it.

"And then I'll show you how to make the best smoked salmon in the world," he added. It was true, I had never tasted any smoked salmon as good as his.

"Perfect." He stirred in a large spoon of brown sugar, squeezed in a lemon and passed me my medicinal hot toddy. My dad was not someone who had ever cooked much. On the very rare times my mother was away, he ordered all of us pizza. I figured he probably knew how to boil an egg, but then again, I wouldn't stake my life on it.

It was unusual he would make me something like this drink, and I was touched. It was another sign that he approved of Franck. I realized at that moment Franck hadn't even gotten a personal tour of my father's gun room. *This was a first.*

We left for the church at quarter to eleven, and by then I was having an extremely difficult time keeping my eyes open. Since when had my eyelids become so heavy? I tended to be like this: I could keep going for a long time, but then I hit an impenetrable wall of fatigue. After that, I could fall asleep anywhere. I chugged down a reheated mug of coffee just before leaving to try and counteract the hot toddy effect.

"Aren't you tired?" I asked Franck from the backseat where I was trying not to nod off on his shoulder. Jayne was fidgeting on my other side, excited to be up so late and that she would be getting a ton of presents the next day.

He stroked my hair off my forehead. "I am, of course, but I'm not sick. Besides, I can't let myself fall asleep. If I did, who else would keep you awake?"

We parked and made our way into the church with me leaning heavily against Franck. That rum toddy must have had a lot of the good stuff in it.

Greg, his parents, and Suzanne were hovering by one of the front rows of pews, waiting to greet us. I was walking none too steadily, but Franck was doing an excellent job of propping me upright.

Greg's parents were an absolutely lovely, soft-spoken South African couple who had emigrated to Canada when Greg was still young. Around them, my own family seemed incredibly loud and strident.

I said a polite hello to them and introduced Franck before sliding into the pew, relieved to be sitting down. Somehow, I ended up on the end of the front pew right beside the central aisle. Franck had a firm arm around my waist to keep me from toppling out.

It seemed forever before a squat minister with fleshy lips made his way down the aisle. I was reminded of why I often agreed with my dad's skepticism about churches and organized religion.

We had to stand up to sing a hymn. I always thought that I would like church a whole lot better if we were just allowed to sit through a service instead of having to hop up and down all the time. If we could just sit still, we could *think*. Perhaps, I considered, the churches didn't actually want people to think too much about what was being said.

I recognized that my mind was getting over-suspicious on me, but I just wanted to be able to sit in my pew, especially as my legs felt full of rum.

The minister took his place at the lectern or whatever it was called in church-ese and began droning on about Jesus and the Virgin Mary. He was not what one would call a scintillating speaker, but rather relied heavily on obscure passages from the Bible and chuckling at his own jokes.

I was doing my best to keep my eyes open, but I started seeing the minister in duplicate, then triplicate ... Surely no one would notice if I just had a little snooze. Franck would poke me when I needed to stand up again.

My eyelids dropped, and almost instantaneously I was sucked into the dark vortex of sleep. I had no sense of time passing and was aware of nothing except strange dreams of Santa Claus and the harmonica lady on Prince Arthur Street.

It wasn't until I felt a sharp—a *very* sharp—poke in the ribs that I woke up with a snort. I looked around me, disoriented. The church was silent, and everyone was staring at me, including the minister.

"I'm getting you out of here," Franck hissed at me. "Your dad gave me the car keys."

The minister started talking again, but without taking his narrowed eyes off me. He did *not* look pleased.

If only we had sat in the back row, we wouldn't have had to scurry up the aisle in full view of everyone's disapproving eyes. Franck had his arm in an iron grip around my waist, I was still woozy with sleep. When we made it through the church door and Franck closed it firmly behind us, he exploded with laughter.

Uh oh. "What happened?" I asked, as I half-walked, half-stumbled through the night air towards my dad's parked car.

"You were snoring so loudly." Franck knuckled tears of mirth from his eyes. "I kept trying to wake you up gently to get you to stop, but you were completely passed out. That pompous priest looked so disconcerted—"

"Oh God," I moaned. I slid into the back seat of the car and Franck got in after me. He gathered me up in his arms, still chuckling.

"I can't believe I snored."

"*So* loudly," Franck said.

"Suzanne is going to be furious with me."

Franck pressed a kiss on my forehead. "No she won't. You were exhausted. Now you can sleep and snore as loud as you want. I don't mind."

"I made Suzanne and Greg look bad in front of their minister and the congregation and Greg's parents."

"No." Franck shook his head. "It wasn't your fault."

I groaned. "What a disaster. I just don't know how to do church properly."

"Luckily the first tenet of Christianity is forgiveness." Franck pulled me closer and smoothed my hair with his warm hand in a hypnotic rhythm. My eyelids began to fall again. My shame was no match for my exhaustion.

"I seem to be testing that out this Christmas," I murmured, and fell back to sleep.

The next morning, Christmas morning, I cornered Suzanne before we even opened stockings and apologized.

She was understandably not thrilled with the scene I had made at midnight mass, but she understood and even began to see its humor. I promised to apologize to Greg's parents that night—they were invited over for Christmas dinner.

Christmas at our house had always been an extravagant event. I had seen the previous year that it was a far bigger deal at our house in Canada than it was in France. In Burgundy, the celebrations were far more focused on the multi-hour, multi-course Christmas meal than presents.

At our house, there were plenty of delicious things to eat, but the centerpiece of Christmas was always the decorated tree in my parents' living room and the sea of brightly wrapped presents underneath.

When I came down to the kitchen, Franck was already drinking a mug of coffee and greeted me as though I hadn't just left his bedroom an hour previously. He could have a career as an actor.

"He got up before me and made a fresh pot of coffee and unloaded the dishwasher and loaded it back up again," my Mom hissed to me as she walked by with a bag of Brussels sprouts. "I think I'll keep him." Franck could not have hit on a better path to my mother's heart.

I poured one for myself and led Franck into the living room.

He recoiled when we turned the corner and got a full view of the room. My mom had done her full-on "Santa" routine at night and now the puddle of presents under the tree had become an ocean. They literally spread halfway across the room. Granted, there were a lot of us: me, Suzanne, Jayne, and my parents, plus Franck and Greg, but still, for the first time in my life it dawned on me just how *much* it all was.

"There are so many presents," Franck said, stunned.

"My mom's side of the family have always done big Christmases," I said. "My grandmother on Salt Spring Island is the same."

"*Merde*," he said quietly. "Were we supposed to get each other presents?"

I shook my head. "We haven't had time to even think about that. Besides, we have no money, and being together is a pretty good present."

He squeezed my hand. "It is."

As we sat down on the couch with our coffees, waiting for the others to dribble into the living room, I thought of the boys that I had known in high school. I couldn't imagine any of them putting so much effort into a relationship with my parents. That was one of the differences, I supposed, between dating a boy and dating a man.

I gave him a tight hug. "Thank God I found you."

He dipped forward to give me a quick kiss. "*Joyeux Noël mon chou.* Can you believe we're here together, celebrating our first Christmas as a couple?"

I shook my head. I still couldn't wrap my mind around how surreal yet how normal it felt to have Franck at home. I realized this relationship with Franck was now officially the longest I'd ever been in.

I wanted to kiss him some more, but I reminded myself I didn't need to give my parents any additional reminders that we were living and sleeping together in Montréal, not when things were going so well. Instead, I just held his hand and drank my coffee, gazing at the colored lights from the Christmas tree reflecting in the metallic wrapping paper of the presents underneath.

Eventually, Franck cocked his head. "How long does it take to open all these presents?"

"I've never paid that much attention. A while."

"How do you have any time left over to eat the meal?"

"Don't forget that the Christmas meal here is much quicker, and it's in the evening, not at lunch."

"But that must be so frustrating for your mom. You said she would be cooking all afternoon."

I'd never considered before how our family's habit of bolting our Christmas dinner impacted my mother, who spent far longer cooking it than we did eating it. Franck would soon see for himself how everything was served at once and had to be devoured before it got cold, in contrast to France where they cleverly served festive meals in leisurely courses, each to be individually savored.

Jayne came bouncing in just then. She was eleven years old, and I wasn't entirely sure if she still believed in Santa Claus or whether she had figured out life's greatest ruse and was just pretending to believe in order to hedge her bets. "Mom says we can start opening the stockings!" she declared with a whoop.

Suzanne came in and sat on the stone fireplace ledge with her mug of coffee. "Can't we wait for Greg?" she said.

He had spent the night at his parents' house—they managed to avoid the whole shared-bed issue in Victoria—when here on vacation, as they both just returned to their childhood homes. The plan was he would come over when the present opening was done at his house.

"Noooooooooo!" Jayne protested. I would have done exactly the same thing when I was eleven. Also, Greg's family were known for moving at a snail's pace compared to my family. It was highly possible they hadn't even gotten out of bed yet. "I can't wait a second longer," Jayne insisted.

I didn't side with either of my sisters. I could understand Jayne's impatience, but given the church debacle last night I decided silence was indeed a virtue.

My mom must have heard, because she came in and stood behind the couch. "Greg can open his when he gets here, Su-zanne," she said. "I don't think Jayne is physically capable of waiting. You wouldn't have been when you were eleven either."

"Fine," Suzanne said.

A little while after the stocking and the present opening got underway, I noticed Franck had stopped opening his gifts and was just staring, his gaze shifting between the frenzied present opening and the living room floor that was increasingly full of torn and crumpled wrapping paper.

I looked at the pile of unwrapped gifts that was steadily grow-ing beside him. He hadn't even finished unwrapping all the things from his stocking that my mother had generously and thoughtfully bought based on the little she knew about him.

"You're falling behind," I whispered to him, half amused and half concerned.

"But ... who bought me all of these things?" He nodded to-wards the new gloves, scarves, and toque, as well as the tube of local chocolates. I remembered in France that the tradition wasn't to do stockings, but to put out a pair of slippers that were filled with a few candies by Père *Noël*.

I shrugged. "Santa Claus."

Franck pursed his mouth.

"OK. OK. My parents, I guess. Well, mainly my mom."

"It's too much."

I eyed his pile of unwrapped and as yet untouched presents from under the tree.

"*Mon amour*," I said. "You're going to have to get used to being spoiled."

chapter twenty-five

In the end, I started unwrapping Franck's presents for him after I had finished unwrapping mine. I piled up his warm sweaters and a complete long john set and books in a teetering pile on the couch beside us.

When it was all over the room was a mess of wrapping paper and discarded ribbon. Franck began collecting up the paper and smoothing it into a pile. "Don't worry about that, Franck," my dad said, coming in from the garage clutching a fistful of black garbage bags. "Just shove all that in here."

Franck's shoulders dropped with relief. He leapt up and threw himself into the clean-up, both to help and, I knew, as a way of dealing with the discomfort of being showered with gifts for the first time in his life.

My mother, headed back to the kitchen where she was putting the finishing touches on brunch. It was only now that I had begun making food for myself that I began to comprehend the miracle that my mother pulled off each Christmas.

She shopped, decorated, wrapped, cooked, and cleaned with hardly any assistance from anyone. The Christmas magic I experienced every year growing up was solely due to her back-breaking efforts. Not only that, but she had to put up with my paternal grandparents every Christmas, and that alone would be enough to qualify for sainthood.

They would be rolling in soon, and like every year they would lose no time in asking my Dad to make them glasses of rum and eggnog, that in their case were mostly rum. We all knew the stages. First they would get tipsy and silly, then drunk and belligerent. Unfortunately for my poor mom, neither of them had a festive bone in their bodies.

Franck made quick work of picking up the wrapping paper, then hurried out to help my mom in the kitchen. Suzanne nudged Greg, who had arrived near the end of the present opening and now sat on the stone ledge beside her. "You're going to have to step up your game with Franck around."

"I can see that," Greg said, with a laugh. "Please get him to stop, Laura."

I chuckled, but I got up too. "I don't think I could even if I wanted to. Besides, I'm realizing that Franck is doing what we should have all been doing all along. Mom does everything herself."

"True," Suzanne said, getting up. "I've been feeling badly about that too. Let's go help."

About a half an hour later the doorbell rang and I went to open it for my grandparents. Within five minutes they both had their eggnogs and were ensconced on the couch, getting slowly soused while they watched the old black and white version of *Scrooge* with Alastair Sim on TV. They said they weren't hungry for brunch, but my grandfather had the foresight to bring the entire bottle of rum into the TV room with him for sustenance.

After brunch I managed to persuade Franck that we could leave the house for an hour to go for a walk, and that my mother would be fine with it as long as we helped her when we got back.

We walked down to Willows Beach, a long stretch of light grey sand that today was dotted with Christmas walkers and dogs wearing little Santa sweaters. There was no hint of snow (there almost never was during Victoria winters) but the wind had picked up and the ocean was fluffy with whitecaps. Seagulls cawed as they wheeled overhead.

We found a relatively dry piece of driftwood and sat down for a moment, our legs stretched out in front of us in the sand, contemplating the blustery, wintery beauty of the ocean.

"When I see how beautiful it is here," Franck said. "I have a hard time understanding why you left."

I took a lungful of the sea air. "Same as you. I wanted to see something different. It felt too comfortable here, too easy after seventeen years in the same place. I appreciate it more now that I've left. It must be the same for you and France, isn't it? What do you miss the most?"

Franck didn't hesitate. "The food and wine."

I couldn't argue with that.

"What did you miss about Victoria when you were in France?"

"The ocean." I didn't hesitate either. I had grown up with the ocean all around me. It was never far, and just knowing I could go to it gave me peace. When I was sad, I went to the ocean, when I was full of joy, I went to the ocean, when I was confused and scared I went to the ocean. It was a part of me, and even though the vineyards of Burgundy had their own rolling beauty, nothing could replace it.

"I can see why," Franck said, gazing out.

"It's different every day," I said, pushing windblown strands of hair out of my eyes. "Not even every day, but every hour, every minute. It changes constantly, just like we do."

Franck nodded.

"I miss my friends and family too when I'm away," I said. "A lot. But somehow, my relationship with the ocean is what I miss the most. It's so simple."

"Like my relationship with Mémé's *blanquette de veau*."

"Exactly."

We both laughed until finally Franck stood up from the log and reached a hand down to me. "Come on, *mon chou*, we should get back to your house and help your mother. Do your grandparents never offer to help or bring any food?"

I shook my head. "Never, but my Grandma Agnes from Salt Spring is the complete opposite—she'd probably bring an entire cow and ten pies and be in there helping with everything. Completely different." I bent over with a rattling cough.

Franck cast me a glance under his lashes. "Maybe you shouldn't have come out. You're still sick."

I shook my head. "I may sound worse, but I'm actually feeling a bit better."

Back at home, Franck made himself completely indispensable. He helped my dad choose the wines, cleaned dishes and dried them as my mom cooked, cut a bushel of onions wearing Jayne's old swim goggles to stop himself from crying, and made my mother fresh pots of coffee to keep her going.

I helped as well, although my main job seemed to subsist of translating between Franck and my mother.

Franck and I set the table in the dining room and I explained to him about the Christmas crackers I was placing above each person's plate. I tried to describe the paper hats inside but ultimately gave up. "You have to see them, or better yet, wear them, to understand."

Before we knew it, it was time to put out all the dishes of food buffet-style on the kitchen island. I managed to get everyone to take their seats, even my soused grandparents who could hardly walk in a straight line by that point in the proceedings. Greg's parents had arrived, and his father had brought his homemade hard sauce for the plum pudding.

Franck was the last one to sit down as he had to wait to bring the dish of stuffing warming in the oven over to the island. My mother declared everyone could come and serve themselves. Franck was left sitting at the table, bewildered, when everyone grabbed their plates and sped into the kitchen. I stopped by his chair, pulled him up and reminded him to bring his plate. At the kitchen island, I lined him up at the end of the serving line.

"I don't understand," Franck said. "How does this work?"

"Just take anything you want to eat, put it on your plate, then you can go back and sit at the table."

"You mean we are supposed to eat everything at once?"

"Yes."

Franck began to panic. "But we worked so hard. Things are going to get cold, and it's just *so much*. There won't be room on the plate."

"I know it makes no sense, but it's the way things are done. I don't really have any explanation, like with the separate bedrooms and the paper hats."

Franck watched everyone piling their plates high with turkey and mashed potatoes and stuffing and gravy and Brussels sprouts and green beans and cranberry sauce like he was watching some wildlife documentary about the mating habits of boa constrictors.

"But they don't even all go together," he whispered to me after a few minutes. "The tastes, I mean."

"You might be surprised."

Franck was the last one to start serving himself. Even Greg's unfailingly polite parents had been quicker on the uptake than my boyfriend. Franck was hesitant about spooning out more than a meager amount of each dish, but I nudged him to take more.

Once we sat down everyone began pulling the ends of their Christmas crackers and reading their lame jokes inside and comparing their toys. My father was the first to perch his silver crepe paper hat from the cracker on his crewcut.

I offered the end of my cracker to Franck. "Grab that little stick thingy and pull when I count to three." He did and jumped when it made a bang.

"Nice one," my father said.

Everyone was putting on their hats. I realized for the first time that we truly did look ridiculous with crepe crowns on our heads.

"What is the tradition behind the crackers and the hats?" Franck asked me.

"I have no idea." I asked the question to the table and everyone shrugged, as clueless as me. None of us knew why we wore paper crowns at the Christmas table except that "It's an English thing."

Franck, of course, didn't keep up with the rest of us at dinner. We all ate faster than him, but he must have found it was good, or at least he was being extremely polite, because he did go back and fill his plate three times.

His hat had slipped down so it was crooked on his head but by the time my mom brought out the plum pudding (yet another English thing) her friend Sandra made her every year, and soaked it with rum and lit it on fire, he was well and truly initiated in our Christmas festivities.

As the blue flames around the plum pudding went on a little too long and the cake began to resemble a lump of charcoal like naughty children got in their stockings, he squeezed my hand. "This is far better than any sociology class."

I watched as my mom served him a plate of the burned plum pudding. She knew I never ate the stuff. "It's an all-senses immersion into a new culture," I said.

He tasted the burnt plum pudding and cocked his head. "It certainly is."

chapter twenty-six

On Boxing Day, Suzanne and Greg and I decided to take Franck up-island to see the beaches in the nearby town of Sooke.

I knew from the year before that there was no such thing as Boxing Day in France, but I thought this British tradition—declaring the day after Christmas a holiday whereby everyone generally sat around, ate turkey sandwiches, and drank copious amounts of coffee—was one of the cleverest inventions of all time.

But this year we eschewed the usual turkey and coffee fest going on at home, and Suzanne, Greg, Franck and I hopped into my parents' car and began the hour-long drive north.

The weather, unfortunately, was what I often thought of West Coast Sullen. Gray, with a low cloud ceiling that seemed to suck up all the light. It was spitting rain.

Franck had been in an odd mood since he got up that morning.

"Are you feeling sick?" I asked him after he got out of the shower. "Don't you want to go to Sooke?"

"I'm fine," he said.

"Indigestion?" I guessed. "That's common the day after Christmas, you know. I'm sure I have some Pepto-Bismol somewhere."

He shook his head. "I don't have a sore stomach."

"Do you not want to go to Sooke then?"

"I do."

"Then what's up?"

"Nothing." He shrugged. "I'm going to get dressed."

But it wasn't nothing. Franck was flat and distant. It drove me crazy that I didn't know why. Had I done something? Said something?

Our first stop in Sooke was a long tongue of land that stretched into the Sooke Harbor. The spit was narrow, but wide enough for a walking path to take us to its end and back. It was an interesting walk, with the ocean on both sides, and I'd been eager to show it to Franck. Granted, it was gray and spitting rain, but on the other hand it was quintessential Pacific Northwest winter weather.

When we parked by the entrance and I told Franck we were stopping to walk out to the end of Whiffin Spit and back, he gave me a forced smile. The whole ride up he had barely said a word except to respond curtly to any questions we asked him or my numerous attempts to get the conversation rolling. He was as downcast as the weather.

I tried not to keep asking him what was wrong but I couldn't help myself. I had been brought up to believe it was my job to make everyone happy. I had learned a hard lesson the previous year with the Ursus Club in Burgundy. They'd forced me to choose between them and Franck and in choosing Franck I realized that it was impossible, and indeed undesirable, to try and please everyone. But this *was* Franck. I loved him, and it was impossible for me to see someone I loved upset or sad and not try to make it better.

As we walked to the end of the spit Greg, Suzanne and I tried to keep up a stilted conversation, while Franck lagged behind in his own world.

By the time we reached the pine tree at the end of the spit that was always decorated by locals with lights and gaudy decorative baubles, I didn't even feel like giving Franck an explanation. Anyway, he didn't ask.

My worry transmuted into annoyance. By the time we'd reached the table at the Point No Point—the restaurant we reserved for lunch that was perched over the ocean and gave a spectacular view of the crashing waves on the rocks below—my annoyance had progressed into full blown fury.

I resented Franck for putting me in such an awkward position in front of my family and for ruining our day with his black mood. When I was upset I made an effort to hide it. Didn't he at least owe me that courtesy?

After lunch, during which the delicious food tasted like dust in my mouth, we took a winding, slippery trail through the moss and rocks down to the beach. Once down there, Franck swerved off from the three of us and walked in a different direction. I watched as he climbed on top of a rock at the end of the beach and stood there, looking out to the ocean, a portrait in self-indulgent melancholy.

Suzanne slid me a glance. "What's up?" She and Greg were watching Franck too, every bit as confused as me.

"I have no idea," I said. "He won't tell me and it's pissing me off."

"Did we say or do something to make him angry?" Greg asked, his eyes heavy with concern.

"Of course not." I scoffed. "He's the one making *me* angry."

Franck showed no signs of decamping from his rock. My exasperation eventually propelled my legs forward. The wind was loud, and Suzanne and Greg were upwind of the rock. I couldn't stand one more second of this. Franck and I were going to have it out on that rock, now.

I clambered up, thankful that my childhood of leaping around beach rocks and driftwood gave me an excellent sense of balance and an instinct about the slippery areas to be avoided.

When I reached the top of the rock, the wind whipped my hair around my face. I called his name. He turned and looked at me with that flat expression he'd been wearing all day: the perfect kerosene for my fire.

"What the hell is wrong with you?" I shouted.

"What do you mean?" Franck asked, his brows drawing in. How could he be perplexed at my question?

"You've been a complete asshole all day," I said. "You're not even making the smallest effort to contribute to the conversation. You're acting thoroughly rude and unpleasant."

I could scarcely believe it, but the shock registering on his face seemed to be sincere. "I'm sorry," he said. "I'm just feeling sad."

"Sad about what?" I demanded. Normally I might have been worried about him being unhappy in Canada, or worse yet in our relationship, but my anger swept all of those concerns away for the time being.

"I got a wave of homesickness this morning." He shrugged. "I can't really explain it, but I just feel ... *mélancholique*."

"Do you regret being here with me?" I demanded.

"No!" The surprise in his face finally broke the mask of gloom he'd been wearing. He looked like my Franck again. "How could you think that?"

"Do you want to go back home to France?" I said. "Is everything here in Canada just too difficult?"

I could understand if this was the case. Our first couple of months in Montréal hadn't exactly been a picnic. It was harder than either of us could ever have imagined.

He shook his head vigorously. "Of course not. Like I said, I'm just feeling sad."

"Well, snap out of it!" I snapped my fingers for emphasis, then regretted it.

"Why?" I was unprepared for Franck's honest confusion.

"Because it's incredibly rude to inflict your moods on others. Being with you today is like being with a walking storm cloud that blocks out every bit of light."

His eyes opened wide at this. "Do you think Suzanne and Greg noticed?"

I let out a laugh so caustic it could rot steel. "Of course they did, Franck! They've been asking me what the hell is wrong with you and wondering if they did or said anything to make you angry."

"I'm so sorry for that," he said. "I honestly thought nobody would notice."

"Are you serious? It's impossible to notice anything else when you're like this. You can at least make an effort to act happy."

Franck cocked a brow. "Act happy?"

"Yes. Act happy."

"But that would be completely dishonest. When one of us is in a bad mood at home, everyone just accepts it. Nobody pays any attention."

"I don't care if it feels dishonest," I said. "It's the polite thing to do. It's rude to act like a complete misery all day."

"Wouldn't it be ruder to lie about your emotions to the people around you?"

It was like arguing with an eel. "So in France you just inflict your moods on everyone around you?"

"There's no question of inflicting," Franck said. "Everyone is like this from time to time. We all just accept that it's part of the human condition and it will pass. Nobody takes it personally or thinks it's anyone's fault. Why would you think that, anyway?"

I thought back to how things were in France. There was some truth in what Franck said. I had seen many of my friends over there—Sandrine and Stéphanie and Hugo and other kids at school—have days where they were sulky and anti-social. It was true; nobody seemed particularly bothered by it. Whenever I commented on it, people just shrugged.

It wasn't isolated to younger people either. I had seen Mémé and Franck's mother Michèle stalk around the house, talking to no-one. Everyone just went on with their lives, unperturbed. If they did comment at all it would be to say something like, "Oh, Mémé's in a mood," in the same neutral way they would report the weather.

"People feel responsible for other people's happiness here," I tried to explain.

"How can we be responsible for someone else's happiness?" Franck asked. "That makes no sense."

Jealousy rose in me, of all things. What a carefree life it would be to not have to worry about fixing other people's moods, or to question whether I had caused them. Still, it wasn't the way things worked here in Canada.

"I can't explain it," I said. "Like why do you eat so many baguettes in France? It's just the way it is. There are cultural differences, and this is a big one."

"So, what am I supposed to do?"

"You have to act like you're happy."

"You mean I have to act differently than how I am feeling?"

"Yes," I said.

"I've never considered trying that." Franck frowned. "I guess I can try—"

"You have to do more than try, you just have to do it." I felt like Yoda training Luke to raise the X-wing fighter out of the swamp on Dagobah.

"I'm not going to be very good at it," he warned.

"Too bad," I said. Jedi masters weren't known for their leniency.

He stared at me with a flicker of a smile on the corner of his mouth. "You can be tough."

My anger hadn't completely gone. "You want to talk about tough? How about having to put up with the way you acted all day? You looked ready to hurl yourself into the ocean."

"No," he said. His lips quivered. "I wasn't thinking of doing that. Too cold."

I just stared at him with hard eyes.

"I'm sorry," he said, repentant at last. "It never even occurred to me that any of you would be bothered by my mood or think at all that it was your responsibility to do anything about it."

"Well, we were, and we did."

We watched each other for at least a minute. The wind kept whipping my hair—damp from the mist—against my face, but I welcomed the sting. "I'm going back down to the beach now," I finally declared. "You can come and join me when you get rid of that black storm cloud over your head.

I stalked back to Suzanne and Greg without looking back. They waited for me with questions writ all over their faces.

"He's just homesick," I explained. "He didn't realize any of us would notice his bad mood."

We shared a glance, and then all burst into laughter. The idea that Franck's mood could possibly go unnoticed, even by someone who was unconscious, was ludicrous.

"Shhhhhh. He's coming," Greg warned.

I turned around to see that Franck had a smile plastered to his face that had the same rictus as a made-up corpse at an open-casket viewing. He really wasn't very good at this.

When he came within earshot he immediately and contritely apologized in broken English to Suzanne and Greg for his mood. Suzanne and Greg both shrugged and tried to downplay it, assuring him it was fine.

When we began to walk back to the car, Franck leaned over and whispered to me. "See. They said my mood didn't bother them."

"They were just being polite," I said through clenched teeth. "They didn't mean it."

Franck shook his head. "*Mon Dieu*, Canada is confusing."

"If it makes you feel any better, so is having a French boy-friend."

chapter twenty-seven

Three days later we went to go visit my grandmother on Salt Spring Island so I could introduce her to Franck. Because she lived on an even smaller island, we ended up back at the Swartz Bay ferry terminal, much to Franck's delight.

"I love this idea of ferry travel," he said, as we drove down from the ramp onto the ferry deck with the dull clunk of metal. There was no trace of his bad mood since that day in Sooke, thank God. Otherwise, I might have wrung his neck.

The boat that made the Salt Spring trip, the *Nootka Queen,* was a far smaller vessel than the ferries that ran between Vancouver Island and the Mainland. I'd been taking it back and forth to Salt Spring from as long as I could remember.

It was even quainter than the bigger boats and Franck was enchanted. He pulled me upstairs to the upper deck where again he insisted on sitting outside. I was more prepared this time, and had worn my heaviest winter parka, gloves, a toque, and a scarf. Luckily, it was a gloriously sunny January day. It wasn't warm by any stretch of the imagination, but the view out to the ocean and past the tiny Piers and Portland islands was worth the chill.

"What's your grandmother like?" Franck asked as we leaned over the railing of the boat.

"She's a character," I said. "She's got friends all over the island. She never stops talking or laughing."

Franck hooked his forearms over the railing. "Tell me more."

I sighed, wondering how to put my maternal grandmother into words. To me, she always seemed slightly larger than life.

"Let's see ... when my grandfather died, leaving her with four young children, she climbed up on the roof whenever it needed repairs on her own. She managed a massive farm with countless animals on it for years single-handedly, while also running a bed and breakfast and taking in foster children."

Franck nodded. This was the information he wanted.

"My favorite story about her was when there was a marauding buck who kept breaking into her massive vegetable garden and eating all her vegetables. Instead of putting up with it or building a bigger fence, she spotted him in her garden, munching away one morning when she was getting dressed. She picked up her rifle from the corner of her bedroom, opened the window, took aim at the buck, and shot it straight between the eyes."

"What?" Franck stared at me in astonishment.

I nodded. "That's not all. After she killed the deer she went into the garden and butchered it and filled her freezer up with venison that lasted a good year or two, then she took the buck's head to the island taxidermist and had it stuffed. The buck's head hangs on the wall of her living room. Even my Dad, who is a lifelong hunter, swears he's never made such a perfect shot. I'll show it to you."

Franck chuckled.

It only took thirty-five minutes to get to Fulford Harbour where the ferry docked, so before we knew it we were climbing back into my mother's Subaru I'd borrowed for the day and driving off the boat. Franck remained transfixed by the scenery that passed us by—winding pastoral roads, the odd cow and sheep, and tiny stone churches built by the early settlers. Vesuvius, the little seaside neighborhood my grandmother had moved to the year before when I had been in France, was on the opposite side of the island, but I knew these roads like the back of my hand.

I pulled into Embe Bakery at the top of the hill going down to Ganges, the island's main town, to buy us bear claws—giant cinnamon-spiced pastries filled with a butter pecan filling. I bought one for each of us plus one for my grandma. She had a wicked sweet tooth like me and I knew she would be expecting it. The bear claws formed a part of the Salt Spring ritual and from

Franck's grin I could tell he approved.

"Maybe we should stop and get some coffee to go with these," Franck said, as we drove down the hill into Ganges.

I shook my head. "My grandma will have coffee on at her place."

"Are you sure?"

"Guaranteed. Trust me."

We drove past the cemetery where my great-grandparents and grandpa were buried, and the island soccer field and the tiny yellow wooden house on the corner that had been converted into the island's movie theater. From the chalk sign out front, I saw *Fried Green Tomatoes* was playing.

I took the branch of the road that led down to Vesuvius Bay, where one could find the warmest water for ocean swimming according to the locals like my grandmother. I pulled into my grandmother's house on the road parallel to the beach. It was easy to find because one of her many friends had painted her a mailbox decorated with big white and brown cows and she had stuck it on a wooden post at the entrance to her driveway.

I honked when I pulled the car to a stop and leapt out. It was incredible, but her beautiful orange rose on the side gate still had a few blooms on it. Vesuvius enjoyed an odd little microclimate, where rhododendrons grew the size of tugboats and roses flowered in January.

I heard the bang of her screen door and she came half-limping (she'd suffered from a bum knee for the past few years) and half charging out to us. She gave me a brief hug but then went over to Franck and put her hands on her hips.

"Hmmm ... so this is your Frenchman, is it?" she demanded.

Franck must have picked up her tone, or maybe his English was getting better, because his eyes glinted with mischief. "*Bonjour*," he said and kissed her cheeks, despite my warnings about *les bises*.

However, my grandma showed no objection. She roared with laughter and patted Franck on the shoulder. "I like the look of you," she said.

I held up the bakery bag. "Got our bear claws," I said.

"Coffee's on." She beckoned into the house with her arm, berating her mongrel dog Gypsy to get out from underfoot. "That dog is as dumb as a post. Can't figure out why I love her anyway."

Franck entered my grandmother's kitchen with an expression of awe. As always, the counters were a joyful clutter of wooden shortbread molds from Scotland, random old cannisters, some half-eaten baking, and canning jars upside down drying on a tea towel.

Grandma reached for three mugs in the cupboard, and finally had to ask Franck for help. At five foot one, she was even more height challenged than me.

Seeing as it was so sunny and we were in Vesuvius, we decided to have our snack on my Grandma's back porch. From there we could see out to the sparkling blue ocean beyond. She had installed at least seven bird feeders around her porch and the birdsong provided us with the perfect accompaniment, as well as the horn from the even smaller ferry boat that did the trip between Vesuvius Bay and Nanaimo, further north up Vancouver Island.

We chatted about this and that and I translated between Franck and my grandmother as best I could, but she talked fast, so I often found I had to summarize or paraphrase.

"Nobody thought you two were going to stay together," she said, licking her fingers after polishing off her bear claw.

"I was well aware of that," I said. "I don't think everyone is necessarily thrilled about it either."

My grandma shrugged. "Nobody was thrilled about me and your grandfather either."

I had forgotten, but now I remembered I had heard stories of there being a big scandal when the two of them had decided to get married. "It was because grandpa was older than you, right?"

She nodded. "He was twenty years older than me, but somehow that didn't seem to matter."

"Your parents were mad though?"

"Furious. My father was more of a softie, but my mother ..." My grandma's normally cheery, open face seemed to close in on itself. "She was not a forgiving woman."

"That must have been difficult," I said. "With all of you living on the island."

She nodded. "Impossible not to cross paths. My father would talk to me and Jack on the sly when my mother wasn't looking, but my mother didn't talk to me until *your* mother was born."

I translated for Franck. He nodded with understanding.

"Ugh. That must have been terrible."

My grandmother nodded. "And then, can you believe it? When my mother deigned to talk to me again at the hospital after your mother was born, she acted as though all of that hadn't happened."

"You mean you never talked about it?"

My grandmother rolled her eyes. "She wasn't much of a talking woman, especially about things like that."

"Did you ever regret it?" I said, thinking of that phone conversation with my parents when Franck and I moved in together. "Making people you loved angry?"

"Never. I would never trade those years I had with your grandfather for anything. Sometimes it takes years, but everyone comes around eventually. You just have to be brave and that's useful training for life anyway."

I translated for Franck. Their eyes met and he grinned at her and nodded. They got along just fine.

After our snack, I gave Franck a tour of my grandma's cottage, filled to the brim with portraits of the queen and my grandfather and great-grandfather Fletcher in their soldier uniforms, as well as the bust of the marauding buck with the bullet hole perfectly placed between his eyes.

I stared at it again, as I had many times throughout my childhood. "Not a millimeter off center," I murmured. "Amazing."

After, we strolled down the road to Vesuvius Bay with Gypsy at our heels. My grandmother brought her cane to turn over rocks on the beach for Gypsy, who gobbled down the tiny salty beach crabs underneath before they could skitter away.

Franck sat down on a large piece of driftwood beside my grandmother and me. He gazed out at the overlapping blue mountains in the distance and the blue sheet of ocean that splayed out in front of us.

"I love this place," he said, intertwining his fingers in mine.

I translated for my grandmother and she winked at me. "He's a keeper."

After Salt Spring the vacation seemed to accelerate. My dad had taken a shine to Franck and the clincher was he had taken him fishing and they had caught six beautiful spring salmon.

My dad confided to me when they got back and were cleaning the fish and readying them to put in his smoker on the rock wall of our driveway. "Franck didn't feel the need to talk all the time. That's a rare thing—someone who realizes one of the best things about fishing is the peace."

I knew for my dad silence in the fishing boat was sacrosanct. "Good," I said. "He had a great time. Can you imagine how cool it is for him to go fishing on the Pacific when he grew up hours from the nearest ocean?"

"He's never fished before?"

"Not ocean fishing. Why?"

"He was a surprisingly deft hand at cutting the plug herring for the bait."

Excellent. Franck continued to score points.

My dad even showed Franck how to smoke salmon and turned over his Little Chief metal-sided smoker so Franck could peer inside. It was not a pretty sight—the smoker was coated with layers of greasy, fatty, dripping tar. "There are the two keys to good smoked salmon," my dad said, indicating with his finger for me to translate. "Demerara sugar and never clean the inside of your smoker."

When it came time to leave, I think my parents were just as sorry to say good-bye to Franck as to me. Maybe a little bit sorrier, if I was going to be honest. He was certainly more help around the house.

Franck's flight to Montréal left Vancouver only twenty minutes before mine, but because I had to change planes in Calgary he arrived three hours earlier than me. The plan was for him to wait at the airport and we would get a taxi back to the apartment together.

We glanced at the screen in the waiting area for Franck's flight once we arrived in the Vancouver airport after a quick hop over from the island on the tiny propeller commuter plane. It showed the weather in Montréal, minus twenty-two with snow and strong winds. Montréal was still in a deep freeze.

Franck gave me a kiss before he got in line to board his flight. "I'll be waiting for you at Dorval," he said. For someone who had taken his first flight only a couple of months before he had adapted to plane travel quickly, and now looked as seasoned as the other travelers.

"Maybe you can find some balloons for me," I joked, thinking of the ones I greeted him with when he'd arrived from France.

"Excellent idea," he said. "*Je t'aime, mon amour.*"

He disappeared through the gate and I went to mine, armed with five trashy magazines and *Heart of Darkness* by Joseph Conrad for one of my English classes.

The day felt long, as it always did when flying back East. Calgary was blanketed in snow and I was heartily glad I didn't have to leave the warmth of the airport. I would have to in Montréal though, but at least I would have Franck with me.

As my plane began its descent into Montréal it began to bounce all over the sky. *They weren't kidding about the strong winds.* It was dark outside, but from the light on the wing I could see snow being whipped against my oval window.

I wondered what the landing conditions would be, and whether Franck's plane had touched down safely.

As we approached the airport the pilot came on with a brief, scratchy message that we would have to be in a holding pattern for a while. I hated holding patterns. The plane banked steeply and jumped around in the sky. My ears plugged and then popped, plugged and then popped. Two people in the row beside me scrambled for their barf bags and used them. The scent of vomit expanded to fill the plane air. An elderly Italian woman sitting two seats over from me took a rosary out of her purse and fingered the beads as she mouthed frantic prayers.

Was I about to die? Fear gripped my stomach and I broke out into a cold sweat.

The circling lasted almost an hour and by the time the pilot told us we were finally landing, my leg muscles ached from the adrenaline coursing through them.

The airplane felt like it kept being blown off course, and when our wheels finally touched the tarmac the plane skidded violently to the right. I heard a scream from further back in the cabin. The pilot, after a long—far too long—stretch of feeling like we were going sideways, somehow managed to straighten the plane more or less back on to the runway as it slowed down.

I peered out my window to see that everything illuminated by the yellow light of the airport was featureless under a thick blanket of snow. The snow gusted right and left so that it was difficult to tell what was falling from the sky and what was being blown around. As far as I could see which, granted, wasn't very far, was that there were no other planes on the surrounding runways or tarmac.

The pilot came on the speaker to say that the airport staff were using their equipment to dig a path for us in the snow as we inched towards the terminal. It took us an entire hour with many stops and starts for the plane to finally get there. He also added that we were the last plane allowed to land that night. Many other flights had been diverted to southern airports and we had somehow squeaked through. I worried that Franck wasn't waiting for me in the terminal, but was instead stuck in Teterboro, New Jersey.

When I finally disembarked the airport, it was almost deserted. I held my breath as I walked through the arrivals door. Was Franck's plane able to land?

I saw him, waiting for me like I had been waiting for him only a few months before, and love and relief filled every cell in my body. Nothing felt quite as frightening or lonely when he was with me.

He wrapped me in a hug and kissed my ear. "What an ordeal," he said. "I couldn't find any balloons, but I did find you chocolates."

He took out a shiny foil box from underneath his puffy winter coat.

I chuckled. "You know me well. I heard most of the planes were diverted. I was so worried yours would be."

He shook his head. "No. We landed just in time, probably because I recited my Ave Maria ten times in a row."

"That must have been it." I rose up on my toes and kissed him again. "There was an Italian woman on my plane that was doing it for my flight. She even had a rosary."

"Lucky for you," he said. "I'll have to teach you how to recite it for when I'm not there."

"Good luck with that," I said. "You saw first-hand how religious my family is."

We found the luggage carousel for my flight. It was the only one that had the screen above turned on, and I stood waiting for my bags to be spat off while Franck filled me in. "I was so worried. All the screens were lighting up red with canceled flights until yours was the only one left, but the arrival time kept being pushed back every few minutes."

"We were circling overhead."

"I think you must have been on the last plane that landed before they shut down the airport to flights."

"They shut down the airport?"

Franck nodded. "There was an announcement just before you came through the arrivals door."

"How was it when you landed?" I leaned against his solid form and yawned.

"Dodgy," he said. "I think they might have already been shutting down the outer runways by then. Were you scared? I was."

I nodded. "I started thinking, when we were being blown around up there that maybe the universe had to serve me up something bad to balance out letting us be together."

"Ah," Franck nodded, knowingly. "Laura's magical thinking."

"I know," I said, rueful. I was trying to break this habit, but it was proving difficult.

Franck grabbed me and wrapped me in a bear hug. "The world doesn't work like that, remember?"

"Right," I said, but we stayed like that for a few minutes while I soaked up his familiar warmth all the same.

The bags took over an hour to come off the ramp. I thought about how nice it would feel to get into bed, but then I remembered how cold our apartment would be—we had turned off the heat to save money before we left.

There was fierce competition for the few remaining taxis. When we walked outside to get into ours, the air was so cold that I felt like my lungs couldn't expand to breathe.

As the taxi slid on the snowy, ice rink of a road out of the airport, we passed a lit-up sign that said "Bienvenue à Montréal!"

A perfect Montréal welcome indeed.

chapter twenty-eight

Our taxi driver was, thank God, a born and bred Montréalais who had been navigating snow drifts and icy streets since he got his driver's license. He was firmly Québécois and kept saying "*Pas de problème*! *Je m'en câlisse de cette neige*!" when faced with yet another impassable street. We half drove, half slid our way back to our apartment. The closer we got, the more I started thinking about the inhospitable home we were heading towards.

He dropped us off at the corner of Saint-Laurent and Prince Arthur, and I glanced up through the blowing snow at our apartment windows. They were dark and looked the exact opposite of welcoming. I was tempted to ask the driver to take us back to the airport and for Franck and me to board the next plane to somewhere with palm trees once the airport opened up again. But no. This was our new reality. We had to face it, and at least we were facing it together.

As I stepped outside the taxi and almost flash froze to the spot, I realized turning the heat off before we left had probably been a West Coaster mistake. We could get away with that in the Pacific Northwest, but here, the pipes … *merde*.

I fumbled with the key in the lock with frozen hands, and we hurried into the protection of the hallway as soon as we could.

Franck and I exchanged a glance.

"Home sweet home," I said with a grimace.

He began to haul his bag and one of mine up the stairs. "Let's get this over with."

Inside our apartment, it was worse than it looked from the

street. Ice had formed on the surface of everything. The windows, the walls, and the toilet seat. The dripping water from the leaky tap had accumulated at the opposite end of the bathtub and was frozen into a solid block of ice.

"Huh," Franck said as we both looked down at it. "I guess there's our proof that the bathtub really *is* tilted the wrong way so it can't drain."

I went to all the thermostats and cranked them up to maximum. Even if it would cost a fortune, we had to thaw this place out before we could ever hope to go to bed. Our sheets were stiff with cold.

"It's hard to come from the West Coast to this," Franck said as he plugged my hairdryer in the wall and began to try and thaw the block of ice that was also lodged in the toilet bowl. "I need to pee."

I shrugged. "I guess you could go pee outside. It's not like anybody's around."

Franck pursed his lips. "Yet somehow, not appealing."

I checked my watch. "Do you think Mazurka's is still open?" Mazurka's was a Polish restaurant on Prince Arthur about two hundred meters from our front door. It was cheap and filling—hence a student favorite. Pierogis were their house specialty. It was open later than many other restaurants, because, as it happened, pierogis were the perfect after-clubbing food. "I doubt it," I said, as I didn't want to get our hopes up. "But if we could go there you can pee and we can eat pierogis while this ice box warms up—"

"Let's go," Franck said. Neither of us had taken off a shred of outerwear yet. "Look, we're already dressed."

It was miserable outside, to be sure, but inside was no better, and at least outside there was the slim possibility of food.

I already had our apartment door open. "Pray for pierogis."

We hurried down the stairs.

Walking outside was difficult with the snow drifts. I was going along, carefully placing one foot in front of the other along what I thought had to be the sidewalk, although it was hard to tell what was what. I sunk into a drift of snow up the middle of my thighs.

"Please let it be open," I muttered into my tightly wrapped

scarf. The wind was howling so loud that Franck couldn't hear me, but I was fairly certain he was praying too.

I was watching where I put my feet so as not to take a header, so when Franck grabbed my forearm urgently my head flew up and I lost my balance until he steadied me again. I followed his finger and he indicated a sole figure, standing on Prince Arthur Street just where it crossed with Saint-Laurent. It was the harmonica lady. She was bundled up and playing her instrument as tunelessly as ever by just sliding it back and forth across her mouth so it just made two different sounds. Side. To side. Side. To side.

It would scarcely have been more surprising to encounter a woolly mammoth on the street corner than her on such a night. Why didn't she go inside somewhere? The streets were almost deserted. There was no one to put money in her open violin case. "How does the metal not stick to her lips in this cold?" I asked Franck.

Franck shook his head. "I have no idea, but it's not safe for her to be out here like this. We should ask her if we can buy her some dinner."

I nodded and approached her, not sure whether she spoke French or English. "Hellobonjour," I said. I had started to adopt the bilingual Montréal greeting. She just stretched her free hand wrapped in what looked like layers of scarves and disintegrating mitts down to her violin case which was rapidly filling with snow. It was strange she had an empty violin case when she was playing a tiny harmonica, but in the list of weird things about her that barely registered. She wanted us to give her some money.

"Come with us," I urged in French. "We'll go somewhere and buy you a warm dinner."

"No!" She shook her head. OK. Definitely anglophone then. "I just want money."

"But it's too cold out here for anyone," I tried to reason with her. "We're worried about you."

She just stretched an imperious bundled hand out to her violin case.

I felt in the back of my jeans pocket where I'd shoved a twenty-dollar bill that my mom had given me for my trip. I put it carefully in her case, and almost immediately it started to be covered with flakes of snow.

She was scowling at me so I backed up. "She doesn't want to come with us," I translated for Franck in case he didn't understand. "But that was a twenty-dollar bill I put in there, which means she could at least go up to Schwartz's for coffee and a smoked meat sandwich if she wants."

We shuffled on, still unsure what to do. I would have thought she would use the twenty dollars to go somewhere and get out of the cold immediately, but I could still hear her reedy harmonica playing monotonously behind us.

"Do you think we should call the police so they can get her somewhere warm?" I asked.

Franck bit his lip. "I'm really not sure."

I was so preoccupied that I didn't see Mazurka's reddish light shining out into the snow-covered street until we had almost arrived. Thank God. Our prayers must have worked. It was still open.

Franck and I took refuge inside as quickly as we could and began to peel off layers of scarves, toques, mittens. The robust Polish woman who always worked the front came out to greet us.

"We didn't think you'd be open," I said. "I'm so glad you are."

She made a disparaging noise in the back of her throat. "Some of the other restaurants around here closed earlier because of the snow so their staff could get home safely. Pfffffftt. What a bunch of weaklings. It is clear they never lived through Communism."

"Right," I said, unsure how to react to this. "That lady at the end of the street playing the harmonica ... do you know her?"

The Polish woman looked at me as if I'd asked a ridiculous question. "The harmonica lady. Everyone knows her."

"It can't be safe for her to be out here playing when it's this cold."

"Pffft," she said. "She can't play the harmonica worth a dime, but she was out doing it last winter in minus thirty. I think she may be a little strange in the head, but she would have done well under the communists—I'll tell you that. She's got grit, that one. A true Montréalais."

I must not have looked convinced, because she patted my shoulder with her large and very capable hand. "I see you're worried. No need. I always bring her all my extra pierogis at the end of the night. We all help her on this street. She seems to have a place to sleep too, if that's what you're concerned about."

I nodded, relieved. Maybe there was more solidarity in a city like this where everyone had to help each other when faced with brutal weather, or maybe it was that, despite what we saw in the news, there were far more good people than bad. Both were probably true.

In any case, it was with a lighter heart that Franck and I sat down at a table in the back of the restaurant and were bathed in the warmth of the place and the lights with red tassels hanging from them. The scents of Eastern European cooking—beets and kirsch and boiled potatoes—enveloped us like a welcome hug.

By the time the piping hot bowls of borscht were placed in front of us, we were feeling more at peace with the world—and with Montréal.

Franck laughed after his first couple of spoonfuls. "Can you feel yourself thawing out too?"

I had been wiggling my toes which had begun to ache. "It's the weirdest feeling. It *hurts*."

"Which toe hurts the most right now?"

I took another spoonful of the ruby red soup and thought about it. "The middle toe of my left foot. It's throbbing. You?"

"My big toe on my right foot. I'm in agony, but I'm very brave. Besides, this borscht is helping."

By the time we each got our plateful of eight cheese-and-potato pierogis each, plus a small metal bowl of sour cream and some friend onions on the side, the world felt like it had righted itself again. It was amazing how good food had that power.

I cut the plumpest pierogi on my plate in half, put some sour cream and onions on top, and popped it in my mouth. I groaned as I bit down on the pillowy, cheesy doughiness.

"Oh my God," I groaned after I swallowed. "These are amazing. This restaurant is a huge plus in the Montréal column."

"Enjoy them," Franck said. "And just don't think about how cold our bed is going to be."

I hadn't thought about that in a while. "I'll be wearing several layers of clothes to bed," I warned. "And probably my toque and gloves too."

"I wonder how long it's going to take to get the place to heat up?"

"It's not like it ever heated up properly. I think there's next to no insulation in the walls and between the floors. Besides, the windows are single paned. It wasn't this cold before we left, so I think we may have to resign ourselves to being freezing most of the time. It's a shame Alison and Sam aren't back from Christmas yet, otherwise we could beg them to sleep upstairs on their floor, at least for tonight anyway."

"I am just praying none of the pipes froze and burst," Franck said. "It's not unlikely, you know."

I frowned. "I know. That was stupid of us."

"It was," Franck agreed cheerfully. "We'll know better next time."

And that was what was wonderful. Even though this city could be hard, we had a future of next times together.

Franck polished off the last of his pierogis and nodded at the waiter to bring the mugs of coffee which came with the set menu we had ordered. It was almost eleven o'clock at night—not usually time to be having a big mug of coffee, but once it got below minus ten outside such rules were waived.

"Ready to head back?" he said when I couldn't possibly drag out my coffee any longer.

"Ugh," I said. It was still going to be freezing in our bed.

"It'll be an adventure, like camping in the Arctic."

"Double ugh."

"It's good for us."

"How is shivering all night good for us?" I said. "I just don't buy it"

"We can snuggle," Franck said, with a cocked eyebrow.

"We can," I said. "But just a warning. I will not be removing any clothes."

Franck winked at me. "We'll see about that."

We left Mazurka's and made our slow trudge back to the apartment. The harmonica lady was still there, but our twenty-dollar bill was gone. She had either pocketed it, or it had been covered up by snow. I hoped her nightly pierogis would be brought to her soon.

We fell back into a semblance of routine, but as it got even colder outside, it began to fully dawn on me just how unacceptable the living conditions were inside our apartment.

Franck went back to his despised job of trying to trick people into going for "free" condo-selling weekends at Mont Tremblant. He was increasingly discontented, so began looking in earnest for something better.

Two weeks after we returned from BC we contacted Denis about the bathtub not draining and the fact that the radiators didn't ever truly heat up the place. Having the heat on maximum brought the apartment temperature to a bit above freezing level, but that was about the extent of it. All we got as a response from Denis was radio silence.

"Either he can't be bothered to fix anything," Franck contemplated one night as we lay shivering in our bed. "Or he's been offed mafia-style."

I thought about this. Both possibilities were plausible. "I don't know what else to do. I guess maybe we should give it a little longer. Denis may be out of town, but if I still don't hear anything maybe I can send him a registered letter or something to get his attention."

Franck nodded. "Also, check the obituaries."

"Too late for that," I sighed. "If he had been knocked off the obituary would only appear for a couple of days. We probably already missed it."

"How about we could go and ask his whereabouts at the 'grocery store' across the street?" Franck and I both hooted with laughter at this. That would be the last thing any sane person would do.

"I always see posters around campus for this free legal clinic at the school. I think it's staffed by the university's law students. Maybe I'll drop in on one of those and ask them how I can light a fire under our landlord's butt."

"Good idea," Franck said and then we both jumped at the sound of someone pounding on the door at the bottom of the stairs.

"What the hell is that?" I asked to the ambient air. The thumps sounded frantic, or furious—I couldn't tell which. "Do you think Denis heard us talking about him?" It was a joke, but I wouldn't put it past him to have installed secret cameras.

"It'll stop." Franck patted my arm under the duvet. "Probably just a drunk student who has the wrong address for a party."

Franck was right. That was a likely explanation. Except the pounding didn't stop, and soon I could hear yelling as well. I couldn't make out the words exactly, but it sounded … persistent.

Franck groaned. "*Bordel de merde*. I'll go down and see what's going on."

I grabbed his arm. "Do you think that's a good idea?"

"I think us getting some sleep is a good idea," Franck said. He hauled himself off our futon and pulled on his ratty bathrobe. I got up and followed him as he shoved his feet in his fake-fur lined winter boots.

Suddenly, I remembered the hockey stick that I'd found on the sidewalk of Milton Street three days previously on my way home from school. I hadn't known what I would do with it at the time, but I had fallen in the habit of carting things left on the sidewalk to our apartment to see if I could find a use for them.

I'd been musing about making a coat hook or something from it, but the hockey stick could serve as a weapon, come to think of it. "Wait," I said to Franck. I ran into the kitchen and grabbed it, then thrust it into his hand.

He looked down at it. "A hockey stick? What am I going to do with this?"

"I clearly need to take you to a hockey game," I said. "They can be used for self-defense, trust me."

The man was still yelling down below, and I could make out his slurring words, even though I couldn't make out exactly what they were. "I think he might be drunk," I said, unnecessarily.

"Yeah," Franck grimaced, then brandished his hockey stick. "But don't worry, I have my hockey stick now. All good."

I kept our door open and peeked around its edge as I watched Franck thump down the stairs in his boots and bathrobe. He opened the door to reveal a large man bundled up with a thick jacket and scarves, leaning heavily against the doorframe.

"Where are the women?" The man bellowed. "I need a woman!"

He was speaking English. Franck couldn't respond in kind, so instead he answered him in French. In Montréal that worked 99.9% of the time. "There are no women here," he said. "What are you talking about? Go away."

"There are women up there. I know it!" The guy staggered backwards.

"You're drunk," Franck said and then raised the hockey stick. "Take off, or I'll use this."

The man eyed the hockey stick with the grudging respect any self-respecting Canadian would give it. Luckily, he didn't realize it was being wielded by a non-hockey playing Frenchman. "Where are the women?" he muttered, backing away and giving a sad sort of sob. "I just need a woman."

Franck watched him stagger away, then turned and came back upstairs. I slammed the door behind him.

"That was bizarre," I said. "Any idea what that was all about?"

"None," Franck said, but then looked down at the hockey stick in his hand. "But maybe we should hang on to this."

chapter twenty-nine

The weather got even colder, and by the end of February there was one day where the temperature dropped to minus twenty-seven degrees, and that didn't even count the wind chill factor. I was desperate for ways to warm up.

Denis had still answered none of our phone calls or messages. Our hot water tank contained roughly two minutes of hot water, and took twenty-four hours to reheat again, so a long, hot shower was out of the question. So was a bath, even if the tub drained, which it didn't.

I was cold all the time. It felt like ice was constantly gnawing on my bones. Only hot drinks, hot food, my classes in the heated amphitheaters and moments in bed with Franck provided any relief. One day I got home from my classes, chilled to the bone. I did twenty jumping jacks but even that didn't warm me up. Maybe I could cook a nice comforting dish for dinner? Franck had been doing basically all the cooking, because besides tuna melts and boiled eggs, I'd never really learned my way around the kitchen. It was high time, I decided, to teach myself.

We still didn't have any money for any complicated or luxury ingredients (not to mention the fact that I didn't have the skill to know what to do with them even if we had). However, I remembered growing up eating split pea soup in the wintertime. My mother would always make several batches and its thick, warm heartiness felt like the perfect thing for a Montréal winter night.

Soup was warm and nourishing and bags of split green beans were dirt cheap. I would surprise Franck, I decided, and went upstairs to borrow a pot from Sam.

She had started seeing a new guy just before Christmas and had been preoccupied with him. I didn't feel I could pop in on her like I used to, but surely needing to borrow a pot wasn't too intrusive. I ended up catching her at a good time. She was drinking tea and studying for an exam the next day. Their apartment looked so cozy and furnished compared to ours. It was nice and toasty, which made sense. If there was no insulation between their floor and our ceiling, as I suspected, we were basically paying to heat their apartment.

"Have you seen or heard from Denis recently?" I asked her as I leaned on the kitchen counter and she kneeled to find her soup pot in the cupboard.

She shrugged. "No, but then again we've been paying our rent on time and we haven't needed to contact him about anything."

"I've been trying to phone him," I said. "I've left so many messages, but he still hasn't gotten back to me."

"Hmmmm," Sam said. "That's weird. What's wrong with your apartment?"

"Hardly any hot water. A bathtub that doesn't drain. Almost no heat. Do you have any of those problems?"

Sam shook her head. "No. Not really. What do you need the pot for?" she asked suspiciously, standing up and holding it against her chest.

Ah. I forgot. She'd been there during my third kitchen-fire incident when we were in high school.

"I'm trying to be more domestic," I said.

"Oh no. Do you have a fire extinguisher?"

I gave her shoulder a little punch. "Oh ye of little faith. I'm starting simple—pea soup. How hard can it be?"

"Can you not burn the crap out of my pot?" she asked with a grin.

"Shut up," I said, taking it from her arms.

"Good luck," she called out, laughing, as I headed back down the stairs to our place.

"I won't need it!" I called over my shoulder.

"Maybe so." She managed to get in the last word. "But if I

smell smoke, I'm calling the fire department."

I would be fine. I was an intelligent woman and it was only pea soup, for heaven's sake.

In the cupboard I knew we had a bag of split peas. I'm not sure why I'd bought them at the time, except that as pea soup was one of Québec's local specialties bags of peas were everywhere. At the time I thought I might eventually do something with them and here I was, being all domestic.

I checked through our cupboard. *Excellent.* There was a box of bouillon cubes left over from a dish Franck had made. I knew enough about eating to be vaguely aware that it was probably tastier to cook the peas with a ham hock, like my mom always did at home, and to make homemade stock, but as I had neither of those things I would just have to make do.

I did have onions though—a whole bag of them. They were super cheap and both Franck and I adored onions. Besides, who didn't love the homey smell of cooking onions when they walked in the door? Franck wouldn't believe his nostrils when he got home from work.

I hummed as I cooked, wishing for my stereo system I'd left back home in Victoria. I'd always loved music and I missed having it play in the background.

Franck was going to be so impressed. Not only was I making dinner, but it was good, typical Québécois comfort food. I knew the French weren't used to eating peas. In fact, I had never come across them even once in my year in Burgundy, but who didn't like peas?

Once I was done frying up the onions into a beautiful caramelized tangle, I checked the recipe on the back of the bag of peas. What a handy thing it was on there. It said to measure in one and a half cups of dried peas. We didn't own any cup measurements. Heck, we barely owned enough cutlery for the two of us to eat. The bag of peas didn't look that big ... Surely it was around two cups and a bit? Anyway, what was I going to do with a few leftover dried peas?

I tore open the bag and dumped the whole thing in with the onions and beef bouillon broth. I stirred the peas into the liquid.

There didn't seem to be enough liquid, so I grabbed my water glass from the kitchen cupboard, filled it, and added a few more glasses of water to the pot. There. Perfect. I brought it to a boil and then lowered the temperature and let it simmer. Only two out of our four stove elements were actually working, but I only needed one. That was something else Denis needed to fix.

I sat down and pulled out some history homework that I'd been putting off.

Franck came in about an hour later, by which time I'd become completely absorbed in my history textbook and its description of the Nazi propaganda machine.

He came into the kitchen, unwrapping the scarf from around his neck, and sniffed the air. "What's burning?"

I leapt up. "Shit! My soup." I'd been so absorbed in my textbook, I'd completely forgotten to stir it.

"You made soup?" Franck took off his mitts and followed me to the stove.

I opened up the lid of the pot. *Was it supposed to look like that?* "Ugh. I didn't stir it, so it looks a little thick," I said. "I just need to add some water."

I grabbed our only wooden spoon off the counter and tried to stir the soup. I strained all my arm muscles, but it would not budge. *Merde.* It was a solid entity now.

Franck was peering over my shoulder. "Should I even dare ask?"

"No."

"What is it supposed to be?"

"Split pea soup and shut up."

"*Vraiment?*" Franck sounded intrigued. "I wouldn't have known. Just how many peas did you put in it?"

"The whole bag," I admitted. "I wanted to surprise you."

"I'm definitely surprised," Franck said, still looking at the congealed green substance in the pot.

"I meant a *good* surprise. I wanted to start cooking," I groaned. "Should we try to eat it anyway?"

Franck took the spoon from my hand and poked the solid mass warily, as if it might spring alive any moment. "With a fork and knife?"

I was about to get mad at him for teasing me, but then I looked back into the pot. Franck's question was valid.

"I don't know," I said. I was disappointed with myself. I was living like an adult now with my boyfriend, but I had no idea how to do the things that most adults did. Cook. Clean. Get the landlord to fix stuff. Balance my check book.

Franck reached over and turned off the stove. I should have thought of that, as the acrid smell was getting stronger.

"I think we may have to dispose of this." Franck tried to break it to me gently.

"No!" I said, "I'm sure if we just …"

"Just what?"

I was sure there was a way we could consume it if even if it didn't look like the most appetizing thing in the world. Maybe we could carve it into slices like a huge pea loaf.

Franck took my hand gently in his. "Look at it, Laura," he said. "How do you think that would feel in our stomachs?"

I hated to admit it, but he was right.

"I was just trying to be more domestic," I whispered.

Franck patted my hand. "Don't worry. Remember how Mémé always says she didn't know how to cook when she was married and first left home? She made tons of mistakes as she learned. We all do."

That was one saving grace. At least Mémé wasn't here to see this debacle.

"Look at it this way," Franck continued. "You learned something, not to put the entire bag of peas in the soup. You can only go up from here."

"What are we going to do with it?" I asked in a hushed tone, as though we were talking about a corpse. "There's not enough room in the garbage can."

Sam's pot was big and was now filled to the brim with rock hard pea soup. On second thought, I wasn't sure if it warranted the moniker of "soup" any longer.

Franck lifted it off the stove. "Surprisingly heavy," he grunted. And this was from the man who had carried my trunk on his shoulder in a blizzard all the way from the university residence.

He walked it to the patio door that swung out to the rusted metal staircase that ran up the back of the building and looked out over that empty patch of snow—which had been grass in the fall.

The snow was thick out there. I gasped at the cold, but somehow I wanted to see what was going to happen to my split pea soup. It was like a burial.

Franck held the pot over the railing upside down and gave it a shake. The contents didn't budge.

"Can you pass me the wooden spoon?" he asked. It was still in my hand, so I passed it over. Franck took it and gave the bottom of the pot several good thwacks, like banging on a drum. Still nothing.

"I'm impressed," he said. "Maybe you have invented something. Congealed pea soup could become some kind of industrial glue."

I didn't dignify that with a response.

Finally, Franck righted the pot again and pounded the bottom on the metal landing. The stairs shook.

He picked up the pot again and hurled it forward, while still holding onto the handles. We both watched as the solid green mass of peas went airborne and landed top down in the snow several feet from the bottom of the staircase. Almost immediately, it half sunk down, leaving only its top layer of black peas visible in a sea of white.

Franck and I peered into the now-empty pot. It was clean. Not a single pea, burnt or otherwise, had been left behind.

We peered down at my attempt at dinner in the snow.

"It's probably going to freeze," Franck said.

"Maybe the animals will eat it. They must be short of food with all the cold and snow, so maybe they'll be happy to find it." I was relieved to think of at least one silver lining to this whole thing, but when I glanced up I saw that Franck was looking down at me with a twitching mouth.

"You don't think the animals will eat it?" I demanded.

"Do you?" he said. "I mean, look at it."

"It could happen!" I said, indignant.

"We'll see."

I sighed deeply. "Now what are we going to have for dinner?"

"Mazurka's?" Franck said.

"Can we afford it?"

"Definitely not."

"Let's go," I said, heading back into the kitchen and grabbing my jacket. "But no talking about my pea soup attempt, agreed?"

"I'm sorry, Laura." Franck shook his head. "You know I don't make promises I can't keep."

chapter **thirty**

That weekend, Franck and I were invited to go to his friend Pascal's for dinner. He lived with his girlfriend Dominique, and I'd be meeting them both for the first time.

Pascal was the only bright spot for Franck at work, and Franck continued to regale me with stories about his antics. Apparently, he would openly mock the smarmy sales boss and chat with the "customers" he called about all kinds of random things.

"How has he not been fired?" I asked as we got on the metro to Old Montréal, where their apartment was.

Franck shook his head. "I can't figure it out. Hey, I saw an interesting job posting today at the employment place. I dropped by after my shift yesterday."

"What was it?"

"It's not glorious or anything, but it's for a polling company called Léger and Léger, polling people around various places in Montréal."

"What kind of things would you be polling?"

Franck shrugged. "The woman at the employment place said there would be a lot of stuff about politics, people's opinions about separatism, politicians, that sort of thing."

"So you wouldn't be selling anything?"

"Nope. As you know, that would be a huge relief."

We found the apartment building. It looked just as derelict as ours. We had that in common with Pascal and Dominique at least. Also, the whole immigrating to Canada thing. I would be the only

Canadian between the four of us, so I was interested if their impressions of my country lined up with Franck's.

Pascal opened the door. He looked pretty much as I expected him to, tall, gangly, and with an expression of wry good humor on his face. He gave me the *bises* and took off my jacket gallantly. I took a moment to be grateful for French men and their good manners. Pascal was older than me, and probably older than Franck. I would guess around twenty-six.

His accent was different. He talked more slowly than Franck and with a far different cadence than either the Burgundians or the Parisians. He was from a town called Colmar in Alsace that Franck told me was incredibly picturesque.

Dominique walked in and I needed a moment to process my shock. She was even older than Pascal—at least thirty and perhaps even a few years older than that.

She was dressed in a red pencil skirt, a silk blouse, pantyhose and high heels. I was nineteen and a student who lived, like most of my fellow students, in jeans, sweaters, and Doc Marten boots. It felt like I was being invited to dinner with someone closer in age to my parents than with me.

Luckily, I managed to hide my surprise well.

As the evening wore on and the excellent bottles of Riesling and sausages and cheese that Pascal's family had managed to smuggle over to him in a series of survival packages were mostly consumed, it came out that Dominique and Pascal had met and proceeded to have a torrid extramarital affair (for her, not for him) when they worked for the same insurance company in Colmar.

Dominique ended up leaving her husband for Pascal, and the scandal was so huge that they decided to move to Canada—at least for a year or two until the gossip died down, maybe longer.

But the most unsettling part of their backstory was the fact that Dominique had a son from her marriage. Her ex-husband wouldn't let Dominique see him after the affair was discovered. They boy was seven years old and living with his father back in Strasbourg.

A custody fight. Affairs. Divorce ... this was true adult stuff that was, thank God, far removed from my student life. Pascal was hilarious and I could see he truly cared about Dominique. They were very nice and hospitable. It just all felt … *off…* like by being with Franck my life had been fast-forwarded to adulthood without me noticing.

The next day on campus didn't help. As I was in line to buy a coffee to keep me awake during my history lecture in one of Leacock Building amphitheaters, I looked up and saw Anne and James ahead of me. Should I make a run for it and pretend like I hadn't seen them? *No. That would be a coward's way out.* Besides. They hadn't done anything wrong.

Like me, they were both wearing jeans and Doc Martens and it hit me that, despite our estrangement, I felt more on the same wavelength with them than the people Franck was making friends with so far out in the working world. I had never given the five-year age gap between Franck and me much thought before, but now that he was out in the real world and I was still living a student existence, it was becoming noticeable.

"Anne. James," I said after they bought their coffees. "How are you guys doing?"

They looked at each other with expressions of animosity on both of their faces.

"We're great," Anne said. "We were wondering if you died."

"No." I laughed, even though I knew that was a jab, not a joke. "Just moved out of residence, which I guess amounts to the same thing."

"How's the amazing Franck?" James asked with a barely contained eye roll.

"He's good." I nodded. "He got a job. It's not great, but it's something."

"And your apartment?" Anne asked.

"Great too," I lied. "All good." We still hadn't heard from Denis and we'd started hearing scratching in the walls we suspected could be a rodent infestation.

"OK well …" Anne said, checking her watch. "We have to get to class, right James?"

He was watching me, but he slid his eyes back to her and

seemed to jerk awake. "Oh. Right. Right. Yes we do."

"OK, it was nice seeing you guys," I called out as they walked off.

They didn't say anything back, or even turn around.

I walked to the history lecture hall, paying little attention to my surroundings, and slid into a seat near the top where I wouldn't have to talk to anybody.

I was full of bullshit. Our apartment sucked. It was freezing and empty. It hurt that my former friends were dismissive of me, though isn't that what I had done to them? I only had myself to blame. I'd abandoned them.

Even if I wanted to, I didn't fit in their student world anymore. I was with Franck, and we lived together in an apartment. We hung out with older people like Pascal and Dominique. People who had jobs and ex-spouses, and sometimes even children.

Where did I fit in? *Is this what being with Franck means*, that I fit with him, but not with the rest of my life anymore?

Franck and I as a couple were between two worlds—the student world and the adult world. I sipped on my coffee. How were we supposed to span that?

Maybe I couldn't have it all—Franck and a life as a student. I hadn't been expecting this sense of dislocation, this grief at having skipped out on something important.

I walked home from my classes feeling bereft but knowing this was one of the rare things that I couldn't talk to Franck about.

Luckily, when he swung in the door, later than usual, he was in such a good mood that he didn't notice I was acting strange.

"I got the new job!" he declared.

"Really? What is it?" I said, pleased despite my melancholy. I knew how miserable he'd been while telemarketing. It constantly preyed on him that he was tricking people.

"At Léger & Léger. That polling company."

"How?"

"I went back to the employment office today and a representative of the company happened to be there updating the ad they had posted. We talked in person and he offered me a job on the spot."

"That's amazing," I said. "Good for you. So, no sales?"

Franck grinned. "No sales." He picked me up and spun me around. "It's excellent timing too because Pascal got fired today and I suspect I was next on the chopping block."

I wondered if Pascal was upset or overjoyed at this inevitability. "What happened?"

"They taped him pretending he was François Mitterand to one of the people on his call list."

I chuckled. I would have paid good money to listen in on that. Pascal was seriously missing his calling by not being a mimic or a stand-up comedian. Despite the age and life gap, I did really enjoy him. "Did the other person on the phone fall for it?"

"Completely."

"Did the person know that François Mitterand is the president of France or did he think it was just a random name?"

"Oh, they knew he was the French president."

"Then how—?"

Pascal told them that the ski weekend at Mount Tremblant was a special gift from the French government in a new campaign to improve solidarity between France and Québec."

"Wow." I whistled. "That takes some nerve."

"Pascal has plenty of that," Franck said. "Although he no longer has a job."

"What's he going to do?"

"I'll call him and tell him about the Léger & Léger job. Maybe he can find something there?"

I nodded. "So when do you start?"

"I'll quit tomorrow at the condo place. They didn't hire us with any kind of contract so we can basically leave whenever we want. I'll start Léger and Léger the day after."

"I'm really, really happy for you."

"And I'll be getting a regular paycheck that isn't as dependent on commissions," he added.

"Does it pay well?"

He shrugged. "It's not good, but it's slightly better than the condo selling, and at least it's all above board. Should we go skating to celebrate?"

I thought about Anne and James and Pascal and Dominique. Maybe we didn't have many friends because we'd been so wrapped up in each other and, well, mere survival that we hadn't really made the effort. Perhaps it was time to remedy that.

"Why don't I go upstairs and ask Sam and Alison if they want to join?"

"That's a great idea." Franck smiled at me.

I ran upstairs and they were both thrilled with the idea. They'd been studying hard and both needed some fresh air and a break. Alison's boyfriend—a lovely exchange student from Vietnam—also wanted to come.

After Christmas, outdoor skating rinks had popped up all over the city. Because it was just assumed that everyone in the city owned at least one (if not several) pairs of skates, there was no spot to rent them.

Luckily, Franck and I had taken the metro to a big second-hand store the weekend before and bought ourselves each a pair of cheap, used skates. They weren't awesome, but then again neither of us were good enough skaters to care and, the kicker, they had only cost five dollars a pair. It wasn't like we needed anything we could pull off a triple axel with.

Alison happened to have a pair of her brother's old hockey skates she could lend to her boyfriend. He confided in me after we had bundled up, threw our ice skates over our shoulders, and headed out onto Prince Arthur, that he'd never done it before.

"I barely have," I reassured him. "It's a myth that all Canadians were born knowing how to skate. Coming from the West Coast, it wasn't something most of us did very often growing up. Not like people here."

Sam had done figure skating for a few years when she was in elementary school—I remember being green with envy over her diamond-encrusted costumes with their flippy little skirts.

The closest rink was on the Carré Saint-Louis between Saint-Laurent and Saint-Denis streets. The city workers had marked out a large rectangle in the middle of the square and flooded it. We laced up our skates and made our way out onto the rink. Franck and I held hands as we progressed in unsteady circles under the different colored lights strung from the tree branches overhead.

Hau, Alison's boyfriend, was clinging to the rink wall as he tested the feel of his blades on the slippery ice. "You didn't tell me this was so hard, Laura!" he laughed.

Alison glided onto the rink just then, started skating backwards and proceeded to execute a flawless jump. I had no idea if it was a double axel or what, but it looked to me like she was competing in the Olympics. She skated up to where Hau, Franck, and I were clutching to the rink wall. "See? It's not hard!" she said, her hands on her hips.

Hau just stared at her. "You're really good," he said. "Why didn't you tell me?"

She shrugged. "I guess I don't think about it much. The competitive skating part of my life is over."

"You're really, *really* good," I said. "Just how competitive were you?"

She shrugged. "I tried out for the Olympic squad."

Sam had skated over, elegant as always, and we all stared at Alison with open mouths.

"No way," I said.

"Yeah," Alison admitted. "I didn't make it, so that was the end of that. It was the best thing that ever happened to me in retrospect. Training for the Olympics is no kind of life. I'm much happier now."

"Skate for us," Hau said to her, looking like he had just seen a miracle. "Please. It's so beautiful to watch."

So Alison did just that. We practically had the rink to ourselves, and the few people sharing it with us stopped and watched as she executed a flawless routine.

Everyone clapped when she was finished.

"Wow," I murmured. "I didn't realize I was in the presence of greatness."

Once Alison was finished, she started to give Hau lessons and tried to convince him to let go of the wall. He didn't look as though he was convinced.

Sam, Franck and I skated around, chatting about my pea soup debacle and school and Europe and the Québécois accent. A contented warmth grew inside me. It was nice to be hanging out with friends that also straddle the world between being a student and being a certified grown-up.

It was time, I realized, for Franck and me to take our relationship out into the world and develop a social life beyond the small unit the two of us formed together. Life was not always easy, and I was finding the same went for serious relationships. They involved choices. I couldn't have it both ways. I couldn't live a traditional student existence and be with Franck, yet I had chosen Franck and would do it again in an instant if faced with the choice.

I liked hanging out with Pascal and Dominique and feeling like we had been instantly transported to France. It's just that I didn't want them to become our only social life. We would have to work on it and this was a solid start. Spinning circles under the lights with Franck, I knew that it was time to expose this—the connection we felt now with our hands interlinked, or when we were separated with a continent and an ocean—to the world.

chapter thirty-one

The new job helped. The hours were regular and while taking polls was not Franck's dream job, and definitely not the optimal use of his Communications degree from the Sorbonne, the people he worked with tended to be young and many of them were also students.

His more regular schedule meant he could also enroll in a Communications course in McGill's Continuing Education program two nights a week, where they studied the theories of Marshall McLuhan, one of Franck's favorite philosophers in media theory. Yes, my boyfriend had favorite philosophers.

Things had settled into a slightly more predictable routine and I felt as though my entire body was taking a deep breath. We started going out with Sam and Alison and their boyfriends and extended groups of friends to the occasional restaurant, party, or club. There was a great place on Saint-Laurent that showed art films in black and white while the crowd sucked back the bonkers cocktails created by the bartenders who were all dressed in silver behind the bar.

One night I returned to Foufounes Electriques—the crazy club with the drag queens that I had gone to with Anne and James on my first night in Montréal. I still had regrets about letting those friendships fizzle out, but I was beginning to accept that I would have to let it go. They wanted me to be the Laura I had been when they first met me—unfettered with a boyfriend—and that was never who I'd been even when Franck was in France. Sometimes moving forward meant letting some people go.

Life in Montréal was finally getting easier. Franck fell in love with the "anything goes" atmosphere of the Foufounes and we spent many nights dancing away there with our group of friends. Conveniently, Schwartz's, that Montréal icon, was right on the way home. I wasn't sure if it closed late or if it never closed. In any case, it was a rare night that we wouldn't slide in after the club and feast on rye sandwiches piled high with their house smoked meat, dipped in copious amounts of yellow mustard and accompanied with a massive kosher dill pickle.

We started to deepen our knowledge of the city beyond the university and the student ghetto. Franck's poll-taking work took him far and wide over the bus and metro network and, better yet, Léger & Léger paid for his transit pass.

One day he came home from his night course and told me, enthralled, they had debated Marshall McLuhan's "medium is the message" theory. I could tell he was delighted to be using his intellect again. "By the way," he added as we were drying the dishes. "We got an invitation to go ice fishing this weekend."

"Ice fishing?" I grew up salmon fishing in the Pacific, so I was not intimidated at all by the fishing part. However, it was minus fifteen outside. I was definitely hesitant about the sitting on the ice part.

"That sounds intriguing," I said. "But won't we freeze? Also, we don't have rods or anything." I looked appraisingly at our hockey stick that stood in its place of honor in the corner of the kitchen. It did its job when Franck had to stomp down the stairs at least every second night to deal with men banging on the door and insisting to be let in, but I still didn't think I could rig it into a decent fishing rod.

Franck leaned against the counter. "Apparently the outing includes everything—the rods and the bait and all that, plus we sit in a little hut that's warmed by a wood stove, so we won't freeze to death. It just costs twenty dollars for the both of us."

Franck and I were hardly rolling in cash. We still hadn't been able to improve on our furniture of milk crates and found in fact that milk crates functioned perfectly well. The monthly deposit from my parents had started arriving again after Christmas and I was certain we had Franck's charm offensive to thank for that. We could afford to go ice fishing if we cut back on some other things. I felt grateful for our situation compared to what it was before Christmas.

"Oh, and we need to bring a six-pack of beer," Franck added. "That's part of the payment."

"Not wine?" Both of us preferred wine to beer any day.

He shook his head. "Apparently beer is *de rigueur* for ice fishing."

"Huh. It's true what they say about learning something every day."

Franck dropped his dishtowel and swept me up in his arms, kissing me all over my face. "And you call yourself a Canadian," he said. "Honestly."

I hit him rather ineffectually with my dishtowel and let myself be ravished with his kisses.

Later I asked. "How are we supposed to get there?"

"He has a car so he can pick us up."

"Who is this guy?" It occurred to me that I didn't even know who had invited us. "He's not, like, a mass murderer or something?"

Franck pursed his lips. "I wouldn't think so."

"That's reassuring."

"Why do you ask?"

"He'll be driving us to an isolated hut somewhere ..." Maybe I had too much imagination, but then again Franck had been known to be a tad too trusting in the past.

He considered this. "No. Not a serial killer I don't think. Besides, the way he talked it sounded like there were a few of us going, not just him and us."

That made me feel better. It would be so much *effort* to murder a bunch of people. "OK. Let's do it. What's this guy's name anyway?"

"Arthur," Franck said. "He's from Montréal but his mother is English Canadian and his dad is Québécois."

"I'd like to be a fly on the wall at their family dinners when they get on the topic of Separatism," I said.

"Not all Québécois are separatists," Franck reminded me.

"No," I said, thinking privately that most of them that I had met were.

On the Sunday morning when Arthur came to pick us up in a rusty old SUV I found Franck had been right, he didn't seem very axe murderer-ish. We commiserated about the language politics that constantly divided Québec and he explained how tricky it was growing up having to straddle both sides of that feud.

With his warm smile, burly build, and beard coming in he looked like someone physically well-adapted to sitting on the ice for hours on end.

I had bundled up in nearly every item of clothing I owned and was given a strange glance by the next person we picked up, Marie. I could smell beer on her breath, and she held an opened can in her mittened right hand. "Salut!" she said to us in French, then nodded down at her can of Molson. "You don't want to start late when ice fishing."

"You mean the fishing?" I clarified in French.

"The fishing!?" she guffawed as she put her seatbelt on. "No. I mean the drinking, *bien sûr.*"

We then picked up a guy named Edmund from Westmount who was definitely on the English side of the equation, and then another girl named Sophie.

They had all brought a six-pack and a several of them had also brought bags of chips and pretzels like we had. Franck, being the proverbial Frenchman, insisted on bringing a saucisson sec from La Vieille Europe and a sharp knife to cut it, as well as a rectangle of comté to cut into cubes.

I had also thought at the time that the knife would be handy as a weapon if we needed it but judging from the good-natured camaraderie in the car, I was sure we wouldn't, except maybe for gutting fish. I was looking forward to showing off my skills as a master fish gutter to Franck. My dad had taught me how to do it when I was around seven and I could gut a Pacific salmon faster than any of my friends.

We pulled into a parking spot near an area of town called Atwater, still in the city, but not our usual stomping grounds.

"What are we doing?" Franck asked, as everyone began to unbuckle their seatbelts.

"We're stopping for a pre-fishing breakfast, *bien sûr!*" Marie declared. I looked up at the restaurant we had parked in front of. It said "Restaurant Greenspot" on a white sign with black square lettering and a Coca-Cola logo beside it. The squared off roof above it was green.

Inside, the scent of baked beans and maple syrup welcomed me as soon as we walked through the door. I sighed in satisfaction. It was a diner like Bens, but this time a grungy, worn-in, well-loved diner.

A waitress who looked as though she had worked the tables there for several decades snapped up plasticized menus for us all and showed us to a big table on the far side of the restaurant.

"I've never been to this place," I said, perusing the items on offer. The restaurant seemed to be Québec food at its finest, specializing in comfort dishes such as pancakes in every form, poutine, baked beans, and yellow split pea soup. Hopefully it was a thinner version than I had concocted, and which still remained, as far as we knew, buried by snow in the patch of grass below our kitchen.

All the faces except Franck's looked up at me in shock. "You've never been to The Greenspot?" Marie asked, sounding horrified. "How is that even possible?"

I shrugged. "I only got here in September, and it's not close to campus."

"But it's an icon," Edmund insisted. "It's the only place to go for hangover breakfasts or pre-fishing breakfasts or Sunday night breakfast-for-dinner when you're dreading to start the week. Where do you go?"

"After the clubs we go to Schwartz's," Franck said.

There was grudging approval from everyone. "That's good too, but The Greenspot is also a must," Arthur said.

I looked around again, the atmosphere warming my heart. "Thanks for bringing us here."

Marie shrugged and then said in French, "You can't go ice fishing without breakfast at The Greenspot. You just can't."

I ordered a stack of pancakes with bacon and a cup of baked beans on the side. I drenched all of it with the huge jug of maple syrup that sat on every table. It was the best maple syrup I'd ever tasted. None of this Aunt Jemima crap that sometimes found its way into our fridge when I was growing up. This was the real amber stuff that came from the maple syrup farms up North. It somehow made everything taste better.

Our conversation was a mix of French and English, most of the sentences were half and half. Despite what the French language activists said, I was discovering the true language of Montréal was this dynamic, fascinating form of functional bilingualism. It made me want to start studying linguistics and write a thesis on it. I didn't know any other place in the world where two languages segued so fluidly in daily conversation.

When we finally rolled out of the Greenspot, bellies full of pancakes and endless mugs of diner coffee, I made a vow to myself to return as soon as possible. This place deserved its icon status, and even though it was a pain to get to I wanted to come back sooner rather than later.

In the SUV I watched out my window as the houses and buildings of the city thinned out, giving way to flat white fields. I'd seen a bit of the countryside on the way to walk around the flagpoles at the border with Franck, but that had been going south. Here it felt like we were headed north, up towards the wilderness.

After at least an hour driving, we came upon a cluster of cars parked in a line in front of a massive stretch of white ice dotted with little wooden huts, some with smoke belching out their metal chimneys.

"We're here!" declared Arthur. "My dad used to bring me here when I was a boy."

In Victoria, frozen lakes were not something that happened in the winter. Sometimes a fringe of ice would gather around the edges, but it was never thick enough to walk on, much to our chagrin.

Here, the lake we parked in front of looked as solid as the road we'd been driving on. It had to be the case, as it was dotted with at least twenty little huts. I trusted the Québécois when it came to their knowledge of ice.

"What's the name of this lake?" I asked Arthur, as we hauled our beers and snacks across an expanse of white.

He shrugged. "No idea. We have a lot of lakes in Québec you know. You could spend a lifetime learning all their names."

Arthur led us to a hut on the far edge of the cluster of little huts. He dug for a key in his pocket and opened the door. "*Bienvenue!*" he said.

I stood there, unsure of what to do. This was completely unlike any form of fishing I had ever known.

Marie glanced down at the six-pack I held between my mitts. "Don't bring that in here," she said. "Leave it outside."

Right. I kept forgetting that in Québec during the winter, the outdoors was one massive freezer. Anything that needed to be kept cold was left out there.

I threw my six-pack down amongst the others that had been tossed haphazardly in the snow drift to the left of the door into the cabin.

"Don't take your jackets off yet," Arthur said. "I have to get the wood stove going first to warm this place up."

"I'll help," Franck said in French.

While Franck and Arthur were busy with that, I surveyed the rest of the cramped space of the hut.

A long wooden bench was placed in front of a slit that had been cut into the ice that went the entire length of the hut. I peered down into it. The ice looked like it ran about a foot and a half deep before I could make out the reflection of lake water. Set up in little holes bored into the ice in front of the open trough were rods with their lines already dangling in the water. The ice part of this was accurate, but I didn't think this activity could really qualify as *fishing*.

"What do you think?" Edmund asked me as he passed me a beer.

"I guess there's no jigging involved?" I said.

"Jigging?" He looked at me blankly.

"Just joking," I said. Of course he wouldn't know that ocean fishing technique. I lifted up my beer in a salute. "Thanks."

Arthur and Franck managed to get a roaring fire started in the woodstove, and the hut began to warm up. There was a bench built into the wall behind us, and we all began discarding mitts and toques and scarves on it.

Arthur waved to the narrower fishing bench. "Have a seat. He opened his bag and took out a Tupperware box of bait that smelled like herring. "Choose a rod, then bait it with one of these."

"What type of fish do we catch here?" I asked.

"Walleye, northern pike, and yellow perch mainly."

I wasn't familiar with any of those. "Are they good to eat?"

"Some of them can be kinda boney, but definitely edible."

I baited my hook, and then baited the hooks of Marie and Edmund, who couldn't figure it out and, I suspected, were grossed out about handling the stinky herring.

After a few minutes of watching my line, still as could be, I shed my coat. It was heating up fast and I deeply regretted wearing long johns on both my top and bottom.

I began to give my line a regular twitch with my finger to make the bait move, and after a while I got a bite. I yelped with excitement. Even if this type of fishing was both odd and tame, a bite was a bite. I hauled up a fish—a tiny fish.

I groaned in disappointment. "Too small to keep."

"No. No!" Arthur said, jumping up and coming up behind me to inspect it. "That's a large one, actually."

Large? I was used to catching ten to twenty-pound salmon.

"Do you need my help to unhook it?" he asked.

I almost laughed. Help? I'd been doing this since I was a child with twenty-pound salmons. "Thanks, but I'm good," I said. I held the fish with a firm grip and twisted the hook out of the cartilage of its mouth.

"Wow. You're good at that," Edmund observed.

"Not my first time at the rodeo."

Franck, when I looked up, was grinning at me.

"Hidden talents," I said and winked at him. "Where did you put that knife you brought for the saucisson? I need it to gut the fish."

"You don't need to gut it," Arthur said. "Just throw it outside."

"What?"

"Just throw it outside in the snow to the right of the door. You'll see."

Franck got up at the same time I did and opened the door for me. The cold outside was bitter, but now it actually felt like a soothing balm after the sauna-like conditions of the hut.

"This is hilarious," I whispered to Franck. "I've never chucked a fish in the snow before, but I guess ... why not? It's as good as any other freezer. I don't understand why we're not gutting them first, though."

Franck chuckled. "My fisherwoman."

"Fisherwomen are still called fishermen, you know."

"But that's not accurate," he said.

"It is," I argued.

But we both shut up to watch as I threw the fish over in the snow. It flash-froze in an instant in a comma-like curve.

I whistled. "I've never seen that before," I said. We shared a complicit smile. We had somehow made it through all those initial struggles to actually start having fun and enjoying real Québécois experiences like this one.

"C'mon." Franck pulled me back inside. "Now I really want to catch one so I can do that."

chapter thirty-two

Weeks went by and the living conditions at our apartment got worse. The heat seemed to be working even less effectively than it had and the scratching in the walls was getting louder. If it was rodents, as we feared, they were breeding.

Our worst suspicions were confirmed one morning, as, on entering the kitchen to make our morning coffee, I was welcomed by a trio of mice all standing on their hind legs having a nice chat in the middle of the kitchen floor.

I didn't scream or shout. They were only mice, but I did let loose an impressive string of curse words in both English and French. This apartment had officially sunk into the "dive" category.

Franck joined me. The mice were still there, not perturbed by my swearing.

From the "*merde*" that slipped out of his mouth I knew he had caught sight of our new roommates too. I grabbed the hockey stick in the kitchen corner and tapped it on the floor beside the mice and began to motion like I was going to treat them like a bunch of hockey pucks. They squeaked and ran under the oven. The thrill of my triumph was temporary.

"Enough is enough," Franck said. "These new roommates are the last straw. We have to do something, Laura."

"Agreed." It was well overdue. I had just been putting it off because things finally felt like they were on a more even keel and I didn't want to rock the boat again. Still, I was sick of putting up with the freezing cold, the lack of hot water, the bathtub that didn't drain, and the hollering men at the building door waking us up almost every night. "We've given Denis every chance to get back to us," I said. "I'll go to that drop-in legal clinic after my classes today."

"I think that's a good idea," Franck said, leaning down and pressing a soft kiss against my neck.

After a while, I said, "Remember how Sam told us the previous renters had taken off without paying rent? At the time it sounded like the most outrageous thing for a renter to do, but now I get it."

"I get it too," he said. "If you're still good to make the coffee, I'm going to go and enjoy my cold shower."

I left the McGill legal clinic extremely satisfied. In my backpack I carried a letter I had drafted up with the trainee lawyer staffing the legal desk. We hit it off immediately. She was from the Okanagan in BC and had a nightmare landlord in her second year. Not Denis, but from what she said negligent landlords in the student ghetto were a dime a dozen. Maybe I would think about a career in law after my English degree. I mean, what else could I do with an English degree that could possibly earn a living?

The letter looked legal and impressive. It began with a large "Without Prejudice" typed in black bold lettering across the top, then laid out the multiple issues in the apartment that made it unhabitable. We included dates we wanted them fixed by, and legal notice that if they were not fixed by those dates we would be withholding rent.

I showed the letter to Franck when he got back from Léger & Léger that evening. He was duly impressed, and he agreed he would send it via registered mail the next day on his way to work.

"The lawyer warned that Denis might not be thrilled."

"I don't give a crap if he's thrilled," Franck said. "As long as we get functional heat and he gets rid of the mice and fixes the rest of it. Besides," He nodded over at the hockey stick in the corner of the kitchen. "We can defend ourselves."

"He's in the mafia," I reminded Franck. "Or at least that's what everyone says. I don't think our hockey stick would be a match for that."

Franck did look briefly cowed by this but rallied. "I can't imagine the mafia kills people just because they insist on having a bathtub that drains."

That night, just like almost every night, we were awoken in the wee hours by a guy pounding on our door and yelling downstairs. We had stopped answering this strange parade of men and were no further along in figuring out where they came from or why they came. We reasoned they would get tired, cold and fed up before we would. That generally proved to be the case.

Franck came home from work the next day and told me he had mailed the letter. All that was left for us was to wait.

The next night, a Wednesday, Franck had just returned home from work when our phone rang.

"I bet it's Denis," I said with satisfaction and picked up the receiver, ready to be forgiving as long as we set some concrete plans for getting some of this stuff repaired.

Instead, I heard a harsh voice in the phone receiver. "You fucking bitch." The words were venomous and slurred. "How dare you go to the lawyers about me? I'm coming to get you and make you fucking regret that."

He hung up and I stared at the receiver in my hand, left with a dial tone and the feeling that all the blood had drained out of my body.

"Who was it, Laura?" Franck demanded, grabbing me by the shoulders. "You look—"

"I think it was Denis." My voice came out strangled. "Actually, I'm sure it was Denis. He threatened me. He called me a fucking bitch and told me that he was coming to get me to make me regret sending him that letter."

Now it was Franck's turn to go pale. "*Putain de merde.*" He clapped a hand to his mouth and began to pace back and forth. "I should have picked up the phone—"

"We need to call the police," I said.

Franck nodded, his eyes huge.

I dialed and got a nice but harassed sounding officer on the phone. I explained the situation to him. "OK, OK," he said. "I'm just taking down notes here. This shouldn't be too much of a problem. The landlord probably got drunk and won't even remember tomorrow, but as a precaution, can you give me the address to your apartment?"

I gave him the address and he paused. "I'm just going to put you on hold for a second, OK?"

"OK."

He came back on the line five minutes or so later, during which time Franck and I flinched at every noise coming from the street below, certain it was Denis or his mafia cronies. We couldn't live like this.

"Is your landlord's name Denis Sadinsky?" the officer asked.

"Yes. That's him. That's who just called me."

"Does he have a key to your apartment?"

"Of course," I said. "He's the landlord."

"OK. Now, you need to listen to me. Are you listening?"

"Yes."

"How fast can you get out of there?" he asked.

"What do you mean? You just said–"

"Forget what I just said," the officer said, impatient. "Denis Sadinsky is a well-known criminal. He's extremely violent and dangerous. You need to get out of there. Now."

"You mean, like, move?" I couldn't believe what I was hearing.

"Yes."

"Tonight?"

"You should already be on the phone to a friend with a truck to help you."

"But where are we going to go?" But after I asked the question, I realized that besides spending the night in prison, the police couldn't help us with that.

"Check into a hotel."

"We don't have the money," I said, more to myself than him.

Move? Now? It was already dark outside and cold. I didn't know anyone with a truck, or anyone in the moving business and a crazed mafioso with his buddies could arrive any minute. Just when I thought things with Franck and me were finally settling into a manageable routine ...

"I'm just going to pass you to my boyfriend," I said. "I have to think."

Franck took the phone, even paler than a few minutes before. He began talking to the police officer in French. I paced back and forth in the bedroom, reeling. Did we really have to move now? Where would we move to? How would we move our stuff?

I remembered I still had this week's copy of the *McGill Daily*, the more subversive of our two student newspapers and the one with a ton of classified ads in the back. I pulled it out and sat on the bed with it, flipping to the back. I traced my finger down the classified sections. *Movers* ...

I found a few numbers. Basically, they sounded like fellow students who had trucks and were ready to do any kind of moving job. *Perfect.* I glanced outside. At almost seven o'clock on a snowy, freezing Wednesday night? I jumped when a car door slammed on the street below. I had to try.

I heard Franck hang up, then came into the bedroom. His eyes were huge. "We have to get out of here," he said. "Laura, I'm so sorry, I never would have encouraged you to do the letter at the legal clinic if I had any idea—"

I shook my head. "Neither of us did," I said. "Besides, we don't have time for that right now. We have to get out of here. I've found a few numbers of movers I can call in here, but first we have to find a place to move to."

Franck watched me. "You sound very ... calm."

"I'm in shock, I think," I clarified. "When I'm like this I get into a super-decisive mode. I can freak out once we're out of here." I stood up. "I'm going upstairs to warn Sam and Alison and to find out if they know anyone with rooms to rent. You can start packing."

I ran upstairs. Franck was already madly filling suitcases when I left.

Sam came to the door quickly.

"Laura!" she said.

I burst in didn't even bother with saying hi before explaining the situation to her and Alison. "You two have to move too. It's not safe for you here."

"Denis?" Sam said. "I can't believe it. He's always so sweet to us."

I waved that away. "The police say he's dangerous."

"Not to us I don't think," Sam said.

"Please," I urged. "Please think about moving. He knows you know me. I couldn't live with myself if—"

Sam grabbed my hand. "You've warned us, Laura and I appreciate that. Truly."

"I still think you should move. Consider it. Also, do you know anyone with a spare room for us?"

Alison thought she might know someone, so she picked up the phone and dialed. I overheard the conversation, and her awkward attempt at explaining the circumstances. Like Franck had done downstairs, I paced back and forth, chewing my thumbnail. I couldn't believe this was happening to us. I felt caught in the middle of some crappy TV drama as one of the hapless victims. Hau came in the room just then from Alison's bedroom and Sam gave him a quick summary of the crisis.

"Are you OK, Laura?" he asked me.

I shook my head. "No. Definitely not."

Alison wrote something down on a piece of paper and hung up the phone. "You're in luck," she said. "My friend Tracy has a spare room in the place she's renting. She's great. The apartment isn't close to here though. It's in Atwater."

"No problem," I said quickly. "I think some distance between us and Denis at this point is a great thing. Can we move in tonight, as soon as I can arrange movers?"

Alison nodded. "Tracy is quick on her feet. She could tell it was urgent so she said to come on over with your stuff as soon as you are able. They're waiting for you. Here's the address."

She handed me the piece of paper. I couldn't quite believe that I would be going to bed, if we were lucky, in an apartment full of strangers in a different part of town.

I hugged both Sam and Alison. "Thank you both *so* much. Alison, you're an absolute life saver. I'm going to miss you. Sam, if Denis asks, tell him you and I got in a fight and you have no idea when or why we left. Play dumb. Even if you don't move, but I wish you would, I don't want any fall-out landing on you."

Sam shook her head. "I feel terrible I got you that apartment."

"No time for that." I gave them both a final squeeze. "Bye, Hau. I hope we can go out again soon to debrief all of this. Keep up with your skating lessons with Alison."

He gave me a slight bow. "Good luck."

I dashed down the stairs. It looked as though in the seven minutes or so I'd been gone Franck had managed to pack up the entire apartment, even going as far as folding up the futon frame and rolling up the mattress and securing it together into a massive roll with duct tape.

I waved the piece of paper at him. "I've got a place for us to go. Now we just need to find some movers."

I grabbed the back pages of the *McGill Daily* and started phoning the numbers in the ads. The first two just went to answering machines, but the third was answered by a groggy sounding guy. In a rush, I explained that we needed to move. Now. I described what we had as far as possessions i.e. not much and said my boyfriend and I would help him get it down the stairs. I added that speed would earn a good tip.

"Wait," the guy said, sounding like he was finally waking up. "Did you do anything illegal?"

"No. Definitely not."

"OK. One hundred bucks cash."

That didn't take much convincing.

"Can you take us by an ATM *en route*?"

He thought about this for a second. "In that case one hundred and fifty bucks cash."

"Deal." We hammered out the rest of the details. We didn't have the money, but it was preferable to being sitting ducks for Denis and his mafia cronies. When I was in this action mindset, indecision wasn't a problem.

I hung up. "Got a mover. He'll be arriving in ten minutes on Prince Arthur."

I looked around the apartment. Besides our things grouped in the front hall, which didn't amount to much, it was as bare and empty as the first time we visited it. It hadn't exactly been an auspicious place for us in many ways but now we were leaving, I felt nostalgic. For better or for worse, this was the first place Franck and I truly lived together as a couple. Life in this apartment had been only a few levels above mere survival, but somehow we were still in love, still together, and we had endured side by side. As I walked through the rooms making sure we hadn't left anything, I bid it a silent good-bye.

I spied the hockey stick in the corner of the kitchen. "The hockey stick isn't coming with us?" I called to Franck, who was stacking up our things in correct carrying order in the front hall.

"Nah. I figured we don't need it anymore. Hopefully at our new place men won't come banging on the door in the middle of the night."

I saw a flash of headlights and ran to the bedroom window to look out at the street below. A small truck was pulling up against the snow piled up at the edge of the sidewalk. "That must be the mover," I said. "Let's do this."

Franck and I took as much we could carry down the stairs and after Franck and I had brief introductions with the two guys who indeed looked to me like university students, they headed back up again with Franck while I stayed in the truck. They seemed slightly jittery too. Maybe they still suspected we were some sort of criminals. Hopefully the sight of our futon and milk crates would alleviate that niggling concern.

Hau appeared outside carrying some of our stuff. "I'll help," he said. "I saw the truck pull up." Between the five of us, we were all moved into the truck within fifteen minutes. That done, we waved good-bye to Hau and I hopped inside the truck on Franck's lap. There were only three seats across.

The driver had just slid his key in the ignition when all of a sudden the street around us was filled with sirens and flashing blue and red lights. *What fresh hell was this?* Three ... No wait, four, squad cars screeched to a stop around us, blocking us in à la *Starsky & Hutch.*

"Fuck. *Merde. Câlisse.* Shit. *Putain.*" Franck and me and the guys swore in a garble of French and English. Were the police coming for us because we were breaking our lease? I broke out into a cold sweat under my winter parka.

"You are criminals!" the younger guys shouted, pointing at us.

"But we're not," Franck protested.

But wait. That made no sense. It was the police who had told us to leave in the first place.

"They've come for us," the other movers muttered. "We're the criminals."

I turned. "What!?" I really didn't need involvement with any other criminals that night.

"We're doing this moving business under the table," the younger looking mover confessed in a shameful rush. He slid down in his seat in a futile attempt to hide. "We don't declare the money we earn. I'll bet the tax department has found out."

I couldn't quite believe that the tax department would dispatch four squad cars for a minor tax infraction.

"We'll see if we can deal with this," I said, and Franck and I got out of the truck. We walked, acting far more bold than we felt, towards the officers.

"Good evening," I said to the closet officer. "Is there a problem?"

"Open the truck!" he barked.

Franck walked gingerly, with his hands up in the air to the back of the truck. He turned the latch on the roll door of the trunk and heaved it open to reveal our futon, kitchen table and chairs, the milk crates, suitcases, and my metal trunk.

"What are you doing?" the cop demanded, sounding so disappointed that I almost laughed.

"We're moving," I said. "What did you think we were doing?"

"I thought you guys were robbing the store." He indicated with his arm over to the mafia grocery store.

I shook my head. "All the food on the shelves there expired like ... three years ago. Why would anyone rob that?"

The police officer sighed; all his aggressiveness evaporated. "Yeah," he agreed. "It's just this part of town is problematic. He pointed a finger to our apartment window. "Do you know last year one of the local mafia guys operated a brothel in there? No end of the trouble we had with that."

Franck and I looked at each other and I could tell we got the flash of understanding at the exact same moment. Ah ha. The men. We'd been living in an old bordello. Now it all made sense. That's why most of the men yelled on and on about "the women."

"We're just moving to a new place," I said. "That's all." I reasoned it was better not to mention that we'd been *living* in that old brothel.

The officer stared at us for a moment, perhaps trying to intuit whether or not we should be trusted. We must have looked hapless enough for him to believe us, because he finally nodded and called his cop friends off.

The sirens went dark and the cop car that had swung in front of the truck crunched away on the icy street. Franck and I hopped back in the cab of the truck.

I wondered idly if we hadn't been blocked by policemen, whether the driver and his friend would have just taken off with all of our stuff in the back. I'd never know, so I decided I might as well give them the benefit of the doubt.

"It's fine," I said to the movers. "They thought we were robbing the grocery store across the street." The two guys looked at me incredulously and then we all burst out in much-needed guffaws.

"Thank God." The driver sighed as he lowered his head to the steering wheel in relief as the police cars drove away. "As you've probably guessed I do this moving thing on the side. I don't exactly have the right permits and stuff."

I shrugged. "Tonight, I really don't care."

"What do you do when you're not moving?" I asked.

"I'm a master's student at McGill."

"I go to McGill too," I said. "What are you studying?"

"Religious studies. Parallels between the Bible and the Quran."

Our black-market mover was also a scholar. This was getting better and better. "That sounds interesting."

"It is," he said. "But it doesn't exactly pay the bills if you know what I mean."

I nodded. I knew exactly what he meant.

"So where are we going?" he asked.

I passed him the address Alison had scribbled on the piece of paper. "OK." He nodded, passing it back to me. "There's an ATM on lower Saint-Laurent we can stop at."

"Perfect." I leaned back against Franck. He slid his arms around me in place of a seatbelt. "God, this has been a weird night," I said.

I felt him chuckle behind me. "If nothing else, it will make a fantastic story."

We pulled away from the corner of Prince Arthur and Saint-Laurent and our crappy apartment and our dangerous, mafia landlord. My brain hadn't quite had the time to catch up to the fact that we were moving away for good and wouldn't be coming back here the next day. It would take a while for it to catch up.

We stopped at the ATM and I took out the cash, and then we continued on. I watched the city lights slip by. I didn't know what to think yet about the events of the past two hours, except that I was grateful Franck was here, holding me firmly against him.

chapter thirty-three

After about twenty minutes we pulled up at the low apartment
building of Alison's friend Tracy's house.

"Welcome to your new home I guess," the driver said. "You
sure they're still up?" I checked my watch. It was midnight.
*Please, God let them still be awake to let us in and tell us where
we can sleep.* I still felt wired, but I knew that once the adrenaline
left my body I would crash.

"I hope so," I said. I climbed out of the cab of the truck while
Franck got out and went to the back with the guys. It was a long
way down to the road—trucks were not designed for people like
me who were only five feet, four inches.

I rang the doorbell and the door was answered by a tall woman with long brown hair and a warm smile. 'I'm Alison's friend
Tracy." She stuck out her hand. "Welcome to our humble abode."

"I can't thank you enough for rescuing us tonight." My adrenaline drained out of me. She seemed nice. "I'll give you the full
story when we get inside, but it turns out our landlord was one
very bad dude. I'm Laura, by the way."

"My pleasure." Tracy opened the door wide to let the movers
move the first load of stuff in. "I'm from the Maritimes and we
are all brought up to help each other out. Come here, I'll show
you your room."

Our room was officially the den, but the remaining roommates—there was another girl and another guy, Tracy told me—
preferred paying less rent than having the use of the den. It was an
enclosed room, but instead of a proper door it had swinging

saloon style doors. Unlockable, and prone to swinging open with the slightest push. This could put a cramp in our love life, but at least here we were safe from Denis. Better yet, I realized once I was inside, it was *warm*.

"Here you go." Tracy waved down on the floor where Franck set down our unfolded futon frame with a grunt. It was a bit of a squeeze, but it fit.

"Perfect," I said.

"I forgot to ask," Tracy said. "Are either of you allergic to cats?"

I shook my head. "No."

"Good, because between us I have one."

I liked the idea of having a pet. It suited this place which was already a thousand times homier than our old apartment. "How lovely."

"My cat is a complete asshole, actually," she said. "But I love him anyway, or maybe a little bit because of it. You'll see."

She pressed a key in my hand. "There's often one of us here, in which case the door will be unlocked, but otherwise this will get you in. Last one out locks up."

I nodded, fatigue creeping up on me quickly.

"If you didn't bring any food for breakfast you can help yourself to my stuff. It's all labeled. Also, the Greenspot is just around the corner."

"The Greenspot?" I reacted as though she said God lived just around the corner. "I'm obsessed with that place."

"Who isn't?" she said. "Now, I'm going to go to bed. I have a teaching practicum tomorrow. Welcome roomies. We'll chat more in the morning."

"Thank you again," I said and after Tracy disappeared into her room I went outside where the movers were talking to Franck. As it turned out, they were offering him a job in the evenings with them.

"You're a natural, man," the smaller mover was saying. "Really strong and fast. We could do with someone like you. Here's my number." He passed Franck a piece of paper. "Call me if you ever want a job."

Franck took it and nodded. After they drove off Franck and I crept to the bathroom, very quietly so we didn't get off on the wrong foot with our new roommates. When we got back to our new bedroom I wanted more than anything to lie down. I realized I wasn't shivering as I stripped out of my clothes and slid beside Franck on our futon.

"I'm warm," I murmured to Franck. "I forgot how nice it is to not feel like an icicle when I hop into bed."

"It's lovely," he agreed and fit his body behind mine. "Do you have to be anywhere early tomorrow?"

I sighed with pleasure. "No, my first class starts at eleven. I need to figure out how to get there, but I'm sure there's a metro I can take. How about you?"

"My shift starts downtown at noon. That means we can sleep in if we want. I think we deserve it."

We didn't speak for a moment as I moved my hand meditatively over his chest. "I'm having a hard time believing that all actually happened."

"Me too. You reacted brilliantly, you know. Decisive and fast."

"You were a ninja at packing and moving."

"We're stronger together," he said, tracing my spine with his fingertips.

"We are." And with that, I was sucked into the vortex of sleep.

I woke up with a piercing pain in my big toe. "What the—?" I sat up to see a small white and gray cat biting my foot through the duvet. I tucked my toes away. "Ow, stop that."

I turned over, but the cat kept clawing at the duvet until he located my feet again and bit my pinkie toe. I gave my feet a little kick to try and dislodge him, but he just meowed and moved over to Franck's feet. He took a big bite of Franck's big toe before I could stop him.

"*Merde*!" Franck bolted upright. I pointed down to the end of the bed, where the cat was having a field day leaping on and trying to bite our feet.

"That must be Tracy's cat," I said. "The asshole."

I got out of bed and picked up the cat, then deposited it outside the swinging doors into what I could see clearly now that it was daylight out, was a larger, furnished living room.

I leapt back in bed with Franck, trying to wrap my mind around the fact that this was our new home. Within seconds, the cat came sauntering back in after pushing the swinging door open with his paws. Like he owned the place, he resumed his attack on our toes.

"I guess that puts an end to our plan for a sleep in." I sighed "But maybe that gives us time to have breakfast at The Greenspot."

"The Greenspot?" Franck perked up immediately.

"Tracy told me it's just around the corner."

Franck went for a shower while I followed the chatter to the kitchen and met one of the remaining two roommates. Tracy was there too.

"Everyone has very different schedules," she said. "Evan, that's the guy you haven't met yet, has a new girlfriend and he sleeps at her place a lot. He's been pretty much living over there the past few weeks but still pays me the rent religiously on the first of every month. My guess is that he has commitment issues and we're his escape plan." She shrugged and took a spoonful of her blueberry yoghurt. "His commitment issues benefit us, so I'm not complaining."

This apartment was completely different from our old one. It was packed with furniture and felt like an actual home. It even had carpet.

"With this many of us we'll be careful with the hot water," I said, thinking how with just Franck and me in our old apartment there hadn't been enough.

Emma, the other girl, waved her hand. "They have huge tanks for these four units. "We never run out. Scald your skin in there if you want. Go for it. Do you want some bread to toast or something?"

"That's super kind of you," I said. "But we were thinking of going to The Greenspot seeing as we're already up." The asshole cat sauntered into the kitchen area and began attacking my bare toes again. Tracy sighed. "His name is Abe. Abe the Asshole. He loves biting toes. Don't say I didn't warn you."

I laughed and picked him up. He began to purr against me. "I just want to thank you for being so kind to us," I said. "Please let us know if there are any rules we can abide by, or anything we can do to make having us here easier."

Tracy grinned. "No need to make any more of those thank you speeches. Pay your rent, clean up occasionally. That's about it."

"I think we can manage that. What's the quickest way to get to campus?"

Emma pointed the butter knife she was holding. "Atwater metro. Just walk two blocks up. You can walk to school too, but it may be a bit cold for you. Alison said you're from the West Coast?"

"Victoria. Island girl born and bred."

"So how are you finding this winter?" she asked.

"Fricking freezing."

"Yeah, you should take the metro. It's a solid forty-minute walk and Sherbrooke and Saint Catherine's are often wind tunnels. OK for us East Coasters, but not for you Westies."

My first instinct was to protest, but it was the truth. This was the first real winter I'd ever experienced. "True," I admitted. Out of the corner of my eye I saw Franck slip back into the bedroom after his shower.

"Your boyfriend seems quiet," Emma said.

"He's not, but he speaks almost zero English. He just emigrated from France. Do you speak French?"

"*Mais bien sûr*," Tracy rattled off in an accent I'd never heard before.

Franck came into the kitchen and I introduced him properly.

Tracy and Franck rattled on in French, with Franck filling her in with no little bit of humor the police ambush of the previous night.

Tracy roared with laughter and I knew it would be fine for me to leave and go have my shower. Franck had already found towels in our bags and had laid one out for me on our bed, which he had made. These little gestures meant so much. I wondered if the mandatory year-long military service he'd done in the Air Force in Dijon was responsible for his behavior, or whether he'd just been brought up that way. Either way, I loved it.

When I came back in the bedroom Franck was there, trying to sort our clothes in some sort of order into the milk crates that we had brought with us and would now serve as makeshift "drawers." The rest of our furniture had gone in the garage that belonged to the apartment.

Franck turned and smiled at me.

"Thanks for making the bed and finding a towel for me," I said.

"No problem." He was still watching me as I dropped my towel and started pulling on my clothes.

He laughed. "Your back is as red as a lobster. Doesn't it hurt to shower with water that hot?"

"Are you kidding? It felt like absolute heaven. Hurt so good." This place was such a wild improvement to our old apartment, despite the cat with the toe fetish. "I haven't been able to have a proper shower and actually feel warm since Christmas in Victoria, and now what are we? March?"

Franck nodded. "March seventh."

"I honestly can't believe we lasted that long in Denis's place."

"I know. Bastard."

"The sooner we forget him, the better," I said, deciding if we didn't change the topic of conversation we might ruin our appetites and that would be a damn shame. "What kind of French accent does Tracy have? It doesn't sound like Québécois, but it doesn't sound like French from France either. I don't think I've ever heard anything like it before."

"It's Acadian," Franck said. "I'd heard people refer to an Acadian accent before, but I always figured it was some sort of myth—maybe something that didn't exist anymore because it had been overtaken by English, but I was wrong."

"It sounds like she's singing when she talks French."

"And the expressions are priceless," Franck said.

"You know, there might be shit people like Denis out there," I said, pulling on my socks. "But there are really good people like Tracy too. I guess somehow that helps reconcile me with having lived in an old bordello run by a mafia kingpin."

"It's a start anyway. Also, don't forget that the Greenspot is just around the corner." Franck patted his stomach. "That's a silver lining, isn't it?"

I pulled on my sweater. "That it is. Speaking of, I'm ready to kill a stack of buttermilk pancakes."

I was stunned how quickly we adapted to our new living situation, aside from the cat, who continued attacking our toes every morning and generally being his asshole self. Our second home was the Greenspot, and the waitress actually began to crack an infinitesimal smile at us every few visits.

We avoided going to the Prince Arthur and Saint-Laurent area, as neither of us particularly wanted to run into Denis. We cooked a spaghetti and meatball dinner for Sam and Alison and Tracy at our new place to thank them. It turned out Alison and Tracy had gone to a university called Mount Allison together in the Maritimes.

Sam filled us in that there had been a raid on the grocery store across the street and a bunch of questionable-looking men had been hauled out from the back, spitting with anger and threatening retribution.

"We've decided we're going to look for another place next year," Sam said. "Even though Denis has acted fine—if a little creepy—towards us, what happened to you has made us nervous."

"I have to be honest," I said. "Sometimes I wake up in the middle of the night worrying about you guys being there still."

"Don't." Alison patted my hand. "Anyway, we'll be moving on in a month."

"What about our old apartment?" I said. "Has he managed to rent it out to anyone?"

'Not that I can tell," Sam said, looking troubled. "But we've noticed a few women in big fur coats coming and going in our stairwell. There is a lot of noise in the middle of the night down there, but it seems empty during the day. I don't know—"

Franck and I shared a look. "The whorehouse is back in business," I concluded.

"What?" Sam demanded.

I couldn't believe I forgot to tell Sam and Alison about the previous iteration of our old apartment. "Before you moved in in September and before we moved in, Denis had been running a bordello in our apartment."

"What!?" Sam gasped. "How do you know?"

"One of the police officers who stopped us the night we moved told us."

That brought us back on the topic of that night, and we gave Sam and Alison the full story of what had gone down, laughing about our poor student movers who thought they were being arrested for not paying their taxes.

"It's all been quite an adventure," Franck said, after the story was told.

"Yes. One I'd rather not repeat," I said.

"I was looking for adventure when I came to Canada," Franck reminded me. "Besides, we learned a lot," he added, always one to look at the bright side.

"I guess we did." We knew better now what to look for in an apartment, such as a big hot water tank and utilities included. Maybe we would even be little bit better at avoiding criminal landlords. The most important thing was that we'd learned Franck and I could survive a crisis without splintering apart.

chapter thirty-four

The snow and cold lasted longer than I could possibly have imagined. Even though I had heard that winters in Montréal lasted the better part of a year, I somehow couldn't truly imagine it. Now I could.

Coming from the West Coast, winter weather after Christmas felt completely unnecessary. The cherry blossoms should be blooming by early February, and there should be T-shirt weather by March. Here in Montréal, we were still in a deep freeze.

Then one morning mid-April, we left the apartment and realized we were boiling under our parkas and gloves and toques. The temperature was hovering around zero, which felt positively balmy. The constant drip of the huge icicles hanging from all the eaves was the soundtrack to our days, and the compacted snow and ice turned into gray slush that we had to slop through on the way to and from school.

That Friday, a group of us including Tracy, Emma, Sam, Alison, Hau and a few others decided to go out to a new restaurant downtown.

I wore my winter parka. It was the evening, after all, and it still hadn't hit two degrees. Yet, walking along Sainte-Catherine, most of the guys wore T-shirts and shorts, and girls strode around wearing spaghetti strapped tank tops as they licked ice cream cones.

"It's not *that* warm out yet," I said in protest.

"It's always like this in Halifax too," Tracy said. I noticed she was wearing a light sweater and no jacket. "As soon as it hits zero the clothes come off."

"Crazy Easterners," I said.

"And proud of it!" Tracy and Alison whooped. Hau and I shared an eye roll.

The snow thawed over the space of a few days. At the beginning, small coins of ground emerged from the white blanket, then large patches, until the snow only clung to the shadowy edges. One night near the end of term we headed out to a party on the Carré Saint-Louis, which meant that we would be in our old neighborhood.

"Do you want to walk by the old apartment?" Franck asked me with a raised brow.

"You read my mind," I said. "I think I'm ready to stop avoiding our old neighborhood. Mazurka's and Schwartz's are there, after all.

Franck grinned. "That is an excellent point."

Even though I was nervous about running into Denis or any of his cronies, it was still light out and the warmer weather meant that Saint-Laurent and Prince Arthur were teeming with people. The soft spring evening gave me confidence.

As we approached, I said. "Besides, we can't let the horrible Denis prevent us from moving freely around our city." We had paid our dues in Montréal, and we had survived. This was *our* town now.

Franck squeezed my hand tighter. "Exactly. Besides, until he gets arrested, Denis is earning far more money running his bordello in that apartment than renting it to us."

"True."

We made our way across the Carré Saint-Louis where the leaves were unfurling in the trees and a few low-key drug deals were going down under the chirping of birds. They had deconstructed the skating rink we used to go to, but I vowed to return to it next winter with Franck. We had started to make memories in this city—memories together—and I wasn't going to let anybody take those away.

The square smelled like damp earth and new leaves. "It's crazy to think that exams are only a week away and that we'll be leaving soon to go back to Victoria," I said.

Franck was only stopping briefly in Victoria on his way to a tree planting job for a tree planting team working out of Prince George in northern BC. It was Tracy, who did that for several summers until she broke her back falling over a tree stump and had to be airlifted out, who hooked up Franck with her old crew.

It was reputed to be one of the most physically grueling jobs in existence, but also well paid if you got in with a good team and a good captain. Besides, we figured, this was probably the best opportunity for Franck to learn English, away from me.

He would be in Victoria only a few days before flying up north. We would be apart all summer, and neither of us was looking forward to that. I had gotten a job working as a customs officer in Victoria's inner harbor, letting people into Canada (or not) via the float planes, ferries, or private boats. I was to report to my training the same day Franck flew to Prince George.

We strolled by Mazurka's on Prince Arthur. The street, which had seemed so desolate the night we'd returned from Christmas in Victoria, with only the harmonica lady in the freezing cold, was now full of chattering people dressed for summer, buskers, and restaurant tables that spilled onto the paving stones. It was just like my first night in Montréal. God, what had happened between then and now could fill a book.

As we neared the intersection with Saint-Laurent threads of the two-note song of the harmonica lady floated over to us.

I sighed in relief. "She survived the winter."

We stopped beside her but as usual she just gestured to her violin case, not recognizing us even though we had been putting money in the case until our middle-of-the-night escape. Out of sight, out of mind, I supposed.

Still, she had popped into my mind frequently on my worst days in Montréal. When I felt sorry for myself about the icy sidewalks or cutting wind or the lack of green, I would think about the harmonica lady and her tenacity. She never complained or stopped. She just played her harmonica.

We strolled across Saint-Laurent and just like that there we were in front of our old apartment building. The mafia grocery store looked dusty and untouched as usual, but it was still open. I concluded the police raid had probably not proved super effective.

The windows of our apartment looked empty. It might have been a dive, but that was where we slept in our makeshift bed together. It was where Franck found out his papers had arrived and where we'd discovered the many uses of a hockey stick. It was also where I finally attempted cooking something besides tuna melts.

"C'mon," I tugged Franck's hand.

"What?" he asked. "We should probably go back to the party."

"I want to see something."

I walked a few steps further to the patch of grass underneath the kitchen stairs. Now the snow had melted, there it was. In the middle of the grass, with only a little bit of snow clinging to it, was my first attempt at pea soup in all its intact glory. Throughout all those harsh winter months, it had held its shape.

"No!" Franck gasped in disbelief. "I don't believe it."

I sighed. "I guess you were right about the animals not wanting it."

"This is fantastic. Seriously, this is the Pea Soup Miracle. It's right up there with the Virgin Mary's apparition at Lourdes."

Heedless of Denis or anyone else, we bent over laughing until our stomachs ached.

Two weeks later our taxi was driving us to the airport. We wouldn't be seeing Montréal again for the next four months and we'd decided we'd worry about finding a new apartment when we returned in late August. In my mind, we'd crossed more than enough hurdles for one year.

Now it was time for summer, the West Coast, and our summer jobs.

Franck and I held hands in the back of the taxi. Just before branching off to the departure area, the taxi passed the huge sign that said, "*Au revoir*! Hope you enjoyed your time in Montréal. Come again soon."

Enjoyment? It hadn't been all enjoyment. There had been pain and frustration and confusion and so much cold as well as the good times. But all the astonishing complexity of real life crazy hadn't broken us as a couple as I had feared. In November when Franck came we faced the daunting challenge of making something real out of what everyone around us believed was fleeting. We had done it, I realized as the taxi pulled up to the airport curb.

Franck and I, a bit bruised, battered and a whole lot wiser, but every bit as much in love, stepped out in front of the Air Canada sign. I squeezed his arm as he paid the driver. We'd become a real couple after these past seven months.

Montréal had forged us.

La Fin

See what happens next when Franck and Laura move to Paris.
Enjoy this sneak peak of *My Grape Paris*,
the bestselling third book in the Grape Series

chapter **one**

The only proof I had that I was supposed to be there in Paris was my temporary student visa and a badly photocopied letter from some unidentifiable administrative office of the Sorbonne.

I scanned the letter I clutched in my sweaty hand. It was the last week in August, but the oppressive humidity made it feel as though we were in the tropics—the perfect weather to be sunning ourselves in Biarritz or Brittany, not tramping around the dog poop-festooned streets of the 5th arrondissement of Paris.

What I could decipher from the letter stated that, after my arrival in France, I should contact my exchange year advisor, Professor Alix Renier-Bernadotte, at the address provided. Just an address. No telephone number or any other contact information. She better be at home.

We found Professor Renier-Bernadotte's apartment a few streets away from the building where I would be taking at least half of my classes. She lived on a narrow, cobblestoned street, just off a much larger street.

The building rose from the sidewalk in the stately style that was synonymous with Haussmann, the designer of modern Paris—gray stone and large symmetrical windows, fronted by ornate ironwork so Parisians wouldn't tumble out onto the street when opening their massive wooden shutters in the morning.

I was already intimidated by this Parisian professor who was supposed to help me register at the Sorbonne, and I hadn't even met her yet.

Franck and I had arrived that morning after more than fifte

hours of travel from Vancouver. This Inter-University Exchange gig—I was being swapped with a French student who would study for a year at my school, McGill University in Montreal, while I studied at the Sorbonne—was already turning out to be more challenging than it looked on paper.

I studied the name tags stuck in the brass buzzer plate mounted on the wall of the apartment building. They were blurred by age and rain. "Does that look like Renier-Bernadotte to you?" I asked Franck, who was lighting a Gitanes. I didn't know how he could smoke in that heat, let alone Gitanes—the cigarette equivalent of pungent Munster cheese.

He took a deep drag and leaned forward to peer at the name I was pointing at. "It looks to me like it says Rognon-Betterave." Kidney-Beets. He rubbed his stomach thoughtfully. "That gives me an idea. If we find a brasserie, they might have veal kidneys in Madeira on the menu. They're a classic dish at Parisian brasseries, tu sais."

I made a gagging noise.

"You think you don't like them because you've never tried them."

"I know I don't like Gitanes, and I haven't tried them either. I can't get past the smell. Same thing with kidneys."

"Completely different. Kidneys are extremely good for you as well as delicious. Smoking is a filthy habit I need to stop."

"At least we agree on that," I said, then nodded at the buzzers. "So, should I buzz Professor Kidney-Beets here?"

Franck shrugged. "You know my opinion. You should wait until your first day of school. All of Paris goes on vacation in August. Haven't you noticed how empty the streets are?"

"Still—"

"I doubt she's here, and even if she is, she won't answer her buzzer. I warned you not to expect the same welcome that McGill provides to the incoming French students."

That was a shame, because at McGill, the incoming French exchange students were treated like royalty. They were appointed a student chaperone as soon as they arrived in Montreal to help them with everything from finding accommodation to registering for courses to meeting other students.

A whole week of special events were put on for the exchange students freshly arrived at McGill. There were scavenger hunts so they could familiarize themselves with the campus and mingle with others, live concerts, and drinks events so their livers could adapt to Canadian beer and the cheap Czechoslovakian wine from the dépanneur. And meetings were set up with various academic advisors so they would have all their questions answered and their timetable completely in order before the beginning of term.

So far, there had been no welcoming committee for me at the Charles de Gaulle airport on our arrival, and the only contact name I had been given was Professor Kidney-Beets, supposedly at this address. As a result, I was pulsing with desperation to connect with her. She was my only shot at feeling less disoriented.

"I have to try," I said. I buzzed on the buzzer.

Nothing.

I buzzed again. Then again.

Franck raised one eyebrow at me. "Does the state of that name tag beside her buzzer look like that of a person who wants students to find them?"

Dignified silence was the only possible response to my boyfriend.

I peered up to the two windows on the fourth floor, where Professor Kidney-Beets' apartment was supposed to be if we had indeed chosen the right buzzer. A curtain twitched and a face dominated by a large pair of glasses glanced down, then the curtain drew shut again.

"She's up there!" I shouted in English, even though Franck and I spoke French together most of the time. "I saw her!" I pointed, just in case Franck misunderstood.

I went back and buzzed the buzzer five more times so there could be no doubt I wanted to see her. I was going to buzz it a sixth time, when Franck reached out and stilled my hand. "Ever heard of getting off on the wrong foot? I don't know who this woman is, but I would bet that it's not a prudent idea to piss her off before the school year even begins."

I stamped my foot and buzzed again three times. The curtain

above didn't even twitch.

Franck took me by the shoulders and pulled me back from the buzzer. "I'm not sure how it is in Canada, but being so persistent when somebody clearly does not want to answer their buzzer is considered rude in Paris," he said gently.

"I'm not the one who is supposed to be advising students and then hiding away in my apartment, leaving them completely abandoned on the street, not knowing what to do or how to choose their courses or—" Tears began to roll down my cheeks. Tears borne of too much travel and too little sleep, and overheating and frustration, and the fact that the reality of this whole year-in-Paris thing was already at loggerheads with my fantasies.

"Come on." Franck took my arm. "Let's go find a brasserie."

"I'm not eating kidneys! I won't!" I heard myself shout like a spoiled, overtired toddler.

"You don't have to," Franck said, stroking the back of my hand. "You're to rest your feet for a while, and there might even be chocolate mousse on the menu for dessert."

"We don't have any money," I wailed. "You're always telling me how everything is so expensive in Paris."

"Not the prix fixe menu at Paris brasseries. They're a bargain. Besides, a good meal raises one's spirits. That's priceless."

I let myself be led up the street, the hope of meeting Professor Renier-Bernadotte's abandoned—for that day anyway.

"Just so you know," I said, "I'll be ordering a carafe of chilled rosé."

"So young, yet so wise." Franck patted my shoulder.

To read on, just go here:
mybook.to/MyGrapeParis

merci

I'm finishing up My Grape Québec during our collective self-isolation for the COVID-19 pandemic. I want to say thank you to all the health care workers who are out there fighting for us on the front lines, today and every day. Doctors, nurses, scientists and researchers saved my life with my liver transplant three years ago, and they continue to be my heroes.

Thank you also to Nyssa Temmel who with her gift of the right lobe of her liver (yeah, you read that right!) has given me the unfathomable gift of three years of life. We are both doing great and every bonus day is a gift.

Thank you to my daughters who bring joy, laughter, and an extra dose of quirkiness every day. Each minute I'm around to be your mom is a lucky one. Thank you to Franck for being my partner and my love through this crazy adventure called life. Your promise to me years ago still holds true – our life together has never, ever been boring.

A special thanks to my parents who managed to take the high road when I moved in with an unknown Frenchman at age nineteen. Now that I am a parent myself, it curls my hair to think of how difficult this must have been for you. To this day I truly admire how you handled it with kindness and a hell of a lot of grace. Thank you for being so awesome and sorry I was so terrifying.

Thank you to my dear friend Pamela Patchet in Montréal for continuing to be my ideal reader as well as just being an incredible human being. The world is so much richer and more beautiful with you in it Pam.

Also thank you to Rachel Ciaves, who is also a wonderful Montrealer who does so much for the PSC community in Canada and the world. Your advocacy and generosity are so appreciated Rachel.

I adore my readers and I'm trying to get this book out to you as fast as possible to read during our collective isolation. You are the fuel that keeps me going and I feel honored to be experiencing this thing called life with you.

Also thanks to our rescue dog Pepper. I appreciate you taking me out for all those head-clearing walks.

Lastly, thank you to the kick-ass city of Montreal. *Je me souviens* indeed.

To join Laura's Grapevine and receive monthly recipes, sneak peeks, and goodies, as well as automatically be entered to win a free week at one of our vacation rentals in Burgundy, France, just click here:

www.laurabradbury.com/enter-to-win

a conversation with **Laura Bradbury**

What inspired you to write My Grape Québec?

In late August 2019 I took our eldest daughter Charlotte back to Montréal to start University at McGill. She was swept into the swing of residence life (in the residence right beside Molson House, no less!) quickly. This left me with the unbelievable indulgence of being able to walk around the city in the warm late-summer air and explore to my heart's content. As I walked kilometers along Sherbrooke and up Saint Laurent to the Plateau and weaved through the streets of the student ghetto, memories came flooding back. My Grape Québec almost wrote itself in those four days, and I would come back to my hotel room every evening and write down all the memories that were teeming in my brain. All that was left for me to do was transcribe them onto my computer.

What importance does Montréal hold for you?

My first year in Montréal was pivotal in my life. It was the year that Franck managed a miracle and came to join me in Montréal. We began our life as a couple, away from our families and the comforts of home. It was brutally hard. We had no money and it was a particularly frigid, long winter marked by severe blizzards. The employment market was dire, and we were both very much trying to figure out this whole grown-up life thing.

The hardship could have broken us and there were more than a few moments I feared it would. It was a trial by fire (or rather ice, seeing as we're talking about Québec) but we somehow emerged at the other side far stronger and for the first time feeling like a solid team.

What do you love about Montréal?

Montréal is like no other city on earth. When I took my oldest daughters back there in the Fall of 2018 to look at Universities, our middle daughter Camille remarked after a few hours in the city "Oh my god Mom, this entire city talks the same way we do at home!". It's true. This crazy mix of English and French prevails – so much so that sentences are often half and half and daily life segues seamlessly between both languages.

It's a vibrant city full of art, culture, and diversity. This means the food scene is second to none, and it's always been that way. Montréalers get out and know how to have a good time, even when it's minus thirty outside. I adore that spirit. There is always something interesting going on in Montréal and no matter what you're into, you'll be able to find it there. I guess the easiest way to explain it is that Montréal is overflowing with heart.

Do you still feel connected to Montréal?

I feel more connected to Montréal than ever. For one of our wedding anniversaries after we moved back to Canada from France, Franck and I went to Montréal just the two of us for a week. We stayed in a little apartment on the Carré Saint Louis. We had a fabulous week – walking up to Little Italy to eat amazing cannolis and drink strong espressos, attending two hockey games, and of course had multiple smoked meat sandwiches and dill pickles at Schwartz's (sadly, Bens was closed by then).

One of my dearest friends Pam lives in Montréal with her family, and she has ended up being a second mom for my daughter Charlotte in Montréal. Spending time with her and her gang is always a treat. Camille is starting McGill in the Fall so Franck and I are thrilled to go and visit both of them and spend more time there as a family. Montréal has not seen the end of the Germains yet!

Did that incident at the end when the police told you to flee the apartment really happen?

I swear to God it did. It was terrifying and disorienting at the time, but still remains one of the craziest stories Franck and I have of our life together (and, trust me, we have quite a few). It was already bad enough when we were told to get out of the apartment immediately at the risk of our lives, but when we were surrounded by cop cars in the moving truck that truly took the whole escapade to a new level. I'll never forget all those flashing lights. Now I can laugh at it.

What are you writing next?

My goal for 2020 was to become a faster, more efficient writer. However, as I answer these questions we are in the middle of the COVID 19 pandemic. As an immunosuppressed post-transplant patient I am self-isolating with my family. Oh, how life laughs at our plans!

I would have thought the isolation would increase my productivity but I'm finding the opposite is true. It's hard to concentrate when it feels as though the world is melting outside my door and I have my three kids home from school and freaked out and bored. Still, I've started writing the second book in my fictional Winemaker's Trilogy and am loving it. Next I'll move on to the third book to finish up that series before moving back to my Grape Books. I've also got a co-authored cookbook entitled Bisous & Brioche (based on my Grape Series) coming out in the Fall 2020 and published by Touchwood Editions. Readers have been asking for this for a long time, so I'm extremely happy to give this to them.

discussion **guide**

1. What is your favorite city in the world? Why?

2. If you were to write a memoir about your life and it had to be of only be on a year of your life, what would it be? What were the defining moments that began and ended that period of time?

3. Do you feel a certain place can have an impact on important relationships in your life? Discuss how this has played out in your life.

4. Do you believe that hardships can forge a relationship just as easily as they can destroy them? Discuss this in the context of your own relationships.

5. Have you experienced that "the one who got away" with any of your past relationships? Have you reconciled and accepted that you didn't take that path, or do you still think about it?

6. What is the worst place you ever lived? Tell stories about that and how you coped and how you eventually got out.

7. Have you ever lived anywhere with extreme weather? Do you have any funny stories of how living in such a place reveals the human spirit?

about **Laura**

Laura Bradbury is the author of the bestselling Grape Series of memoirs recounting her life in France with her French husband and their three franco-Canadian daughters. She has branched out into fiction with her Winemakers Trilogy and has also co-authored a cookbook Bisous & Brioche, published by Touchwood Editions in Fall 2020. Splitting her time between Vancouver Island, Canada and Villers-la-Faye, France Laura still runs three vacation rentals in the vineyards of Burgundy, France with her Franck. Laura is now enjoying renewed health after a life-saving liver transplant in March 2017 (due to the rare auto-immune condition called PSC) and loves traveling, walking her rescue dog Pepper, reading, beachcombing on the local beaches, and doing everything she can to support PSC research and campaign for an opt-out organ donation system in Canada.

find **Laura** online

Website
laurabradbury.com

Facebook
facebook.com/AuthorLauraBradbury

Instagram
instagram.com/laurabradburywriter

Pinterest
pinterest.ca/bradburywriter

Bookbub
bookbub.com/authors/laura-bradbury

Sign up for my Grapevine Newsletter and enter to win a free week
in Burgundy
www.laurabradbury.com/enter-to-win

Made in the USA
Middletown, DE
30 October 2020

22981558R00175